# FARMERS' ALMANAC ™

*Calculated for the United States*
*for the year of our Lord*

# ⧗ 2 0 0 1 ⧗

BEING THE FIRST AFTER BISSEXTILE, OR LEAP YEAR, AND UNTIL THE
## FOURTH OF JULY
THE 225TH YEAR OF THE INDEPENDENCE OF THE
## UNITED STATES

Containing early America at its best, delightfully threaded through with
a measure of good humor, amusing anecdotes, wise-old weather predictions,
helpful hints and good reading for every member of the
family done on a high moral plane.

EDITED BY PETER GEIGER, PHILOM.
AND MANAGING EDITOR, SONDRA DUNCAN

COPYRIGHT © 2000 BY ALMANAC PUBLISHING COMPANY   NO. 1815862

ISSN: 0737-6731

Address all correspondence to:
FARMERS' ALMANAC
P.O. Box 1609, Lewiston, Maine 04241

# CONTENTS

# FEATURE ARTICLES

# PHILOSOFACTS

• The new year lies before you like a spotless track of snow; be careful how you tread on it, for every mark will show.

• When you point a finger at others, you are pointing three at yourself.

• The milk of human kindness furnishes the cream of society.

• Go the extra mile–it's never crowded.

• The past is precious; the future is fantasy; the present is priceless.

• The squeaky wheel doesn't always get the grease; sometimes it gets replaced.

• A narrow mind and a wide mouth usually go together.

• If you'd like to have some company, just leave the house messy.

• Conversation is the art of telling people a little less than they want to know.

• Remember–the heavier the load, the more you take things for granite.

• The goal of criticism is to leave the person with the feeling that he or she has been helped.

• Nothing makes time go faster than buying on it.

• In diagnosing the illness of society, many are willing to write the prescription, but few are willing to take the medicine.

• Getting an idea should be like sitting on a pin; it should make you jump up and do something.

• One sure way to make a person worry is to tell him or her not to.

• Only some of us can learn from other people's experiences; the rest of us have to be the other people.

• Don't be too anxious to give your children what you didn't have, as you might neglect to give them what you did have.

• Many so-called open minds should be closed for repairs.

• Half of our troubles come from wanting our own way. The other half comes from being allowed to have it!

• Diplomacy is the art of letting someone else have your way.

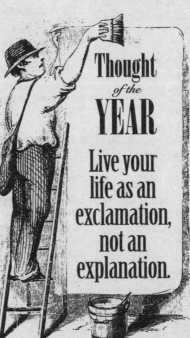

Thought *of the* YEAR

Live your life as an exclamation, not an explanation.

*Greetings* We are pleased to offer warm greetings through this Almanac, part of an Almanac family that has mellowed for more than a century and a half in the fine traditions of early America. Like a friendly clasp of hands, it is a symbol of our sincerest good wishes. You will find in its pages anecdotes and information that should be helpful throughout the year and be a guide to pleasant living.

**We hope it will find a convenient and important place in your home.**

## ≋ 2001 ≋

### JANUARY
| S | M | T | W | T | F | S |
|---|---|---|---|---|---|---|
|   | **1** | 2 | 3 | 4 | 5 | 6 |
| 7 | 8 | 9 | 10 | 11 | 12 | 13 |
| 14 | **15** | 16 | 17 | 18 | 19 | 20 |
| 21 | 22 | 23 | 24 | 25 | 26 | 27 |
| 28 | 29 | 30 | 31 |   |   |   |

### FEBRUARY
| S | M | T | W | T | F | S |
|---|---|---|---|---|---|---|
|   |   |   |   | 1 | 2 | 3 |
| 4 | 5 | 6 | 7 | 8 | 9 | 10 |
| 11 | 12 | 13 | 14 | 15 | 16 | 17 |
| 18 | **19** | 20 | 21 | 22 | 23 | 24 |
| 25 | 26 | 27 | 28 |   |   |   |

### MARCH
| S | M | T | W | T | F | S |
|---|---|---|---|---|---|---|
|   |   |   |   | 1 | 2 | 3 |
| 4 | 5 | 6 | 7 | 8 | 9 | 10 |
| 11 | 12 | 13 | 14 | 15 | 16 | 17 |
| 18 | 19 | 20 | 21 | 22 | 23 | 24 |
| 25 | 26 | 27 | 28 | 29 | 30 | 31 |

### APRIL
| S | M | T | W | T | F | S |
|---|---|---|---|---|---|---|
| 1 | 2 | 3 | 4 | 5 | 6 | 7 |
| 8 | 9 | 10 | 11 | 12 | 13 | 14 |
| 15 | 16 | 17 | 18 | 19 | 20 | 21 |
| 22 | 23 | 24 | 25 | 26 | 27 | 28 |
| 29 | 30 |   |   |   |   |   |

### MAY
| S | M | T | W | T | F | S |
|---|---|---|---|---|---|---|
|   |   | 1 | 2 | 3 | 4 | 5 |
| 6 | 7 | 8 | 9 | 10 | 11 | 12 |
| 13 | 14 | 15 | 16 | 17 | 18 | 19 |
| 20 | 21 | 22 | 23 | 24 | 25 | 26 |
| 27 | **28** | 29 | 30 | 31 |   |   |

### JUNE
| S | M | T | W | T | F | S |
|---|---|---|---|---|---|---|
|   |   |   |   |   | 1 | 2 |
| 3 | 4 | 5 | 6 | 7 | 8 | 9 |
| 10 | 11 | 12 | 13 | 14 | 15 | 16 |
| 17 | 18 | 19 | 20 | 21 | 22 | 23 |
| 24 | 25 | 26 | 27 | 28 | 29 | 30 |

### JULY
| S | M | T | W | T | F | S |
|---|---|---|---|---|---|---|
| 1 | 2 | 3 | **4** | 5 | 6 | 7 |
| 8 | 9 | 10 | 11 | 12 | 13 | 14 |
| 15 | 16 | 17 | 18 | 19 | 20 | 21 |
| 22 | 23 | 24 | 25 | 26 | 27 | 28 |
| 29 | 30 | 31 |   |   |   |   |

### AUGUST
| S | M | T | W | T | F | S |
|---|---|---|---|---|---|---|
|   |   |   | 1 | 2 | 3 | 4 |
| 5 | 6 | 7 | 8 | 9 | 10 | 11 |
| 12 | 13 | 14 | 15 | 16 | 17 | 18 |
| 19 | 20 | 21 | 22 | 23 | 24 | 25 |
| 26 | 27 | 28 | 29 | 30 | 31 |   |

### SEPTEMBER
| S | M | T | W | T | F | S |
|---|---|---|---|---|---|---|
|   |   |   |   |   |   | 1 |
| 2 | **3** | 4 | 5 | 6 | 7 | 8 |
| 9 | 10 | 11 | 12 | 13 | 14 | 15 |
| 16 | 17 | 18 | 19 | 20 | 21 | 22 |
| 23 | 24 | 25 | 26 | 27 | 28 | 29 |
| 30 |   |   |   |   |   |   |

### OCTOBER
| S | M | T | W | T | F | S |
|---|---|---|---|---|---|---|
|   | 1 | 2 | 3 | 4 | 5 | 6 |
| 7 | **8** | 9 | 10 | 11 | 12 | 13 |
| 14 | 15 | 16 | 17 | 18 | 19 | 20 |
| 21 | 22 | 23 | 24 | 25 | 26 | 27 |
| 28 | 29 | 30 | 31 |   |   |   |

### NOVEMBER
| S | M | T | W | T | F | S |
|---|---|---|---|---|---|---|
|   |   |   |   | 1 | 2 | 3 |
| 4 | 5 | **6** | 7 | 8 | 9 | 10 |
| **11** | 12 | 13 | 14 | 15 | 16 | 17 |
| 18 | 19 | 20 | 21 | **22** | 23 | 24 |
| 25 | 26 | 27 | 28 | 29 | 30 |   |

### DECEMBER
| S | M | T | W | T | F | S |
|---|---|---|---|---|---|---|
|   |   |   |   |   |   | 1 |
| 2 | 3 | 4 | 5 | 6 | 7 | 8 |
| 9 | 10 | 11 | 12 | 13 | 14 | 15 |
| 16 | 17 | 18 | 19 | 20 | 21 | 22 |
| 23 | 24 | **25** | 26 | 27 | 28 | 29 |
| 30 | 31 |   |   |   |   |   |

*Dear Readers,*

There is something very special about editing a publication that now reaches into a third century. Looking at the pages of dog-eared, older editions of the *Farmers' Almanac*, I realize that, while the world is a very different place from what it was in 1818 when the first Almanac was printed, in some ways it's the same. For example, in 1923, the fifth editor of the *Farmers' Almanac*, William Jardine, expressed a concern of his stating, *"Don't allow the old-fashioned neighborliness to be forgotten in these days of telephones, automobiles, trolleys, and daily mail. The good custom of visiting is too rapidly disappearing in many communities; the newcomer is apt to be neglected and not made to feel welcomed."* Jardine's worry reflected many people's apprehensions in the early 1900s. And, as we enter this new millennium, some may argue that Jardine's fear is a concern of today's world. With technological devices replacing face-to-face communications, some aspects of our lives are becoming less personal. On the other hand, telephones, E-mail, automobiles, and airplanes have enabled us to meet and to keep in touch with neighbors in other communities, states, and countries. In reality, life is what we make of it. All of us share the responsibility to embrace technology in a manner that enables us to work, communicate, and do things more effectively. We also have a responsibility to not let it replace the invaluable aspect of a personal touch (human interaction).

It is because of human interactions that our country once again has a Dollar Coin. Our kudos go out to Jim Benfield and The Coin Coalition for their unrelenting fight to introduce such a coin. In 1990, the *Farmers' Almanac* also championed the idea of a dollar coin, and even made suggestions on how it could succeed in the areas that the Susan B. Anthony dollar failed. Good things take time, and this coin was worth the wait.

Last year many of you wrote to us regarding Caleb's Weatherbee's article on the 100 most memorable weather events. In our article, we stated that during the Great Tri-state Tornado of 1925, many died in Murfreesboro, Tennessee. But (as many of you pointed out) it should have stated that many died in Murphysboro, Illinois. In addition, our article also spoke of a new, national, 24-hour record of 77 inches of snow that fell January 11 and 12, 1997, in Montague, New York. However, last year the National Weather Service took away that record, stating that the local snow spotter did not properly measure the snowfall. So the old 24-hour record of 75.8 inches of snow, set in Silver Lake, Colorado, on April 14-15, 1921, still stands.

Speaking of the weather, Caleb reveals some very interesting predictions for the upcoming year (starting on page 92 ) and shares some insights on a warming trend.

Managing Editor Sandi Duncan and I enjoyed the opportunity to ring in the year 2000 with an abundance of interviews, including ones on CNN, *NBC Nightly News*, National Public Radio, and many of the local programs that invited us to be their guests. Each interview is an opportunity for us to interact with you. Speaking of interactions, our Web site— www.farmersalmanac.com—is a great way to communicate with us. While it may not be face-to-face communications, we believe that Jardine, may he rest in peace, would smile if he knew how easy it is for people in this day and age to be neighborly.

Thank you, dear readers, for yet another year in *Farmers' Almanac* history.

*Faithfully,*

Peter E. Geiger, Philom.
For David Young, Philom.

*The 2001 Edition of the*
# FARMERS' ALMANAC™

ORIGINATOR:
DAVID YOUNG, PHILOM.
(1781-1852)

EDITOR:
PETER GEIGER, PHILOM.

MANAGING EDITOR:
SONDRA DUNCAN

CONTRIBUTING EDITORS:
RICHARD LEDERER
MARY BETH MORRIS

GRAPHIC DESIGNER:
RICHARD PLOURDE

ASTRONOMY:
JOE RAO,
SONIA KARNES,
HART WRIGHT COMPANY

SENIOR COPY/RESEARCH
EDITOR:
LYLE BLOOM

COPY EDITORS:
KAREN DAISE
NANCY MOYER
DORIS VIOLETTE
WADE WALKER

ADMINISTRATIVE
ASSISTANT:
LOUISE ST. PIERRE

PUBLISHER:
ALMANAC PUBLISHING
COMPANY

EDITORIAL, PUBLISHING,
ADVERTISING OFFICE:
P.O. BOX 1609
LEWISTON, MAINE 04241
Phone: 207-755-2000
Fax: 207-755-2422
E-mail: questions@farmersalmanac.com
Web site: www.farmersalmanac.com
Advertising: advertising@farmersalmanac.com

## Unscramble the Almanac term and WIN a FREE Magnet!

# FARMERS' ALMANAC WORD SCRAMBLE

For the past several years, we've challenged readers to find a hidden object within the pages of the
*Farmers' Almanac*. This year we decided to challenge you to a word scramble.

Unscramble the letters in the balloon above to
make a term used in this Almanac, and you could
win a FREE *Farmers' Almanac* Important Numbers
Magnet. This colorful refrigerator magnet allows you
to personalize it with important telephone numbers.

**Hurry! Only the first 1,000 people to respond
correctly will win this FREE magnet.**

Only letters will qualify; please, no phone calls,
E-mails or faxes. Mail your letters to:

*Farmers' Almanac* **Word Scramble
Box 1609, Lewiston, ME 04241**

# NAMING A *National Dessert*

C ritics love them. People crave them. Contests revolve around them, and social gatherings specialize in them. What are they? Desserts—those sweet indulgences that top off a meal.

Americans love their desserts. And why shouldn't we? Everywhere we turn we are hit in the taste buds with signs, ads, and places to buy double-layer chocolate cakes, brownie sundaes, homemade apple pies, strawberry cheesecakes, pastries, and other mouth-watering treats. We all know the consequences of eating too many sweets, but that forbidden, almost sinful quality adds to their allure and attraction.

But before you put this Almanac down and head to the kitchen to see what home- or store-baked goodies you might find, stop to think about what *one* dessert is most American and why? While favorite desserts vary with everyone's taste buds, your editors at the *Farmers' Almanac* feel that our country needs a "National Dessert."

### A Country Of Symbols

The United States portrays its strong image through a variety of symbols—national anthem, motto, seal, bird, flag—yet there is no designated national food of any type. Mention France and images of light, flaky croissants and rich pastries might come to mind. Germany may conjure up thoughts of sauerkraut and sausages, Italy pasta, and Switzerland chocolate. But what about the USA?

### A Melting Pot

Perhaps it is because of our melting pot image, our being made up of so many different people from various ethnic and cultural backgrounds, that makes it hard for anyone to relate one certain dish to our country. Yet, it is due to this great medley of peoples that we are able to enjoy such a palatable assortment of foods

(and desserts). To help narrow a national food down, we decided to focus on the sweetest course, dessert.

### Mom's Apple Pie

Thanks to the expression "As American as apple pie," many might suggest that apple pie is or should be our National Dessert. But why is apple pie considered so American? Apples were not native to this country. Perhaps our claim to it relates to the legend of Johnny Appleseed, who walked throughout the Midwest sowing apple seeds from a sack by his side. Or it may refer to another popular but inaccurate legend that gives credit to George Washington's cook for inventing apple pie during the General's stay at Valley Forge. Whatever the reason, should apple pie be our *official* dessert?

## Piece Of The Pie

Looking back at America's history, desserts have appeared as the last course for hundreds of years. Wild berry or fruit pies and tarts date back as early as 1640. Cakes were being baked long before the Revolutionary War, with the most prominent being the fruit, cheese, spice, and pound cakes. Pudding and candies were a popular treat in the days of early settlers, and recipes for cookies can be found in a 1796 cookbook by Amelia Simmons entitled *American Cookery*. And speaking of patriotic, Thomas Jefferson has been credited with championing the idea of ice cream.

## Have Your Cake And Eat It Too

Turn the pages forward hundreds of years, and desserts—in even more enticing flavors and varieties—are being served throughout the country. So how, with this array of delectable dishes, do we pick one to become our National Dessert?

Well, after tons of taste testing, recipe searching, and dessert-lover polling, we've come up with a list of 5 savory desserts; one of which we believe should be our National Dessert. Now, as self-indulgent and sinful as these dishes might be, a national dessert should say something about our country and its people (besides the fact that indulging in sweets is a popular pastime for us Americans!).

## Cast Your Vote

Here are 5 appetizing contenders for a National Dessert. Cast your vote by marking an X next to your choice (please choose only one) on the ballot below. Fax or mail it to us (you can photocopy it if you don't want to tear it out of your Almanac), or send us your choice by regular or E-mail, or check out our Web site for an online voting booth.

After we name our National Dessert in next year's *Farmers' Almanac*, we'll be looking for the best recipe for this national treat!

---

### A National Dessert should meet one if not all of these criteria:

1. PATRIOTIC—does it include ingredients that are native to America? Or does it have ties to a historical event, pastime, or person?
2. MAJORITY RULES— just like our country, we need to be diplomatic in choosing our National Dessert, so when you cast your vote keep in mind that in addition to your taste buds, this dessert should be a popular choice among most Americans.
3. ACCESSIBLE—while cherries jubilee may be the crème de la crème of the party, our National Dessert should be something readily available for purchase, or easily made.
4. DELICIOUS—of course, the National Dessert should just plain taste great!

---

### ✗ My choice for the National Dessert is...

❑ Strawberry Shortcake

❑ Chocolate Cake

❑ Apple Pie

❑ Ice Cream

❑ Cheesecake

❑ Other _____

*Please choose only one! All votes must be received by March 1, 2001*

---

Mailing address: *Farmers' Almanac* Dessert Poll, Mt. Hope Ave., Box 1609, Lewiston, ME 04241 • Fax: 207-755-2149 • E-mail: desserts@farmersalmanac.com
Web site: www.farmersalmanac.com

# 1834 Almanac's Cure For Using Tobacco

**Antitobacco campaigns date back many years. This was found in an 1834 copy of a FARMERS' ALMANAC:**

*Ye, who are chewing, snuffing, smoking,*
*Think or think not that I am joking,*
*When I declare the solemn fact is,*
*All may leave off this tempting practice,*
*Let every one the process try,*
*To beg off all and never buy.*

## CHOCOLATE LOVERS TAKE NOTE!

**What is chocolate?** It's a bean ... well, sort of. Chocolate is a processed form of *Theobroma cacao*, or the cacao bean.
**How is edible chocolate made?** The cacao beans are fermented, cleaned, roasted and shelled, then ground to produce cocoa butter and a nonalcoholic paste called "chocolate liquor." The "liquor" is refined, then "conched" (kneaded) and mixed with sugar, vanilla, and additional cocoa butter.

# Everything you always wanted to know about HICCUPS, and more!

**HICCUPS** (sometimes known as hiccoughs). What are they? They're annoying—embarrassing—funny (at times)—and sometimes painful. And yet, all of us at one time or another, most often without any warning, are afflicted with these funny sounding, annoying things that feel like they come from somewhere near our stomachs.

## BUT WHAT ARE THEY, REALLY?

Hiccups are defined as a sudden, involuntary inhalation that is stopped abruptly by the voice box closing, producing a short, sharp sound. Why this happens is almost as big a mystery as the cure. Most people seem to get hiccups when they eat too fast, swallow too much air, eat hot, spicy foods or liquids, or have an imbalance of carbon dioxide in their bloodstream.

*continued*

**CURES** There are thousands of "cures" (we even found some remedies in *Farmers' Almanac*s from the 1800s!) for the hiccups out there, some of which people swear by, and others that seem to remedy these annoying sounds for only 2 out of 10 people. Consensus is to try as many remedies as possible to find the one (or two) that works, and then keep using it! **Here are a few of the hundreds of hiccup cures we found (If you have a cure not listed here, E-mail us at: hiccups@farmersalmanac.com):**

➤ Swallow some water while holding your nose and ears. After taking a mouthful of water, place your thumbs on your ears (push them shut gently) and your pointer fingers on your nostrils (pinch them shut). Then swallow the water. Repeat, if necessary.

➤ Hold your breath and count to ten. If that doesn't work, try coughing, sneezing, or gargling. This alters your air intake.

➤ Drink upside down! This may seem awkward, but try bending over and taking a drink of water while your head is next to your thighs.

➤ Drink water fast (without taking a breath between gulps).

➤ Breathe into a paper bag. This allows you to breathe in your own air, which contains carbon dioxide. However, don't do this for more than a minute, as recycling your own air can cause you to black out.

➤ BOO! If another person has the hiccups, help him or her break the cycle of the diaphragm contractions. Give that person something else for their body to respond to; such as a "Boo!" or "Hey, look over there!"

➤ Suck on crushed ice.

➤ Try chewing a piece of gum.

➤ Swallow a teaspoon of sugar.

➤ 1834 *Farmers' Almanac* Cure–place 4 drops of cinnamon oil on a lump of sugar. Hold it in your mouth until it (sugar or hiccup) is gone.

**WHY DO SOME OF THESE UNIQUE REMEDIES WORK?** The general goal for a cure is to increase carbon dioxide levels in the blood or to disrupt/overwhelm the nerve impulses causing the hiccups. This is done by holding your breath, drinking upside down, eating sugar, etc. Since your body isn't used to some of these sensations, it stops concentrating on what's going on in your diaphragm, and pays attention to the new sensation.

Most of the time, hiccups only last a few minutes, but if they persist for a long time or seem to be happening on a frequent basis, contact your healthcare provider.

# Hunter's Secret Teriyaki Marinade

1/3 cup oil
1/4 cup soy sauce
2 cloves garlic, chopped or pressed
1/4 cup honey
2 tbsp. vinegar
2 tbsp. minced onion
2 tbsp. ginger
Dash of pepper

Mix all ingredients well. Great marinade for many meats, but it is especially good for venison. Let meat set as long as possible in marinade before cooking.

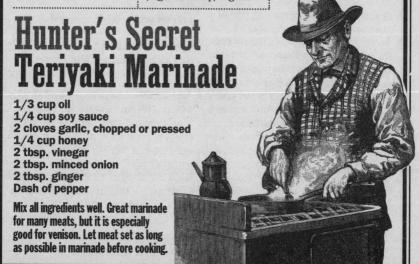

# Make *your* own Tea

N ext time you're in the mood for a cup of soothing hot tea, or a glass of refreshing iced tea, why not head to your garden? Herbal teas, which have grown immensely in popularity, can be made from herbs grown in a backyard, patio, or kitchen herb garden.

**HOW?** Fresh or dried herbs can be used for tea. Just remember to keep dried herbs in an airtight container.

**A general method for making herbal teas calls for 1 teaspoon of dried herbs per 6-oz. or 8-oz. teacup of boiling water; or 2-3 teaspoons\* of fresh herbs per cup (crush the leaves before adding boiling water.) Place the herbs in the cup first, then pour in the water. Cover the cup and leave for 5 minutes before straining out the herbs and drinking.** When making iced tea, follow the same method. Remove the herbs once steeped. Cover the container and then put it in the refrigerator to cool. To sweeten, add a little honey or sugar, and for added effect, add a sprig of the fresh herb as a garnish.

Here are a few of the more popular herbs used for teas, and tips on how to turn them into a delicious drink:

**Mint** is a popular flavor for tea drinkers. There are many varieties of mint, including spearmint, peppermint, orange mint, and more. Experiment with all of them to find your favorite flavor. To make the tea, use whole mint leaves, slightly crushed (use method listed).

**Chamomile** is another tasty herb for making tea. But this tea requires the flowers only, not the leaves of the plant. Steep for not more than 3 to 4 minutes, using 1 teaspoon of dried flowers, or 3 teaspoons of fresh, to a 6-oz. or 8-oz. cup of boiling water.

**Bergamot** herbs make a sweet, citrus-flavored tea. It is best made by using 1 teaspoon of dried flowers per cupful, and simmering gently for 5 or 6 minutes.

**Lavender** is not only a popular aromatherapy herb, but also a flavorful herb for tea. Use the flowers and steep according to the general method listed.

**Lemon verbena** is a tea for the lemon lover. For best results, use fresh leaves, about 1 tablespoon per 6-oz. or 8-oz. cup of boiling water. Steep for at least 5 minutes.

**And for those who enjoy soft drinks better...try this Ginger Ale Spritzer.** You'll need: 2 sprigs of crushed mint, a pint of ginger ale, pitcher, ice, and one lemon. Place the crushed mint in a pitcher filled with ice. Then add the juice from half of a lemon. Pour a pint of ginger ale into the pitcher, slice up remaining lemon, and add to the drink. Stir and serve immediately.

\*If making tea for the first time, you may want to experiment with the amount of herbs you use. Go for weak at first, as you can always make it stronger.

## BY RICHARD LEDERER
Contributing Editor

# DOING A NUMBER
# ON ENGLISH

Recently, some organizations in Germany joined forces to compile a list of the hundred words that best reflect the 20th century, *AIDS, beat, bikini, camping, comics, computer, design, . . . Holocaust, image, jeans, pop, . . . single, sex, star, stress* are just some of the English words that became part of the German language during the past hundred years and are featured in the list.

That's just one piece of evidence that English has become the closest thing that humankind has ever had to a universal language.

"I think that language is a mirror of history, and these words reflect that," said Karin Frank-Cyrus, head of the Society for German Language. "The English language has become a *lingua franca*, a language that the whole world understands."

It is said again and again these days that there are lies, damnable lies and statistics. Nonetheless, Americans are fascinated by statistics and take a special interest in facts that can be quantified. Allow me, then, to do a number on our glorious, uproarious English language. **Here are some essential facts about our English tongue, expressed statistically:**

# PERCENTAGE OF...

... the world's population 30 years ago who spoke English: **10.**

... the world's population who now speak English: **20.**

... those people who learned English as a second (or third or fourth) language: **51.5.** China has more English-speaking people than the United States.

... the world's English-speaking people who live in the largest English-speaking country, the United States: **20.**

... students in the European Union studying English: **83.**

... people in the European Union who are fluent in English: **75.**

... nonnative persons around the world who are fluent in English: **25.**

... all books in the world printed in English: **50.**

... international telephone calls made in English: **52.**

... radio programs broadcast worldwide in English: **60.**

... global box office receipts from films in English: **63.**

... global E-mail in English: **68.**

... international mail and telexes written and addressed in English: **70.**

... global computer text stored in English: **80.**

... Internet home pages in English: **85.**

... the 12,500 international organizations in the world that make use of the English language: **85.**

... those international organizations that use English exclusively: **33.**

... words in English that are borrowed from languages other than the original Anglo-Saxon: **75.** Borrowed words in English versus Anglo-Saxon words, expressed as a ratio: **3:1.**

... English words made from Latin word parts: **50.**

... the average English-speaking person's conversation made up of the most frequently used 737 words: **96.**

... all English words used throughout history that no longer exist: **85.**

# NUMBER OF...

... languages in the world: **approximately 3,000**.

... countries or territories in which English has official status: **87.**

... words listed in the Oxford English Dictionary: **616,500.**

... words added to English each year: **5,000.**

... words in the largest dictionaries of German, the world's second largest language: **185,000.**

... words in the largest dictionaries of Russian, the world's third largest language: **130,000.**

... words in the largest dictionaries of French, the world's fourth largest language: **100,000.**

... words the average English-speaking person actually recognizes: **10,000 to 20,000.**

# PUZZLES & BRAINTEASERS

## WHAT IS IT?

• What is the beginning of eternity; the end of time and space; the beginning to every end; and the end to every place?

• What lives in winter, dies in summer, and grows with its roots upwards?

• What is bought by the yard, but worn by the foot?

• What can you put in a person's left hand which he or she cannot possibly put or take in his/her right hand?

## COLOR QUIZ:
Which is greener: a STOPLIGHT or a 7-UP bottle?

## GRAMMATICAL QUIZ:
*Which is correct to say:* **"The yolk of the egg are white,"** or **"The yolk of the egg is white"**?

## *Light as a feather*
*What is light as a feather, but something no one can hold for very long?*

## How can it be?
A woman from New York married 10 different men from that city, yet she did not break any laws. None of these men died, and she never divorced. How was this possible?

## NUMBER FUN
What is the final number in the sequence below?

| 4 | 5 | 6 | 7 | 8 | 9 |
|----|----|----|----|----|----|
| 61 | 52 | 63 | 94 | 46 | ?? |

## Is a CAR a CAR?
When does a car cease to be a car?

## WET *then* DRY
What dries as it gets wet?

Give up? The answers are on page 55

# 12 Great Reasons to Own a Mantis Tiller

**1. Weighs just 20 pounds.** Mantis is a joy to use. It starts easily, turns on a dime, lifts nimbly over plants and fences.

**2. Tills like nothing else.** Mantis bites down a full 10" deep, churns tough soil into crumby loam, prepares seedbeds in no time.

**3. Has patented "serpentine" tines.** Our **patented** tine teeth spin at up to 240 RPM – twice as fast as others. Cuts through tough soil and vegetation like a chain saw through wood!

**4. Weeds faster than hand tools.** Reverse its tines and Mantis is a precision power weeder. Weeds an average garden in 20 minutes.

**5. Digs planting furrows.** With the optional Planter/Furrower, Mantis digs deep or shallow furrows for planting. Builds raised beds, too!

**6. Cuts neat borders.** Use the optional Border Edger to cut crisp edges for flower beds, walkways, around shrubs and trees.

**7. Dethatches your lawn.** Thatch on your lawn prevents water and nutrients from reaching the roots. The optional Dethatcher quickly removes thatch.

**8. Aerates your lawn, too.** For a lush, healthy carpet, the optional Aerator slices thousands of tine slits in your lawn's surface.

**9. Trims bushes and hedges!** Only Mantis has an optional 24" or 30" trimmer bar to prune and trim your shrubbery and small trees.

**10. The Mantis Promise.** Try any product that you buy directly from Mantis with **NO RISK!** If you're not completely satisfied, send it back to us within one year for a complete, no hassle refund.

**11. Warranties.** The entire tiller is warranted for two full years. The tines are guaranteed forever against breakage.

**12. Fun to use.** The Mantis Tiller/Cultivator is so much fun to use gardeners everywhere love their Mantis tillers.

### For FREE details, call
### TOLL FREE 1-800-366-6268

# Helpful Hints

## Prevent Panty Hose RUNS with Salt!

Prevent panty hose from getting "runners" by doing the following: hand wash new panty hose and drip-dry. Then mix 2 cups of salt in 1 gallon of water, and soak the washed and dried panty hose in the mixture for 3 to 4 hours. Drip-dry again.

## ACTIVE Children?

Busy children should drink at least 6 glasses (8 oz. each) of fluid a day. Water is best and juice is also good. Avoid soda as it causes bloating, nausea, cramps, and can dehydrate.

### Recycled coffee mugs
Chipped, colorful mugs or cups make great planters.

### Homemade insecticide
Rubbing alcohol is a good insecticide for mealy bugs. Simply dip a cotton swab in alcohol and then touch each bug with the cotton tip. Repeat if necessary.

### Cooking tip
Rinse pan in cold water before scalding milk to prevent sticking.

### Best buy
When batteries go on sale, buy by the dozen. The shelf life of batteries is about 5 years.

## Like Fish But NOT Its Odor?

To remove fish odors from hands, use one teaspoon baking soda to one quart of water.

### Frost-free mirrors
No garage? If winter weather tends to leave your car covered by frost, try covering the side-view mirrors with plastic bags. To attach the bags, use clothes pins. The mirrors will be frost-free in the morning (one less place to scrape!).

## PROTECT YOUR SPRING CROCUSES!

Squirrels like to eat crocus bulbs that have been newly planted. To protect them, place a screen or chicken wire over planted bulbs. Remove it when the bulbs begin to sprout.

# Helpful Hints

## To prevent frostbite
Dress in layers. Clothing should fit loosely. Be certain to cover your head, neck, face, and ears. Don't forget to protect your hands and feet. Mittens are best, and wool socks are recommended. Get enough fluids before venturing out in the cold, as dehydration increases your chances of frostbite or hypothermia. Safeguard your skin (face, ears) with a waterproof skin cream.

## Laundry tip
Wash delicates in baby shampoo.

## NO BROWN FRUIT!
To keep APPLES and BANANAS from turning brown in a salad, drizzle PINEAPPLE juice over them.

## Wrapping paper tip
When wrapping a large package or gift, measure the item with a piece of string before cutting. Then use the string to cut the correct amount of paper.

## No more sticky mess
To remove the sticky substances left by cellophane tape, price tags or labels, rub the spots with pure lemon or orange extract. This also works well for stuck-on chewing gum.

## No more scrubbing
Next time you have a baked-on, messy cooking pan, fill the cooled pan with water, place a fabric softener (dryer) sheet in the water, and then let it soak overnight. The next morning, you'll be able to remove the sticky, baked-on food easily, without a lot of scrubbing.

## Greaseless hands
Put your hand inside a waxed sandwich bag when greasing your baking pans or casserole dishes.

## Quicker Grilling Time

Love to barbecue but hate how long it takes? Try microwaving, boiling, or steaming foods before you head to the grill. It reduces grilling time, but still gives food that grilled flavor.

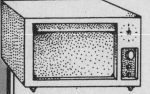

## Best microwave muffins
Use double paper muffin liners to microwave muffins as they will help absorb moisture.

## Tastes and smells great
Add a great scent to yellow or white cake by placing a rose geranium leaf in the bottom of the cake pan before pouring in the batter.

## Fish on the grill
For an easy, yet tasty, grilled fish, simply wrap the fish, a slice of lemon, and a sprig of dill in a piece of foil. Then grill.

## Homemade, Gentle
## KITCHEN CLEANER
For a gentle but effective kitchen cleaner, blend 1 cup of salt with 1 cup of baking soda. Store in a covered container. This works wonderfully as a scouring powder.

## • AUTUMN •

### Fresh Apple Omelet

1/4 cup sugar
1/4 tsp. cinnamon
3 tbsp. flour
1/4 tsp. baking powder
Dash of salt
2 eggs, separated
3 tbsp. sugar
3 tbsp. milk
2 egg yolks, well beaten
1 tbsp. lemon juice
1 large unpared red apple,
    thinly sliced

Mix together sugar and cinnamon, and set aside. Sift flour, baking powder and salt into a small bowl. In a medium bowl, beat egg whites until foamy. Gradually add in sugar, beating until stiff peaks form. Beat together milk and egg yolks until smooth, then add to flour mixture. Fold in lemon juice and egg whites. Pour batter into a preheated, buttered, oven-proof 10-inch skillet, spreading evenly. Arrange apples on top and sprinkle with sugar-cinnamon mix. Bake in 375°F oven for 10 minutes or until top is glazed. Cut into wedges and serve warm.

— Peter Bruno,
Somerville, New Jersey

### Cranberry Meatballs

2 lbs. ground beef
1 cup bread crumbs
1/4 tsp. pepper
1/4 tsp. garlic salt
1 medium onion, chopped
1/2 cup parsley
2 tbsp. soy sauce
1 cup cranberry sauce
1 cup ketchup
1 tbsp. lemon juice
2 tbsp. brown sugar

Mix ground beef with bread crumbs, pepper, garlic salt, chopped onion, and parsley. Form into meatballs and place in a 9" x 12" baking pan. Combine soy sauce, cranberry sauce, ketchup, lemon juice and brown sugar. Pour sauce over meatballs and bake for 45 minutes at 350°F.

— Marion Schwab,
Bethlehem, Pennsylvania

## • WINTER •

### Breakfast Scones

3 cups packaged biscuit mix
2 tbsp. sugar
1/2 cup chopped raisins or
    cranberries
1 cup milk
*Glaze (optional)*
3 tbsp. sugar
1/4 tsp. cinnamon
1 tbsp. butter, melted
1 tbsp. cream or milk

Combine biscuit mix, sugar and raisins, and mix well.

With a fork, stir in milk to make soft dough. Drop heaping tablespoons of the dough, 1 inch apart, on a greased cookie sheet. Bake 15 minutes in an oven pre-heated to 425°F. Serve warm. Glaze if desired. Cream together glaze ingredients to make a paste. Brush over warm scones. Bake 2 minutes longer, until lightly browned. Serve warm.

— Jane Martin,
Wilmington, Delaware

### Hamburger Soup

1 lb. ground beef
8 oz. tomato sauce
3 cups water
3 carrots, peeled and sliced
1 onion, chopped
3 medium potatoes, peeled
    and cut into 3/4" cubes
1 tsp. garlic powder
1 cup uncooked macaroni
1 small package frozen corn
1 small package frozen
    mixed vegetables
Salt and pepper

Brown beef in large soup pot. Drain well. Add tomato sauce, water, carrots, onion, potatoes, garlic powder and macaroni. Bring to a boil and simmer, stirring occasionally, until vegetables are cooked and macaroni is done. Add corn and mixed vegetables. Simmer until vegetables are tender. Add salt and pepper to taste.

— Charles Hanover,
Williamsport, Pennsylvania

## • SPRING •

### New Orleans Baked Carrots

8 or 9 carrots, peeled and
   cut into strips
1/2 cup onion, chopped
1/2 cup raisins
1 apple, peeled, cored and
   chopped
2 tbsp. honey
2 tbsp. butter, melted

Mix all ingredients in a
large bowl. Pour into a
casserole and cover. Bake
at 375°F for 40 to 45 minutes or until tender.

— Grace Weston,
Baton Rouge, Louisiana

### Daffodil Dip

1/2 cup mayonnaise
8 oz. package cream
   cheese, softened
1/4 cup fresh parsley,
   chopped
2 tbsp. onion, chopped
1 hard-boiled egg yolk,
   pushed through a sieve
Pepper to taste

Gradually add the mayon-
naise to cream cheese, mixing well. Add parsley
and onion. Sprinkle with
sieved egg yolk. Makes
2 1/2 cups. Serve with raw
vegetables.

— Sharon Smith
Fort Myers, Florida

### Chocolate-Covered Easter Eggs

1/2 lb. butter, melted
2 lbs. confectioners' sugar
1/4 cup cold mashed pota-
   toes
1 tsp. vanilla
1/2 cup peanut butter
1/2 lb. semisweet choco-
   late bits

Thoroughly mix melted
butter, sugar, mashed potatoes, vanilla and peanut butter. Shape into an egg with
a teaspoon. Chill at least 2
hours or overnight. Melt
chocolate bits in double
boiler and dip cooled eggs.
Allow to chill 1 hour.

— Leigh Kale,
Summit, New Jersey

## • SUMMER •

### Strawberry Spinach Salad

1 package fresh spinach
1 pint strawberries
*Dressing*
1/2 cup sugar
2 tsp. sesame seeds
1 tbsp. poppy seeds
1 1/2 tsp. onion, chopped
1/4 tsp. Worcestershire
   sauce
1/2 tsp. paprika
1/2 cup vegetable oil
1/4 cup cider vinegar

Wash spinach and chop into
bite-sized pieces. Wash
and hull strawberries. Place
both in a bowl.

*Dressing*
Mix together sugar, sesame
seeds, poppy seeds, onion,
Worcestershire sauce, pa-
prika, vegetable oil and
cider vinegar. Toss with
spinach and strawberries,
then serve. Raspberries can
also be used.

— Deborah Morris,
Pennington, New Jersey

### Summer Squash Au Gratin

3 to 5 summer squash, cut
   into 1/4" to 1/2" rounds
1 cup green pepper chunks
1/2 cup onions, sliced thin
2 tbsp. olive oil
1 cup croutons
2 large tomatoes, chopped
Salt and pepper to taste
3/4 cup sharp cheddar
   cheese, grated

In a skillet, heat olive oil
over high heat and gently
sauté the squash, green
pepper and onion for 2-3
minutes. Add the croutons,
tomatoes and salt and pepper. Mix well, and continue
to cook for an additional
minute. Remove from heat
and place in a suitable
casserole dish. Top with the
cheese and place about 8"
under preheated broiler
until the cheese has just
melted. Serve as a side dish
or a light lunch!

— Donna Ponte,
West Gardiner, Maine

# PONDER THIS

❖ All the pet care books advise that it is important to have plenty of clean, fresh water for your dog. I did that. And the first thing my dog did when she got outdoors was to take a long drink out of a mud puddle!

❖ Who wouldn't like to have a golf club that gave you an extra 10 yards every time you hit the ball? Unless it was a putter.

❖ In the Stone Age, the hand that cradled the rock ruled the world.

❖ Winter in the northern United States is Mother Nature and Old Man Winter having a good old-fashioned snowball fight.

❖ You can't buy friendship, but enemies can sure cost you a bunch.

❖ The class was studying math. The teacher said, "I am going to introduce you children to something different. If 'X' is three carrots, and 'Y' is four potatoes, then 'A' is twice as many as 'Y'. Can anyone tell me what this is called?" Johnny: "It sounds like a recipe for alphabet soup to me."

Married in January's chilling time,
Widowed you'll be before your prime.
Married in February's sleety weather,
Life you'll tread in tune together.
Married when March winds shrill and roar,
Your home will be on foreign shore.
Married 'neath April's changeful skies,
A checkered path before you lies.
Married when bees over May blossoms flit,
Strangers around your board will sit.
Married in merry month of June,
Life will be one honeymoon.
Married as July's flower banks blaze,
Bitter-sweet memories in after days.
Married in August heat and drowse,
Lover and friend in your chosen spouse.
Married in gold September glow,
Smooth and serene your life will flow.
Married when leaves in October thin,
Toil and hardships for you begin.
Married in veils of November mist,
Fortune your wedding ring has missed.
Married in days of December cheer,
Love will shine brighter year after year.

❖ WEDDING WEATHER LORE ❖

If choosing a date for the "big day" isn't hard enough, here's an old weather rhyme about getting married.

*By Michelle L. Gabriel, a freelance author in Waipahu, Hawaii*

# The lost art of doing nothing!

**H**ave you ever stopped to think about what a busy time we live in; rushing here and there, filling every waking moment with some type of chore or activity? Granted, not all activities are work or chore related; however, whatever happened to the days, hours, or even minutes of doing absolutely nothing? Have those times disappeared with the 1900s, or have we just forgotten how refreshing and how invigorating doing nothing can be?

While it is difficult to avoid or escape the hustle and bustle of our everyday lives, it is also important that we take some time out for doing absolutely nothing at all. But, because our society often frowns upon idle time, we have all become very proficient at filling every possible gap of free time with some distraction or activity. And thanks to modern conveniences, which, in one way or another, help take care of many of our daily survival needs (pizza delivery, microwave dinners, automatic washers and dryers,

**Are afternoons of lying in the grass pondering cloud shapes, evenings of watching sunsets, or mornings of counting snowflakes as they hit the window-pane all but extinct? Will we ever spend another hour or even a minute alone with our own thoughts? What incredible daydreams will never be had because we just simply do not have the time?**

etc.), we can get involved in more activities than ever (sometimes doing several at one time). Combine those activities with the advances in home entertainment equipment and we wind up with more and more ways to distract ourselves, and use up any and every quiet moment we might find.

Today, it seems as though we have fewer and fewer opportunities to do nothing, even if we wanted to. That seems to be even more reason to make the most of the little spare time we do have. You may really enjoy all the things you do to fill up those precious and few moments, but have you ever thought about just enjoying these times by NOT DOING ANYTHING?

Yet, many of us fear we will become bored if we do nothing. So, in a desperate attempt to not experience that boredom, we just keep searching for more activities to fill our precious free time.

But there are some real benefits of doing nothing. Think about how mentally and physically rewarding it is to stop and release the stress, fears, and worries of everyday life. The art of doing nothing gives us a time-out from everything—work, chores, responsibilities, and even favorite pastimes— and grants us the peace and joy of a few quiet moments to ourselves. It affords us the opportunity to shut down the conscious side of our brain (the thinking, logical side), and put the more creative other side to work (the side that enables us to hope, dream, and set lofty goals that we may or may not someday achieve).

## Interested?

If you feel that life is moving too fast and would like to rediscover the lost art of doing nothing, there is hope. And two good features about

doing nothing are that it doesn't have to cost a fortune, and it can be done right in your own home.

While some of you will immediately throw yourselves down in the grass of your backyards and start cloud watching, others may need practice before you can just lie there. If you need them, there are some definite steps you should follow (even doing nothing can have a training process). For some, the training will be mandatory, and may take only a few minutes, or a few months. Everyone will train in his or her own way. Regardless, you have to take the training seriously. There won't be an exam or anything, but the right training will reap the most fulfilling do-nothing time.

Finally, we will put doing nothing into practice. This may involve several baby steps, like finding ways to do nothing, losing our guilt about doing nothing, and even defending our right to do nothing. So, if you are still ready to give it a try, here are a few steps.

## Accept the need to do nothing

First, you must recognize that you really do need to slow down and make time for yourself. Sometimes we are so busy taking care of things for others that we don't take any time to recharge ourselves. You need to recognize this, and to see that life is too short to occupy every waking moment with activity. Ask yourself a few key questions like "When was the last time I spent an afternoon stretched out on a hammock, or spent an evening soaking in a tub?" What you ask about and how you answer will also be a good indicator for deciding if that something is how you would enjoy doing nothing.

*continued*

Evaluate all of the activities and chores that keep you busy during the day and consider which one or ones can be sacrificed (or pushed aside) so you can have some time for doing nothing. Pick the activity you like doing the least. This may pose a problem if that task is crucial to everyday survival (such as cooking, or going to work), so you may have to pick your second least favorite, one that will not adversely affect your life (or the lives of your family). Do not feel guilty about it. Finding the time to do nothing can be more important than doing that chore.

## Figure out how

Step two is figuring out how to do nothing—what it is that will enable us to take that time out for ourselves. To help clear your mind, you might choose to look at photos, listen to soft music, conjure up a memory of a happy time in your life, or even read about this subject. There is information out there on how to do nothing. One author has taken this topic very seriously and has published an entire book on the subject. In her book, *The Art of Doing Nothing: Simple Ways to Make Time For Yourself,* Veronique Vienne has written ninety-six pages about ways to make time to slow down and enjoy our lives. If you are the kind of person who has to read all about it first, this book could be an excellent way to get started. If not, there are still plenty of ways to figure out how to do nothing (and enjoy it).

Another way is to ask other people what they would do if they had to do nothing for an hour and wanted to make the time enjoyable. Remember to tell them sleeping is not permitted.

You may want to make a list to keep with you, in case you have a chance to do nothing sometime and can't easily think of a way to make that time enjoyable.

## Acceptance within and without

Finally, you have to accept that it's OK to do nothing. Now is the time to deal with any internal guilt you may have. Your conscience may be telling you, "I just can't do nothing," when there is a house to be cleaned, clothes to fold, a yard to mow, snow to shovel, paperwork to file, or E-mail messages to answer. You may feel guilty about abandoning your favorite TV show in favor of bird-watching. Relax! You will get to those chores and activities, all in due time. You need to remember that doing nothing is good for your well-being, and that there is nothing wrong with doing nothing.

When you start to favor doing nothing over one of your previous activities, other people's reactions may become an obstacle. You need to be prepared to educate them on the beauty of doing nothing. They may not see things your way at first, but persistence will usually pay off.

One approach for convincing people you are not crazy might be to invite a friend or family member to do nothing with you. Ask your best friend to join you to watch the leaves fall off the maple tree, or invite your spouse to watch a sunset with you. After they realize what a relaxing time they had, maybe they will join your crusade and introduce more people to this art of doing nothing.

After you have taken the steps to perfect doing nothing, you must not lose sight of this newfound hobby. You may need to repeat one of the steps occasionally, in order to remind yourself just how important and beneficial this art can be. The important thing is to just enjoy it! Doing nothing can be as relaxing and as satisfying as the funniest sitcom, most interesting Web site, or most challenging video game. Don't feel abnormal because watching logs burn down in the fireplace, counting geese flying south for the winter, or lying in a meadow daydreaming makes you feel on top of the world.

There is no better time than the present to put these steps into action and start doing nothing. How often in your life is someone going to tell you to go do nothing? So, go take advantage and get started. And the next time you have a stressful commute home or have spent a long day chaperoning multiple children at the mall, don't turn to the TV or computer for comfort. Sit down and do nothing at all.

... the character Raggedy Ann™ was created by Johnny Gruelle, an illustrator, cartoonist, and father? During the lengthy illness of his daughter, Marcella, he painted a new face on an old rag doll that Marcella had discovered in her grandmother's attic. He named the doll Raggedy Ann, after two poems, "The Raggedy Man" and "Little Orphant Annie," written by his friend James Whitcomb Riley. Gruelle told Marcella stories of Raggedy Ann's adventures to entertain her. After Marcella's death, Gruelle wrote, illustrated, and published the stories as a 25-book series. In 1918, he also began making and selling the very recognizable Raggedy Ann doll.

\* \* \*

... Mr. Potato Head™ was the first toy to be advertised on TV?

\* \* \*

... Silly Putty™ (that bounceable clay-like toy that comes in a plastic egg) was discovered by accident? During World War II, the General Electric Company was attempting to find a substitute for rubber, and inadvertently discovered Silly Putty.

## did you know

## Beware of Package Size!

 The size of a package can be deceptive. Sometimes the **"King," "Giant,"** and **"Family"** sizes are not bargains. Read the package carefully to find out how much you are buying. Compare the prices per ounce or per pound between different sizes and different brands.

**Do you know what "NET WEIGHT" means?**

All packaged items must indicate their "Net Weight," which is the weight of the product without the weight of its packaging, wrapping, or the containers used for prepackaging. Meat, cheese, fish and other items sold at deli counters are also weighed according to their net weight.

## Did you know?

**Another reason to avoid sunburn is that the burn can significantly slow your skin's ability to release excess heat.**

## Ever wonder where the X in Xmas came from?

It's not what you may think. The "X" is not an attempt to get away from associating "Christ" with Christmas; its origin is actually very religious in nature. It seems that the Greek word that gives us the English word "Christ" started with the letter "chi" or "X." The word "Xmas" itself was used as early as the mid-1500s.

## Make the E in E-mail stand for EFFICIENCY

You've got mail!

While E-mail allows instant communication, many of us spend more time than needed reading and responding to electronic messages. Here are a few tips on using E-mail more efficiently:

• Limit the number of times you check your E-mail. Twice a day may be the most efficient.

• Keep your personal and business E-mail separate. Limit or restrict personal E-mail to your home and work E-mail to your workplace. Avoid the temptation to check your personal E-mail address during the work day.

• Filter out the unsolicited E-mail advertisements you may receive. Many of these unwanted messages allow you to refuse their future E-mailings by replying to the first message.

• Organize addresses and messages with address book features and folders.

• Keep your messages simple. If a reply is needed, a simple "yes" or "no" will suffice in most cases.

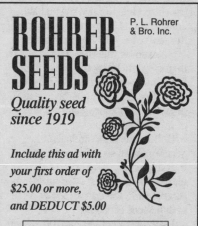

**HAVE A WEATHER-RELATED QUESTION?**
If so, write to Caleb's Comets, *Farmers' Almanac*,
P.O. Box 1609, Lewiston, ME 04241. Or E-mail:
caleb@farmersalmanac.com. Not all questions will
be published; however, all will be answered.

# CALEB'S COMETS

### ❓ Why do you sometimes see the Moon during the day?

Actually, you can see almost any celestial object in the daytime sky, provided the object is bright enough and large enough. The Moon fills both requirements.

As another example, the planet Venus is readily visible in the daytime, especially when near its greatest brilliancy. Unfortunately, Venus is nothing more than a speck in the sky, so you have to know EXACTLY where to look against the "sea of blue sky" in order to see it.

Supernovae (massive stars that blow themselves to bits at the end of their lives) have also been visible in the daytime. Two examples are the Guest Star of AD 1054 in Taurus, and Tycho's Star of 1572 in Cassiopeia.

Brilliant meteors (fireballs) have, on occasion, been seen flaring across the daytime sky. One such meteor blazed a path above the Grand Tetons in August 1972, and was witnessed by tens of thousands of people.

Lastly, a few comets have been seen in the daytime. The Great Comets of 1843 and 1882 were readily visible even when next to the Sun. (They likely were at least 100 times more brilliant than a full Moon; the 1882 comet was, in fact, compared to the flame emitted by a smelting furnace!)

### ❓ How does it decide to rain or snow? Sometimes the air temperature is 32° F and we get rain, while other times it's 33° F and it snows?

Much depends not only on the temperature at ground level (where you happen to be), but also on the temperature of the air above you. Sometimes — especially during March and April— there can be a layer of very cold air several thousand feet above you. As the atmosphere warms, this cold layer of air becomes increasingly unstable, which can eventually cause some form of precipitation. If at the higher altitudes it is below freezing, the precipitation falls as snow. Near the ground, there might be a very shallow layer of warmer-than-freezing air. As the snowflakes descend through the warmer air, they don't have enough time to fully melt; instead they turn into very large snowflakes (sometimes the size of silver dollars!). In such very special conditions, you can have a snow fall, even if your backyard thermometer is reading well above freezing.

This is reversed when there is a very shallow layer of below-freezing air near the ground, while the air several thousand feet above you is unusually mild and warm. Precipitation that falls is liquid (rain). Upon falling into the shallow, cold layer near the ground, either it freezes upon contact with surfaces, forming a glaze (freezing rain), or the raindrop itself freezes before hitting the ground (sleet).

### ❓ How do people know when it will be a full Moon?

Astronomers determine the moment of a full Moon based on the Moon's position in relation to the Sun. When the Moon is exactly opposite in the sky to the Sun (180 degrees apart), it is deemed a full Moon. At that moment, the Sun is setting in the west and the Moon is coming up in the east, and the Moon's disk is fully (100%) illuminated. Some hours before or after the moment of full Moon, the Moon is ever-so-slightly out of round and its illumination is only 99.8% of full. Most folks, however, refer to the Moon as full not only on the day it is actually full, but also on the day before, since it is hard to see the difference.

### ❓ I've heard that there is a theory that crops shouldn't be planted until the three ice men come. I think this refers to three saint's days in May. Do you have any details on this lore?

The "Three Ice Men" to whom you refer are most likely Saint Mammertius, Saint Pancratius and Saint Gervatius whose respective feast days occur on May 11, 12, and 13. They are also sometimes referred to as the "Three Chilly Saints." An old French saying states that: "St. Mammertius, St. Pancratius and St. Gervatius do not pass without a frost." You could presume that in Europe's not-too-distant past, parts of it were rather cold through the middle of May. Hence, the legend of the Three Ice Men (or Three Chilly Saints) was created.

# HOW OUR
# WEATHER
# FORECASTS
## ARE MADE

Our weather forecasts are made by **"Caleb Weatherbee"** by means of a long-standing (and secret) formula which goes back to the early 1800s, when the *Farmers' Almanac* was founded. The very first weather prognostications were made by David Young, the Almanac's first editor. In this formula, many factors are taken into consideration: Sunspots, Moon Phases, etc. It has been passed from calculator to calculator and has never been revealed. The formula itself is locked in the heart and mind of its calculator.

**Experience is the best teacher in choosing quality, but here are a few pointers on buying some fruits and vegetables.**

TIPS ON BUYING FRESH FRUITS AND VEGETABLES

**ASPARAGUS:** Stalks should be tender and firm, tips should be close and compact. Choose the stalks with very little white as they are more tender.

**BERRIES:** Select plump, solid berries with good color. Avoid stained containers, indicating wet or leaky berries. Berries such as blackberries and raspberries with clinging caps may be under-ripe. Strawberries without caps may be too ripe.

**BROCCOLI, BRUSSELS SPROUTS, AND CAULIFLOWER:** Flower clusters on broccoli and cauliflower should be tight and close together. Brussels sprouts should be firm and compact. Smudgy, dirty spots may indicate insects.

**CABBAGE AND HEAD LETTUCE:** Choose heads heavy for size. Avoid cabbage with worm holes, lettuce with discoloration or soft rot.

**CUCUMBERS:** Choose long, slender cucumbers for best quality. May be dark or medium green, but yellowed ones are undesirable.

**MELONS:** In cantaloupes, thick close netting on the rind indicates best quality. Cantaloupes are ripe when the stem scar is smooth and space between the netting is yellow or yellow-green. They are best when fully ripe with fruity odor. Honeydews are ripe when rind has creamy to yellowish color and velvety texture. Immature honeydews are whitish-green. Ripe watermelons have some yellow color on one side. If melons are white or pale green on one side, they are not ripe.

**ORANGES, GRAPEFRUITS, AND LEMONS:** Choose those heavy for their size. Smoother, thinner skins usually indicate more juice. Most skin markings do not affect quality. Oranges with a slight greenish tinge may be just as ripe as fully colored ones. Light or greenish-yellow lemons are more tart than deep yellow ones. Avoid citrus fruits showing withered, sunken, or soft areas.

**PEAS AND LIMA BEANS:** Select pods that are well-filled, but not bulging. Avoid dried, spotted, yellowed, or flabby pods.

# EMBEDDED IMAGES

***Rotate this page...*** In addition to the chalice there are **4** things to look for. How good are you at spotting these? Answers are on page 55.

## ❦ SIGNS OF THE TIMES ❦

Sign on an electrician's truck: "Voltswagon."

Sign in a shoe repair store: "We bring back departed soles."

Seen on a garden supply store window: "Let your mind go to seed."

Sign in a photo lab: "Some day your prints will come."

Sign on a barbershop window: "It's longer than you think."

Sign on a diaper delivery truck: "We offer bottom prices."

# A Gardener's

By **Eliot Tozer**

Freelance author for the National Gardening Association

It's late fall. The sky is blue, and the sun is bright. Then your local weather forecaster ruins everything with these chilling words: "Possible frost tonight." Once the initial panic subsides, reason sets in. Frost is a local event, and it's possible to predict with considerable certainty whether it will hit the plants in your garden. So relax, walk outside, and pay attention to these six signs that predict the likelihood of frost. Then, if necessary, spring into action.

**1. LOOK SKYWARD.** Frost (also called white or hoarfrost) occurs when air temperatures dip below 32°F and ice crystals form on plant leaves, injuring, and sometimes killing, tender plants. Clear, calm skies and falling afternoon temperatures are usually the perfect conditions for frost. If temperatures are falling fast under clear, windy skies—especially when the wind is out of the northwest—it may indicate the approach of a mass of polar air and a hard freeze. A hard or killing frost is based on movements of large, cold air masses. The result is below-freezing temperatures that generally kill all but the most cold-tolerant plants.

But if you see clouds in the sky—especially if they are lowering and thickening—you're in luck. During the day, the sun's radiant heat warms the earth. After sunset, the heat radiates upward, lowering temperatures near the ground. However, if the night is overcast, the clouds act like a blanket, trapping the heat and keeping air temperatures warm enough to prevent frost.

**2. FEEL THE BREEZE.** Wind also influences the likelihood of frost. In the absence of wind, the coldest air settles to the ground. The temperature at plant level may be freezing, even though at eye level it isn't. A gentle breeze, however, will prevent this settling, keeping temperatures higher, and saving your plants. Of course, if the wind itself is below freezing, you'll probably have fried green tomatoes for tomorrow's supper.

**3. CHECK THE MOISTURE.** Just as clouds and gentle winds are your friends, so humidity and moisture. When moisture condenses out of humid air, it releases heat. Not much heat, true, but perhaps enough to save the cleomes. If the air is dry, though, the moisture in the soil will evaporate. Evaporation requires heat, so this removes warmth that could save your peppers.

**DO CONSIDER DEW** The dew point is the temperature at which the air is totally saturated with moisture and begins to condense. Television and radio meteorologists may state the dew point temperature during routine forecasts. The more moisture the air contains, the higher the temperature will be when the moisture starts to condense as dew, producing heat. And, obviously, the higher the temperature, the less chance of frost. For example, a dew point of 43°F almost certainly means no frost that night. Interestingly enough, frost is more likely to form on a dry evening when the air temperature is a warmish 50°F and the dew point is a low 33°F than when the air temperature is a cooler 43°F and the dew point is 41°F.

# Guide to Frost

**4. CHECK YOUR GARDEN'S LOCATION.** This can have a tremendous influence on the likelihood that an early frost could wipe out your garden, while leaving your next-door neighbor's untouched. As a general rule, the temperature drops 3°F to 5°F with every 1,000-foot increase in altitude. The higher your garden, the colder the average air temperature, and the more likely your plants will be hit by an early freeze. So gardening on a hilltop isn't a great idea, but neither is gardening at the lowest spot on your property. Since cold air is heavier than warm air, it tends to sink to the lowest areas, causing frost damage. The best location for an annual garden is on a gentle, south-facing slope that's well heated by late-afternoon sun and protected from blustery north winds. A garden surrounded by buildings or trees or one near a body of water is also less likely to become frost covered.

**5. SCRUTINIZE THE SOIL.** Your garden's soil type affects the amount of moisture it holds and your plants' ability to withstand cold weather. Deep, loose, heavy, fertile soil releases more moisture into the surrounding air than thin or sandy or nutrient-poor soil. The more humid the air is, the higher the dew point will be, and the less likely that frost will form on those plants. Heavily mulched plants are more likely to become frosted, since the mulch prevents moisture and heat from escaping out of the soil and warming the surrounding air. (Light-colored mulches, such as hay or straw, have the additional disadvantage of reflecting sunlight and heat during the day.)

**6. KNOW YOUR PLANTS.** The plant itself determines its likelihood of frost damage. Immature plants still sporting new growth into the fall are most susceptible—especially the new growth. Frost tolerance tends to be higher in plants with maroon or bronze leaves, because such leaves absorb and retain heat. Downy- or hairy-leaved plants also retain heat. Compact plants expose a smaller proportion of their leaves to cold and drying winds. By the same token, closely spaced plants protect each other.

## What's a Gardener to Do?

So you've checked the weather conditions and decided that, yes, Jack Frost is coming, and protecting your plants is worthwhile. You'll want to do two things. First, cover your plants, both to retain as much soil heat and moisture as possible and to protect them against strong winds, which can hasten drying and cooling. Use almost anything to cover plants: newspapers, bushel baskets, plastic tarps, straw, or pine boughs. Spun-bonded fabric row covers will protect plants down to 30°F, polyethylene row covers to 28°F. Cover the whole plant before sunset to trap any remaining heat. Lightweight coverings such as row covers and newspaper should be anchored to prevent them from blowing away.

*continued*

Second, keep the soil moist by watering your plants the day a frost is predicted. Commercial fruit and vegetable growers leave sprinklers on all night to cover plants with water. As the water freezes, it releases heat, protecting the plants, even though they're covered by ice. To prevent damage, the sprinklers need to run continuously as long as temperatures remain below freezing.

And as you survey your garden's fading glory, you may take heart from the experience of John Loudon, a 19th-century British horticulturist. Loudon stuck four stakes into a plot of grass to support a cambric handkerchief six inches above the surface and found that the temperature beneath the handkerchief remained 9°F higher than the temperature of the surrounding air. Yes, you can beat the frost—at least for a few nights.

This story was orignally published in *National Gardening Magazine*.
Contact NGA's Web site at **www.garden.org** for more articles on a variety of gardening topics, weekly gardening tips, and to have your gardening questions answered.

| COLD TEMPERATURE EFFECTS ON PLANTS AND VEGETATION |
| --- |
| **FROST:** Damage depends upon length of frost duration. |
| **LIGHT FREEZE:** 29°F to 32°F / -2°C to 0°C  Tender plants killed with little destructive effect on other vegetation. |
| **MODERATE FREEZE:** 25°F to 28°F / -4°C to -2°C  Wide destruction on most vegetation with heavy damage to fruit blossoms and tender semihardy plants. |
| **SEVERE FREEZE:** 24°F / -4°C and colder  Heavy damage to most plants. |

# AVERAGE FROST DATES

The dates listed here are normal averages for a light freeze/frost in selected towns. The definition of a light freeze is when the temperatures are between 29 and 32 degrees F. During a light frost, tender plants may be killed, with little destructive effect on more hardy vegetation.

There is a **50% probability** that a frost may occur **after the spring date** and **before the fall date listed** (as well as a 50% chance one could happen earlier in the spring or later in the fall). Frost dates were taken from *Climatography of the U.S. No. 20, Supplement No. 1*, published in 1988 by the National Climatic Data Center, National Oceanic and Atmospheric Administration.

| CITY | LAST SPRING FROST | FIRST FALL FROST | CITY | LAST SPRING FROST | FIRST FALL FROST |
|------|-------------------|------------------|------|-------------------|------------------|
| Birmingham, AL | Mar 29 | Nov 6 | Sandpoint, ID | May 20 | Sep 17 |
| Mobile, AL | Feb 27 | Nov 26 | Chicago, IL | Apr 14 | Nov 2 |
| Fairbanks, AK | May 17 | Sep 6 | Galesburg, IL | Apr 22 | Oct 15 |
| Juneau, AK | May 16 | Sep 26 | Mount Vernon, IL | Apr 14 | Oct 21 |
| Flagstaff, AZ | Jun 13 | Sep 21 | Quincy, IL | Apr 15 | Oct 21 |
| Phoenix, AZ | Feb 5 | Dec 15 | Springfield, IL | Apr 17 | Oct 19 |
| Tucson, AZ | Feb 28 | Nov 29 | Evansville, IN | Apr 9 | Oct 26 |
| Jonesboro, AR | Mar 29 | Nov 5 | Indianapolis, IN | Apr 22 | Oct 20 |
| Pine Bluff, AR | Mar 19 | Nov 8 | South Bend, IN | May 1 | Oct 18 |
| Escondido, CA | Feb 19 | Dec 10 | Cedar Rapids, IA | Apr 29 | Oct 7 |
| Red Bluff, CA | Feb 22 | Dec 1 | Davenport, IA | Apr 14 | Oct 27 |
| Sacramento, CA | Feb 14 | Dec 1 | Fort Dodge, IA | May 2 | Oct 6 |
| San Bernardino, CA | Feb 23 | Dec 8 | Great Bend, KS | Apr 17 | Oct 24 |
| Tahoe City, CA | Jun 17 | Sep 15 | Topeka, KS | Apr 21 | Oct 14 |
| Aspen, CO | Jun 14 | Sep 7 | Bowling Green, KY | Apr 13 | Oct 21 |
| Denver, CO | May 3 | Oct 8 | Frankfort, KY | Apr 22 | Oct 21 |
| Glenwood Springs, CO | May 22 | Sep 25 | Lexington, KY | Apr 17 | Oct 25 |
| Danbury, CT | Apr 30 | Oct 6 | Owensboro, KY | Apr 10 | Oct 21 |
| Hartford, CT | Apr 25 | Oct 10 | Alexandria, LA | Mar 5 | Nov 16 |
| Norfolk, CT | May 14 | Oct 2 | Hammond, LA | Mar 15 | Nov 10 |
| Dover, DE | Apr 9 | Oct 28 | Monroe, LA | Mar 9 | Nov 7 |
| Lewes, DE | Apr 13 | Oct 27 | Augusta, ME | Apr 28 | Oct 8 |
| Wilmington–New Castle, DE | Apr 13 | Oct 29 | Lewiston, ME | Apr 27 | Oct 15 |
| Jacksonville Beach, FL | Feb 14 | Dec 14 | Portland, ME | May 10 | Sep 30 |
| Tallahassee, FL | Mar 12 | Nov 14 | Baltimore, MD | Mar 26 | Nov 13 |
| Augusta, GA | Mar 28 | Nov 6 | Hagerstown, MD | Apr 18 | Oct 18 |
| Columbus, GA | Mar 21 | Nov 9 | New Bedford, MA | Apr 6 | Nov 10 |
| Savannah, GA | Mar 10 | Nov 15 | Springfield, MA | Apr 19 | Oct 15 |
| Boise, ID | May 8 | Oct 9 | Worcester, MA | Apr 27 | Oct 17 |
| Idaho City, ID | Jun 25 | Aug 31 | Adrian, MI | May 4 | Oct 7 |
| Moscow, ID | May 23 | Sep 23 | Gaylord, MI | May 28 | Sep 18 |

# AVERAGE FROST DATES

| CITY | LAST SPRING FROST | FIRST FALL FROST | CITY | LAST SPRING FROST | FIRST FALL FROST |
|------|-------------------|------------------|------|-------------------|------------------|
| Kalamazoo, MI | May 1 | Oct 14 | Muskogee, OK | Apr 1 | Nov 2 |
| Grand Rapids, MN | May 26 | Sep 16 | Tulsa, OK | Mar 30 | Nov 4 |
| Willmar, MN | May 4 | Oct 4 | Eugene, OR | Apr 24 | Oct 25 |
| Hattiesburg, MS | Mar 17 | Nov 8 | Klamath Falls, OR | Jun 7 | Sep 22 |
| Tupelo, MS | Apr 1 | Oct 25 | Portland, OR | Apr 3 | Nov 7 |
| Vicksburg, MS | Mar 13 | Nov 18 | Allentown, PA | Apr 21 | Oct 18 |
| Jefferson City, MO | Apr 26 | Oct 16 | Johnstown, PA | Apr 27 | Oct 14 |
| Mexico, MO | Apr 21 | Oct 18 | Block Island, RI | Apr 10 | Nov 11 |
| Poplar Bluff, MO | Apr 6 | Oct 23 | Kingston, RI | May 8 | Sep 30 |
| Bozeman, MT | May 30 | Sep 16 | Charleston, SC | Feb 17 | Dec 10 |
| Helena, MT | May 18 | Sep 18 | Columbia, SC | Mar 30 | Nov 1 |
| Superior, MT | May 22 | Sep 18 | Florence, SC | Mar 23 | Nov 4 |
| Grand Island, NE | Apr 29 | Oct 9 | Eureka, SD | May 16 | Sep 23 |
| North Platt, NE | May 11 | Sep 24 | Hot Springs, SD | May 18 | Sep 20 |
| Scottsbluff, NE | May 7 | Sep 29 | Chattanooga, TN | Apr 5 | Nov 1 |
| Las Vegas, NV | Mar 7 | Nov 21 | Knoxville, TN | Mar 29 | Nov 6 |
| Reno, NV | Jun 1 | Sep 16 | Memphis, TN | Mar 23 | Nov 7 |
| Concord, NH | May 23 | Sep 22 | Nashville, TN | Apr 5 | Oct 29 |
| Keene, NH | May 19 | Sep 25 | Amarillo, TX | Apr 14 | Oct 29 |
| Nashua, NH | May 17 | Sep 24 | Austin, TX | Mar 3 | Nov 28 |
| Cape May, NJ | Mar 30 | Nov 10 | Lubbock, TX | Apr 8 | Nov 1 |
| Lambertville, NJ | Apr 28 | Oct 15 | San Antonio, TX | Mar 3 | Nov 24 |
| Sussex, NJ | May 9 | Oct 2 | Cedar City, UT | May 20 | Oct 2 |
| Trenton, NJ | Apr 6 | Nov 7 | Logan, UT | May 7 | Oct 12 |
| Gallup, NM | May 26 | Sep 29 | Ogden, UT | May 4 | Oct 13 |
| Lordsburg, NM | Apr 22 | Oct 30 | Burlington, VT | May 11 | Oct 1 |
| Albany, NY | May 7 | Sep 29 | Montpelier, VT | May 18 | Sep 23 |
| Elmira, NY | May 14 | Oct 2 | Newport, VT | May 20 | Sep 24 |
| Lake Placid, NY | Jun 4 | Sep 11 | Fredericksburg, VA | Apr 21 | Oct 15 |
| Central Park, NYC | Apr 1 | Nov 11 | Norfolk, VA | Mar 23 | Nov 17 |
| Syracuse, NY | Apr 28 | Oct 16 | Richmond, VA | Apr 10 | Oct 26 |
| Watertown, NY | May 8 | Oct 6 | Seattle–Tacoma, WA | Mar 24 | Nov 11 |
| Asheville, NC | Apr 10 | Oct 24 | Spokane, WA | May 4 | Oct 5 |
| Greensboro, NC | Apr 11 | Oct 27 | Clarksburg, WV | May 3 | Oct 10 |
| Raleigh–Durham, NC | Apr 11 | Oct 27 | Oak Hill, WV | May 3 | Oct 10 |
| Bismarck, ND | May 14 | Sep 20 | Wheeling, WV | Apr 25 | Oct 27 |
| Grand Forks, ND | May 20 | Sep 20 | Appleton, WI | May 2 | Oct 13 |
| Akron–Canton, OH | May 3 | Oct 18 | Milwaukee, WI | May 5 | Oct 9 |
| Cincinnati, OH | Apr 14 | Oct 27 | Oshkosh, WI | May 8 | Oct 4 |
| Youngstown, OH | May 6 | Oct 14 | Casper, WY | May 22 | Sep 22 |
| Enid, OK | Apr 4 | Nov 3 | Rock Springs, WY | May 25 | Sep 16 |

# Planting & Gardening Calendar

NOTE: Each month the Moon passes through the 12 zodiac signs.
There are good signs and bad signs for planting, and each sign has a specific function.
This chart reflects the best time for planting and gardening where climate permits.

| | ABOVEGROUND CROPS | ROOT CROPS | SEED BEDS | TRANSPLANT | FLOWERS | KILL PLANT PESTS | SET EGGS |
|---|---|---|---|---|---|---|---|
| **JAN** | 1, 2, 5, 6, 24, 28, 29 | 9, 10, 15, 16, 17, 18, 19, 23 | 9, 10, 18, 19 | 1, 24-31 | 9, 10, 15, 16, 17 | 11, 12, 13, 14, 25, 26, 27 | 3-17 |
| **FEB** | 1, 2, 5, 6, 24, 25, 28 | 12, 13, 14, 15, 19, 20 | 5, 6, 14, 15 | 23-28 | 5, 6, 12, 13 | 7, 8, 9, 10, 11, 21, 22, 23 | 2-15 |
| **MAR** | 1, 5, 6, 24, 28, 29 | 11, 12, 13, 14, 15, 18, 19, 20, 23 | 5, 6, 13, 14, 15 | 1, 24-31 | 5, 6, 11, 12 | 7, 8, 9, 10, 21, 22 | 3-16 |
| **APR** | 1, 2, 24, 25 | 7, 8, 9, 10, 11, 15, 16, 20, 21 | 1, 2, 10, 11, 28, 29 | 23-29 | 1, 2, 7, 8, 9, 28, 29 | 3, 4, 5, 6, 17, 18, 19, 30 | 2-15 |
| **MAY** | 5, 6, 22, 25, 26 | 7, 8, 12, 13, 17, 18, 21 | 7, 8, 25, 26 | 22-28 | 5, 6, 25, 26 | 1, 2, 3, 4, 14, 15, 16, 27, 28, 29, 30, 31 | 1-14, 31 |
| **JUNE** | 1, 2, 3, 4, 22, 23, 28, 29, 30 | 5, 8, 9, 10, 13, 14, 15, 18, 19 | 3, 4, 5, 22, 23, 30 | 21-26 | 1, 2, 22, 23, 28, 29 | 11, 12, 24, 25, 26, 27 | 1, 13, 29, 30 |
| **JULY** | 1, 2, 20, 25, 26, 27, 28, 29 | 5, 6, 7, 10, 11, 12, 15, 16, 19 | 1, 2, 19, 20, 28, 29 | 20-26 | 19, 20, 25, 26, 27 | 8, 9, 21, 22, 23, 24 | 1-14, 28-31 |
| **AUG** | 2, 3, 22, 23, 24, 25, 26, 29, 30, 31 | 7, 8, 11, 12, 13, 16, 17 | 16, 17, 24, 25, 26 | 18-24 | 16, 17, 22, 23 | 4, 5, 6, 18, 19, 20, 21 | 1-11, 27-31 |
| **SEP** | 18, 19, 20, 21, 22, 25, 26, 27, 30 | 3, 4, 8, 9, 12, 13 | 12, 13, 20, 21, 22 | 17-23 | 12, 13, 18, 19 | 1, 2, 14, 15, 16, 17, 28, 29 | 1-10, 25-30 |
| **OCT** | 1, 16, 17, 18, 19, 23, 24, 28, 29 | 2, 5, 6, 9, 10 | 9, 10, 18, 19 | 16-22 | 9, 10, 16, 17 | 11, 12, 13, 14, 15, 25, 26, 27 | 1-10, 25-31 |
| **NOV** | 15, 16, 19, 20, 21, 24, 25, 26, 29 | 1, 2, 5, 6, 12, 13, 14, 30 | 5, 6, 14, 15, 16 | 15-21 | 5, 6, 12, 13 | 7, 8, 9, 10, 11, 22, 23 | 1-8, 23-30 |
| **DEC** | 16, 17, 18, 21, 22, 23, 26, 27 | 3, 4, 9, 10, 11, 12, 13, 30, 31 | 3, 4, 11, 12, 13, 30, 31 | 14-21 | 3, 4, 9, 10, 30, 31 | 5, 6, 7, 8, 19, 20 | 1-8, 23-31 |

# Why wait ten months?

## Now you can have rich, dark compost _in just 14 days!_

With the amazing Compos-Tumbler, you'll have bushels of crumbly, ready-to-use compost — _in just 14 days!_ (And, in the ten months it takes to make compost the old way, your ComposTumbler can produce _hundreds of pounds_ of rich food for your garden!)

Say good-bye to that messy, open compost pile (and to the flies, pests, and odors that come along with it!) Bid a happy farewell to the strain of trying to turn over heavy, wet piles with a pitch-fork.

### Compost the Better Way

Compost-making with the ComposTumbler is neat, quick and easy!

Gather up leaves, old weeds, kitchen scraps, lawn clippings, etc. and toss them into the roomy 18-bushel drum. Then, once each day, give the ComposTumbler's _gear-driven_ handle a few easy spins.

### The ComposTumbler's Magic

Inside the ComposTumbler, carefully positioned mixing fins blend materials, pushing fresh mixture to the core where the temperatures are the hottest (up to 160°) and the composting bacteria most active.

After just 14 days, open the door, and you'll find an abundance of dark, sweet-smelling "garden gold" — ready to enrich and feed your garden!

### NEW SMALLER SIZE!

Now there are 2 sizes. The 18-bushel original ComposTumbler and the NEW 9.5-bushel Compact ComposTumbler. Try either size risk-free for a full year!

**See for yourself! Try the ComposTumbler risk-free with our 1-Year Home Trial!**

**Call Toll-Free 1-800-880-2345**

## NOW ON SALE— SAVE UP TO $115!

## ComposTumbler®

_The choice of more than 250,000 gardeners_

☐ YES! Please rush FREE information on the ComposTumbler, including special savings and 1-Year Home Trial.

Name _____

Address _____

City _____

State _____ ZIP _____

MAIL TO: **ComposTumbler**
160 Koser Rd., **Dept. 45080C**
Lititz (Lancaster Co.), PA 17543

© 2000 PBM Group

*by*
# Joe Rao
*Farmers' Almanac*
## ASTRONOMER

## From Strawberries to Wolves,

# The Moon has it covered.

## Ever hear of a Full Strawberry Moon? How about a Wolf or Harvest Moon? Read on...

Full Moon names date back to Native Americans, of what is now the northern and eastern United States. The tribes kept track of the seasons by giving distinctive names to each recurring full Moon. Their names were applied to the entire month in which each occurred. There was some variation in the Moon names, but in general the same ones were current throughout the Algonquin tribes from New England to Lake Superior. European settlers followed that custom and created some of their own names.

Since the lunar month is only 29 days long on the average, the full Moon dates shift from year to year. Here is a listing of the full Moon names, as well as the dates for each full Moon during 2001.

■ **THE FULL WOLF MOON** January 9th, 3:24 p.m. EST Amid the cold and deep snows of midwinter, the wolf packs howled hungrily outside Indian villages. Thus, the name for January's full Moon. Sometimes it was also referred to as the Old Moon, or the Moon After Yule. Some called it the Full Snow Moon, but most tribes applied that name to the next Moon.

For those living in the Maritime Provinces of eastern Canada or the northeastern United States, the rising of the Wolf Moon of 2001 will coincide with the closing stages of a lunar eclipse. For these regions, the shadow of the Earth will be slipping off the Moon's disk as the Moon emerges from the east-northeast horizon.

■ **THE FULL SNOW MOON  February 8th, 2:11 a.m. EST** Since the heaviest snow usually falls during this month, native tribes of the north and east most often called February's full Moon the Full Snow Moon. Some tribes also referred to this Moon as the Full Hunger Moon, since harsh weather conditions in their areas made hunting very difficult.

This year's Full Snow Moon arrives almost at the same time that the Moon is at perigee (closest point to the Earth, 221,748 miles). The Moon's perigee will occur at 5 p.m. EST on February 7. Such a near coincidence of a full Moon with perigee will result in dramatically high and low ocean tides. Any coastal storm around this time will almost certainly aggravate coastal flooding problems. Such an extreme tide is known as a perigean spring tide.

While this will also be the biggest and brightest full Moon of 2001, the distance variation is not readily apparent to observers who view the Moon directly.

····················································································

■ **THE FULL WORM MOON  March 9th, 12:23 p.m. EST** As the temperature begins to warm and the ground begins to thaw, earthworm casts appear, heralding the return of the robins. The more northern tribes knew this Moon as the Full Crow Moon, when the cawing of crows signaled the end of winter; or the Full Crust Moon, because the snow cover becomes crusted from thawing by day and freezing at night. The Full Sap Moon, marking the time of tapping maple trees, is another variation. To the settlers, it was also known as the Lenten Moon, and was considered to be the last full Moon of winter.

····················································································

■ **THE FULL PINK MOON  April 7th, 10:21 p.m. EST** This name came from the herb moss pink, or wild ground phlox, which is one of the earliest widespread flowers of the spring. Other names for this month's celestial body include the Full Sprouting Grass Moon, the Egg Moon, and—among coastal tribes—the Full Fish Moon, because this was the time that the shad swam upstream to spawn.

In 2001, this is also the Paschal Full Moon, the first full Moon of spring, and the Moon that sets the date of Easter: The first Sunday after the first full Moon of spring is, in most cases, observed as Easter (April 15, 2001).

····················································································

■ **THE FULL FLOWER MOON  May 7th, 8:52 a.m. EST** In most areas, flowers are abundant everywhere during this time. Thus, the name of this Moon. Other names include the Full Corn Planting Moon, or the Milk Moon.

····················································································

■ **THE FULL STRAWBERRY MOON  June 5th, 8:39 p.m. EST** This name was universal to every Algonquin tribe. However, in Europe they called it the Rose Moon.

····················································································

■ **THE FULL BUCK MOON  July 5th, 10:03 a.m. EST** July is normally the month when the new antlers of buck deer push out of their foreheads in coatings of velvety fur. It was also often called the Full Thunder Moon, for the reason that thunderstorms are most frequent during this time. Another name for this month's Moon was the Full Hay Moon.

····················································································

■ **THE FULL STURGEON MOON  August 4th, 12:55 a.m. EST** The fishing tribes are given credit for the naming of this Moon, since sturgeon, a large fish of the Great Lakes and other major bodies of water, were most readily caught during this month. A few tribes knew it as the Full Red Moon because, as the Moon rises, it appears reddish through any sultry haze. It was also called the Green Corn Moon or Grain Moon.

····················································································

■ **THE FULL FRUIT OR BARLEY MOON  September 2nd, 4:43 p.m. EST** The names Fruit and Barley were reserved only for those years when the Harvest Moon is very late in September, or (as in 2001) in October. This year's most extreme apogee (the Moon's farthest distance from Earth, 252,493 miles) occurs nearly 11 hours earlier, at 6 p.m. on September 1st.

*continued*

■ **THE FULL HARVEST MOON** October 2nd, 8:48 a.m. EST This is the full Moon that occurs closest to the autumn equinox. In two years out of three, the Harvest Moon comes in September, but in some years (such as this year) it occurs in October. At the peak of harvest, farmers can work late into the night by the light of this Moon. Usually the full Moon rises an average of 50 minutes later each night, but for the few nights around the Harvest Moon, the Moon seems to rise at nearly the same time each night: just 25 to 30 minutes later across the U.S., and only 10 to 20 minutes later for much of Canada and Europe. Corn, pumpkins, squash, beans, and wild rice—the chief Indian staples—are now ready for gathering.

■ **THE FULL HUNTER'S MOON** November 1st, 12:41 a.m. EST With the leaves falling and the deer fattened, it is time to hunt. Since the fields have been reaped, hunters can easily see fox and the animals which have come out to glean.

■ **THE FULL BEAVER MOON** November 30th, 3:49 p.m. EST This was the time to set beaver traps before the swamps froze, to ensure a supply of warm winter furs. Another interpretation suggests that the name Full Beaver Moon comes from the fact that the beavers are now actively preparing for winter. It is sometimes also referred to as the Frosty Moon. In 2001, this Moon can also be called a "Blue Moon." *(See explanation below.)*

■ **THE FULL COLD MOON; OR THE FULL LONG NIGHTS MOON** December 30th, 5:40 a.m. EST During this month the winter cold fastens its grip, and nights are at their longest and darkest. It is also sometimes called the Moon before Yule (although in 2001 this full Moon comes just after Christmas). The term Long Night Moon is a doubly appropriate name because the midwinter night is indeed long, and because the Moon is above the horizon for a long time. The midwinter full Moon has a high trajectory across the sky because it is opposite a low Sun.

## WHAT IS A BLUE MOON?

For more than half a century, whenever two full Moons appeared in a single month (which happens on average every 3 1/2 years), the second has been christened a "Blue Moon." In our lexicon, we describe an unusual event as happening "Once in a Blue Moon." This expression was first noted back in 1821 and refers to occurrences that are uncommon, though not truly rare.

Under that rule, in 2001, the full Moon of November 30 should be christened a Blue Moon, though the Moon on that night will look no different than any other full Moon. On past occasions, usually after vast forest fires or major volcanic eruptions, the Moon has reportedly taken on a bluish or lavender hue. Soot and ash particles, propelled high into the Earth's atmosphere, can sometimes make the Moon appear bluish (but that should not be the case for this year's Blue Moon).

### Why "Blue" Moon?

For the longest time nobody knew exactly why the second full Moon of a calendar month was designated as a Blue Moon. One explanation connects it with the word "belewe" from the Old English, meaning, "to betray." Perhaps, then, the Moon was "belewe" because it betrayed the usual perception of one full Moon per month.

However, in the March 1999 issue of *Sky & Telescope* magazine, author Phillip Hiscock revealed one somewhat confusing

# PHASES OF THE MOON

■ **NEW MOON** The Moon is not illuminated by direct sunlight.

■ **WAXING CRESCENT** The visible Moon is partly, but less than one-half, illuminated by direct sunlight while the illuminated part is increasing.

■ **FIRST QUARTER** One-half of the Moon appears illuminated by direct sunlight while the illuminated part is increasing.

■ **WAXING GIBBOUS** The Moon is more than one-half, but not fully, illuminated by direct sunlight while the illuminated part is increasing.

■ **FULL MOON** The visible Moon is fully illuminated by direct sunlight.

■ **WANING GIBBOUS** The Moon is less than fully, but more than one-half, illuminated by direct sunlight while the illuminated part is decreasing.

■ **LAST QUARTER** One-half of the Moon appears illuminated by direct sunlight while the illuminated part is decreasing.

■ **WANING CRESCENT** The Moon is partly, but less than one-half, illuminated by direct sunlight while the illuminated part is decreasing.

origin of this term. It seems that the modern custom of naming the second full Moon of a month "blue," came from an article published in the March 1946 *Sky & Telescope* magazine. The article was "Once in a Blue Moon," written by James Hugh Pruett. In this article, Pruett interpreted what he read in a publication known as the *Maine Farmers' Almanac* (no relation to this *Farmers' Almanac*, published in Lewiston, Maine), and declared that a second full Moon in a calendar month is a "Blue Moon."

However, after reviewing the *Maine Farmer's Almanac*, Hiscock found that during the editorship of Henry Porter Trefethen (1932 to 1957), the *Maine Farmers' Almanac* made occasional reference to a Blue Moon, but derived it from a completely different (and rather convoluted) seasonal rule. As simply as can be described, according to Trefethen's almanac, there are normally three full Moons for each season of the year. But when a particular season ends up containing four full Moons, then the third of that season is called a Blue Moon! To make matters more confusing, the beginning of the seasons listed in Trefethen's almanac were

fixed. A fictitious or dynamical mean Sun produced four seasons of equal length with dates which differed slightly from more conventional calculations.

So, basically the current use of "Blue Moon" to mean the second full Moon in a month can be traced to a 55-year-old mistake in *Sky & Telescope* magazine. But now a question: just when should we celebrate the next Blue Moon? According to the long-forgotten rules of Trefethen's almanac, the next Blue Moon will come on November 19, 2002.

But what about the Blue Moon scheduled for November 30th of this year? Unfortunately, with many years of popular usage now behind it, the second-full-Moon-in-a-month rule is like the proverbial genie that can't be forced back into its bottle. So which then should we use? Perhaps, as some suggest, we should celebrate by both the Trefethen and Pruett methods of determining in what year a Blue Moon will occur. As the late Charles A. Federer, founder of *Sky & Telescope,* noted: "Even if the calendrical meaning is new, I don't see any harm in it. It's something fun to talk about and it helps attract people to astronomy."

# BEST DAYS IN 2001

The best days listed here are based on both the phase of the Moon and its position in the zodiac. Many people believe that if you do the tasks on the dates listed, you will get the best results possible.

| | JAN | FEB | MAR | APR | MAY | JUN |
|---|---|---|---|---|---|---|
| Bake | 3, 4, 24, 30, 31 | 5, 6, 26, 27 | 5, 6, 25-27 | 1, 2, 23, 28, 29 | 5, 6, 25, 26 | 1, 2, 22, 23, 28, 29 |
| Can Fruits and Vegetables | 9, 10, 18, 19 | 14, 15 | 13-15, 23 | 10, 11, 20, 21 | 7, 8, 17, 18 | 5, 14, 15 |
| Dry Fruits and Vegetables | 11, 20-22 | 8, 16-18 | 16, 17 | 12-14, 22 | 9-11, 19, 20 | 6, 7, 16, 17 |
| Jams/Jellies | 18, 19 | 14, 15, 21, 22 | 13-15, 21, 22 | 10, 11, 17-19 | 7, 8, 14-16, 21 | 5, 11, 12, 18, 19 |
| Cut Firewood | 1-8, 24-31 | 1-7, 23-28 | 1-8, 24-31 | 1-6, 23-30 | 1-6, 22-31 | 1-4, 21-30 |
| Cut Hair | 1, 2, 15-17, 20-22, 25-29 | 12, 13, 16-18, 21-25 | 11, 12, 16, 17, 21-24 | 7-9, 12-14, 17-21 | 5, 6, 9-11, 14-18 | 1, 2, 6, 7, 11-15 |
| Mow to Increase Growth | 1-8, 24-31 | 1-7, 23-28 | 1-8, 24-31 | 1-6, 23-30 | 1-6, 22-31 | 1-4, 21-30 |
| Mow to Retard Growth | 9-23 | 8-22 | 9-23 | 7-22 | 7-21 | 5-20 |
| Castrate Farm Animals | 1, 2, 20-29 | 16-25 | 16-24 | 12-21 | 9-18 | 6-15 |
| Dig Holes | 1-8, 24-31 | 1-7, 23-28 | 1-8, 24-31 | 1-6, 23-30 | 1-6, 22-31 | 1-4, 21-30 |
| Dig Post Holes | 9-23 | 8-22 | 9-23 | 7-22 | 7-21 | 5-20 |
| Harvest | 16-23 | 14-22 | 16-23 | 15-22 | 15-21 | 13-20 |
| Pick Apples and Pears | 3, 4, 30, 31 | 7, 26, 27 | 7, 8, 25-27 | 3, 4, 23, 30 | 1, 27-29 | 24, 25 |
| Prune Trees | 23, 24 | 19, 20 | 18-20 | 15, 16 | 12, 13 | 8-10 |
| Wean | 1, 2, 20-29 | 16-25 | 16-24 | 12-21 | 9-18 | 6-15 |
| Hunt | 1, 24-31 | 23-28 | 1, 24-31 | 23-29 | 22-28 | 21-26 |
| Quit Smoking | 11-14, 20-22 | 8-11, 16-18, 21, 22 | 9, 10, 16, 17, 21, 22 | 12-14, 17-19, 22 | 9-11, 14-16, 19, 20 | 6, 7, 11, 12, 16, 17, 20 |

# Best Days in 2001

The best days listed here are based on both the phase of the Moon and its position in the zodiac. Many people believe that if you do the tasks on the dates listed, you will get the best results possible.

| JUL | AUG | SEP | OCT | NOV | DEC | |
|---|---|---|---|---|---|---|
| 20, 25-27 | 2, 3, 22, 23, 29-31 | 18, 19, 25-27 | 16, 17, 23, 24, 30, 31 | 19-21, 27, 28 | 16-18, 24, 25 | **Bake** |
| 10-12, 19 | 7, 8, 16, 17 | 3, 4, 12, 13 | 2, 9, 10 | 5, 6, 14 | 3, 4, 11-13 | **Can Fruits and Vegetables** |
| 13, 14 | 9, 10 | 5-7, 14, 15 | 3, 4, 11, 12 | 7-9 | 5, 6 | **Dry Fruits and Vegetables** |
| 8, 9, 15, 16 | 4-6, 11-13 | 2, 8, 9 | 5, 6 | 1, 2, 14, 30 | 11-13 | **Jams/Jellies** |
| 1-4, 20-31 | 1-3, 18-31 | 1, 17-30 | 1, 16-31 | 15-29 | 14-29 | **Cut Firewood** |
| 3, 4, 8-12, 25-27, 30, 31 | 1, 4-8, 22, 23, 27, 28 | 1-4, 18, 19, 23, 24, 28-30 | 16, 17, 20-22, 25-29 | 12, 13, 17, 18, 22-26 | 9, 10, 14, 15, 19-23 | **Cut Hair** |
| 1-4, 20-31 | 1-3, 18-31 | 1, 17-30 | 1, 16-31 | 15-29 | 14-29 | **Mow to Increase Growth** |
| 5-19 | 4-17 | 2-16 | 2-15 | 1-14, 30 | 1-13, 30, 31 | **Mow to Retard Growth** |
| 3-12, 30, 31 | 1-8, 27-31 | 1-4, 23-30 | 1, 2, 20-29 | 17-26 | 14-23 | **Castrate Farm Animals** |
| 1-4, 20-31 | 1-3, 18-31 | 1, 17-30 | 1, 16-31 | 15-29 | 14-29 | **Dig Holes** |
| 5-19 | 4-17 | 2-16 | 2-15 | 1-14, 30 | 1-13, 30, 31 | **Dig Post Holes** |
| 13-19 | 12-17 | 10-16 | 9-15 | 8-14 | 7-13 | **Harvest** |
| 3, 4, 21, 22, 30, 31 | 1, 18, 19, 27, 28 | 23, 24 | 20-22, 30, 31 | 17, 18, 27, 28 | 14, 15, 24, 25 | **Pick Apples and Pears** |
| 5-7 | 2, 3, 29-31 | 25-27 | 23, 24 | 19-21 | 16-18 | **Prune Trees** |
| 3-12, 30, 31 | 1-8, 27-31 | 1-4, 23-30 | 1, 2, 20-29 | 17-26 | 14-23 | **Wean** |
| 20-26 | 18-24 | 17-23 | 16-22 | 15-21 | 14-21 | **Hunt** |
| 8, 9, 13, 14, 17, 18 | 4-6, 9, 10, 14, 15 | 2, 5-7, 10, 11, 14-16 | 3, 4, 7, 8, 11-15 | 3, 4, 7-11 | 1, 2, 5-8 | **Quit Smoking** |

# WRIGHT'S FISHING CALENDAR

**B – BEST    G – GOOD    F – FAIR    P – POOR**

Mo.(Morning) and Ev.(Evening) give the best time of day, but are subject to change by local conditions, such as high winds, storms, or cold. These forecasts are based on fishing experiences over many years.

| Day | JAN | FEB | MAR | APR | MAY | JUN | JUL | AUG | SEP | OCT | NOV | DEC |
|-----|-----|-----|-----|-----|-----|-----|-----|-----|-----|-----|-----|-----|
| 1 | B ev | F mo | F ev | B mo | P mo | P mo | G mo | F mo | B mo | B mo | G ev | F ev |
| 2 | B mo | F mo | P mo | B mo | F mo | F mo | B mo | G mo | B ev | B ev | G ev | F ev |
| 3 | P mo | P mo | P mo | P mo | F mo | B mo | F mo | G mo | B ev | F ev | F ev | B ev |
| 4 | P mo | P mo | P mo | F mo | G mo | B mo | F mo | B ev | B ev | F ev | F ev | B ev |
| 5 | F mo | B mo | B mo | G mo | F mo | B ev | G ev | B ev | F ev | G ev | B ev | P ev |
| 6 | G mo | B mo | B mo | G mo | F mo | F ev | G ev | B ev | P ev | F ev | B ev | P ev |
| 7 | F mo | F mo | F mo | F ev | B ev | F ev | G ev | B ev | P ev | P ev | P ev | F mo |
| 8 | F mo | F ev | F mo | F ev | B ev | G ev | B ev | B ev | F ev | P ev | P mo | F mo |
| 9 | B ev | G ev | G ev | F ev | F ev | F ev | G ev | P ev | F ev | B mo | P mo | P mo |
| 10 | B ev | G ev | G ev | B ev | F ev | F ev | B ev | P ev | P mo | B mo | F mo | P mo |
| 11 | F ev | G ev | F ev | G ev | P ev | G ev | B ev | F ev | P mo | P mo | F mo | G mo |
| 12 | F ev | P ev | F ev | P ev | F ev | G ev | B ev | F mo | B mo | P mo | P mo | F mo |
| 13 | F ev | P ev | G ev | P ev | F ev | B mo | P mo | F mo | B mo | F mo | P mo | P ev |
| 14 | F ev | G mo | G ev | P ev | G ev | B mo | P mo | P mo | P mo | F mo | F mo | P ev |
| 15 | P ev | G mo | G ev | F mo | G mo | B mo | F mo | P mo | P mo | P mo | F ev | P ev |
| 16 | P mo | P mo | P mo | F mo | G mo | P mo | F mo | G mo | P mo | P ev | F ev | P ev |
| 17 | P mo | P mo | P mo | G mo | B mo | P mo | P mo | G mo | P ev | P ev | P ev | F ev |
| 18 | G mo | P mo | F mo | G mo | B mo | F mo | P mo | P ev | P ev | F ev | P ev | F ev |
| 19 | G mo | F mo | F mo | G mo | P mo | P mo | G mo | P ev | P ev | G ev | F ev | G ev |
| 20 | P mo | F mo | F mo | B mo | P mo | P mo | G ev | P ev | G ev | P ev | F ev | G ev |
| 21 | P mo | F mo | G mo | G mo | P mo | P ev | P ev | F ev | G ev | P ev | F ev | B ev |
| 22 | P mo | F mo | F mo | P mo | P ev | G ev | P ev | P ev | G ev | P ev | G mo | B mo |
| 23 | P mo | F ev | G mo | P ev | P ev | G ev | F ev | P ev | P ev | F mo | G mo | B mo |
| 24 | P ev | G ev | G ev | P ev | P ev | P ev | F ev | G ev | P mo | F mo | B mo | P mo |
| 25 | F ev | G ev | P ev | P ev | B ev | P ev | P ev | G mo | F mo | G mo | B mo | P mo |
| 26 | F ev | P ev | P ev | P ev | B ev | F ev | P ev | G mo | F mo | G mo | B mo | F mo |
| 27 | G ev | P ev | P ev | P ev | P ev | F mo | P mo | P mo | F mo | G mo | F mo | G mo |
| 28 | B ev | F ev | F ev | B ev | P ev | P mo | G mo | P mo | G mo | B mo | F mo | F mo |
| 29 | B ev |  | F ev | B ev | P mo | P mo | G mo | F mo | B mo | B mo | G mo | F mo |
| 30 | P ev |  | P ev | P mo | F mo | G mo | P mo | G mo | B mo | F mo | G ev | B ev |
| 31 | P ev |  | P ev |  | F mo |  | P mo | G mo |  | F mo |  | B ev |

# ANGLER'S ALMANAC

## To help you keep track of the "Big Ones" and the "Best Spots" for fishing.

Record your fishing adventures here, next to the Wright's Fishing Calendar. Next year, you can refer to the *Farmers' Almanac* and be reminded of your favorite fishing holes!

| DATE | TIME OF DAY | WEATHER | LAKE OR BROOK | BAIT OR LURE | NO. FISH HOOKED | TYPE(S) | LENGTH | WEIGHT |
|------|-------------|---------|---------------|--------------|-----------------|---------|--------|--------|
|      |             |         |               |              |                 |         |        |        |
|      |             |         |               |              |                 |         |        |        |
|      |             |         |               |              |                 |         |        |        |
|      |             |         |               |              |                 |         |        |        |
|      |             |         |               |              |                 |         |        |        |
|      |             |         |               |              |                 |         |        |        |
|      |             |         |               |              |                 |         |        |        |
|      |             |         |               |              |                 |         |        |        |
|      |             |         |               |              |                 |         |        |        |
|      |             |         |               |              |                 |         |        |        |

# Getting back to nature with... HERBS

**As medicine marches into the new millennium with genetically engineered drugs and artificial organs, so does a countertrend rejecting anything artificial.**

More and more people want to go back to a more "natural" approach to health. Organically grown produce and "all-natural" products fill grocery store shelves. A highly educated population, seeking to be in harmony with Mother Earth, is turning increasingly to holistic medicine, the healing traditions of Native Americans, and folk remedies. This growing demand accounts for the reemergence of one of the oldest methods of healing—herbal medicine.

As part of a natural health style, herbal supplements have become popular health tonics for self-medication. These supplements usually are sold as dry powders in capsules, as tinctures, or as ingredients in other health products. They are not subject to the regulations that the FDA has imposed on pharmaceuticals, and the active ingredients in herbs do have side effects and will interact with other medications. In addition, not all herbal products are standardized in potency.

Five top-selling herbs—ginseng, echinacea, St. John's wort, garlic, and ginko biloba—are listed here, along with some of the claimed health benefits and risks associated with them.

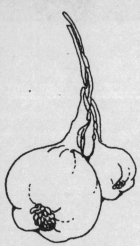

**BY MIKE WILSON**
*Freelance author located in Lexington, Kentucky.*

☛ **CONSULT YOUR DOCTOR** Herbs are medicines, so consult your physician before undertaking any herbal self-medication. And remember to mention herbal supplements when healthcare practitioners ask you what medications you are taking. Read the labels and try to find reliable products with standardized potencies. By using herbal medications, you can obtain their benefits "naturally."

## GARLIC

You may think that garlic only makes food taste good and breath smell bad, but there is good evidence that eating one to two cloves a day can reduce cholesterol and LDL cholesterol oxidation, part of the process that begins plaque buildup that clogs arteries. Garlic also may help block certain cancers, reduce blood pressure, and inhibit blood clotting. Raw garlic even has antiviral and antibacterial effects.

While odorless garlic can be purchased in capsule form, powdered garlic capsules may not work as effectively as raw garlic. Garlic seems to have some definite benefits with few side effects. However, because of its anticoagulant effect, there may be an interaction with blood thinners like warfarin.

## GINKO BILOBA

Ginko biloba, very popular in Germany and increasingly popular in America, is a derivative of the ornamental ginko tree. It works as an antioxidant and inhibits blood clotting. It is promoted as stimulating cognitive abilities by improving blood circulation. Many people like the idea of remaining mentally sharp, and take ginko biloba to help.

However, the blood-thinning properties of ginko biloba suggest that it should not be combined with aspirin or pharmaceutical blood thinners. There have been a few reports of spontaneous bleeding attributed to it, and suggestions that it may impair fertility.

## GINSENG

Ginseng grows wild in woodland areas of both America and Asia. Ginseng root has long been popular in Asia as an "adaptogen" or tonic (good for everything), and as a sexual stimulant. Ginseng is a member of the species *Panax*, a species name with the same root as the word "panacea."

Does ginseng work? Many people think it does. Traditionally, wild ginseng is considered the best, but the growing demand for it has led to its commercial cultivation. Wisconsin is where most of the cultivated ginseng in America is grown.

While ginseng has been highly valued in the East for 2000 years, western scientists are divided on its effectiveness. Some authorities warn of side effects that include asthma attacks, raised blood sugar levels, high blood pressure, and heart palpitations. Ginseng also has an anticoagulant effect and should not be combined with blood thinners.

## ECHINACEA

Echinacea, or coneflower, is not only a favorite herbal today, but years ago it was also a popular medicine among Native Americans, and one of the most popular ingredients in American medicines before the advent of antibiotics. Three types of echinacea are used medicinally— *E. angustifolia, E. pallida* and *E. purpurea*, with the roots of *E. angustifolia* and *E. pallida*, and the above-ground parts of *E. purpurea* considered the most efficacious (check the label).

*continued*

Believers claim that echinacea can prevent or cure the common cold. Studies on its effectiveness have had mixed results, but there is evidence that it can lessen the effect of a cold if it is taken at the first sign of any symptom.

Echinacea enhances the immune system by, among other things, stimulating disease-fighting leukocytes, and inhibiting the release by bacteria of enzymes that injure cells. It also reduces inflammation on the cellular level.

Germany has approved echinacea use for colds. Authorities there say echinacea may be used safely for up to eight weeks, but some studies show it is most effective when used only a week or two at a time. It should be avoided by those with an autoimmune disease, rheumatoid arthritis, lupus, tuberculosis or multiple sclerosis.

## ST. JOHN'S WORT

St. John's wort is found in many parts of the world. It blooms near the Feast of St. John, June 24, and has long been a folk remedy. Currently, St. John's wort is used as a treatment for depression, and can be purchased over the counter for one-quarter the price of prescribed antidepressants. It is widely prescribed in Europe, and has been studied there much more than in the United States. European studies (most of which do not meet U.S. standards) have found St. John's wort as effective for treating mild to moderate depression as many pharmaceutical antidepressants.

St. John's wort has ten or more pharmacologically active ingredients, but hypericin, found in the plant's leaves and flowers, appears to slow the breakdown of serotonin, a neurotransmitter that helps brain cells communicate with each other. (Low levels of neurotransmitters, such as serotonin, can cause depression.) Some pharmaceutical antidepressants work the same way. However, it may take 4 to 8 weeks to notice any effect from the use of the herb.

St. John's wort should not be taken during pregnancy or with other antidepressants, nor by those with bipolar disorder or serious depression. St. John's wort also increases a user's sensitivity to the sun, and may impair fertility. In all events, it is an inadequate substitute for proper therapy.

# Dry, cracked, lips?

### What causes chapped lips?

The biggest culprit is the weather. Dry winter winds, changes in temperature and humidity (often caused by indoor heat), and exposure to sun (winter and summer) can cause your lips to become dehydrated and crack. Licking or biting your lips is another reason why they become chapped.

### Here are some ways to beat chapped lips.

### How to protect your lips from chapping

Unlike your skin, your lips do not produce natural oils to protect them against drying. Here are some steps you can take to keep your lips looking and feeling good from season to season:

■ **First and foremost, do NOT lick or bite them. When lips start drying out, the automatic reaction is to add moisture to them by licking. Don't! Licking actually enhances the drying and biting your lips makes them even worse.**

■ **Apply lip balm (or lipstick) before going out into the elements. Reapply it several times while outside.**

■ **Use a lip balm that has a sunscreen in it. The sun is very damaging to your lips, especially when it's reflecting off snow.**

■ **Avoid flavored lip balms for use on children. The tastier the lip balm is the more likely kids will want to lick it off their lips.**

■ **Cover your lips with a scarf or a ski mask when spending time outdoors in cold weather.**

■ **Drink additional fluids. Some experts suggest consuming several ounces of water every few hours.**

■ **Use a humidifier at home and in the office during the winter months.**

■ **Make sure your diet includes enough vitamin B and iron (or take a multivitamin every day) as a deficiency of these vitamins can play a part in scaling on the lips and cracking at the corners of your mouth.**

### How to soothe chapped lips

Rub your finger over the side of your nose. Then wipe your finger on your lips. Your face contains the oils which your lips are lacking. This oil will help your lips.

Slather on a thick coating of petroleum jelly or bag balm. Both of these products seal in the moisture and form a barrier on your lips. Apply often.

Try yogurt. Sometimes, if the corners of your mouth have become chapped and cracked, you might have a yeast overgrowth that can be caused by antibiotics or stress. The acidophilus in yogurt can help kill the yeast and cure your chapped lips.

# Skeeter's SCIENCE POTPOURRI

## POP QUIZ

**1.** What Greek philosopher founded the first recorded botanical garden in Athens, and was given the title "Father of Botany" by the famous 18th-century Swedish botanist Linnaeus?

A) Pythagoras
B) Plato
C) Archimedes
D) Aristotle

**2.** Which one of the following is not, botanically speaking, a true berry?

A) Tomatoes
B) Raspberries
C) Grapes
D) Bananas

**3.** If you were stranded in the Sonoran Desert of southwestern Arizona, which cactus could provide you enough water to survive?

A) Saguaro
B) Barrel
C) Prickly Pear
D) All of the above

*Answers on page 58*

**4.** Ten of the eleven plants that furnish 80% of the world's food . . .

A) Are monocotyledons (contain one seed leaf)
B) Are in the grass family
C) Include nine of the ten most economically important crops in the world
D) All of the above

**5.** Approximately 80% of the world's supply of cordage fiber in ropes and twine comes from the leaves of what plant?

A) Hemp
B) Eucalyptus
C) Agave
D) Bamboo

**6.** What is the term for the percentage of solar radiation that is reflected by the earth's surface?

A) Albedo
B) Refraction
C) Solar Oscillation
D) Subsidence

**7.** Who wrote "Water is the driver of nature"?

A) Charles Darwin
B) William Shakespeare
C) Leonardo da Vinci
D) Gregor Mendel

**8.** If at 78%, nitrogen is the most abundant gas in our atmosphere, and oxygen is another 21%, what percentage does carbon dioxide ($CO_2$) account for?

A) 10%
B) 3.5%
C) 0.35%
D) 0.035%

**9.** What is the pH number of distilled water in a cup or glass?

A) Less than 7
B) Exactly 7
C) More than 7
D) None of the above

**10.** Which of the following are cold-blooded animals?

A) Salamander
B) Frog
C) Crocodile
D) None of the above

# ❋ FAVORITE TOMBSTONE ❋

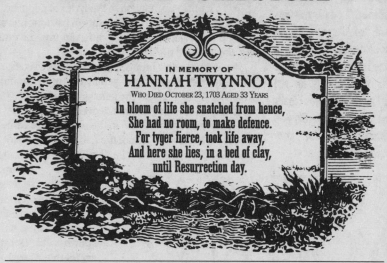

IN MEMORY OF
## HANNAH TWYNNOY
WHO DIED OCTOBER 23, 1703 AGED 33 YEARS

In bloom of life she snatched from hence,
She had no room, to make defence.
For tyger fierce, took life away,
And here she lies, in a bed of clay,
until Resurrection day.

---

### PUZZLES AND BRAINTEASERS ANSWERS FROM PAGE 16

**WHAT IS IT?** The letter E. An icicle. Carpet. His/her right elbow. **GRAMMATICAL QUIZ** Neither, the yolk is yellow. **NUMBER FUN** 18, square the top numbers, then reverse the digits. **IS A CAR A CAR?** When it turns into a driveway. **COLOR QUIZ** A 7-UP bottle of course! A stoplight is red! **WET THEN DRY** A towel **LIGHT AS A FEATHER** Your breath. **HOW CAN IT BE?** She was a justice of the peace.

## *Try This Tongue Twister*

**"Silly Sara" by Danielle DeFosse, a sixth-grade student at Montello
Elementary School, Lewiston, Maine**

Silly Sara sings softly to her sleepy sister,
She sometimes shares secrets with her sympathetic sibling.
Sara sips soda on Saturday afternoons.
She slurps her Sunday soup when sitting slouched on the sofa,
Then she slips away to slide down slippery slopes in Switzerland.
Screams shriekingly at scary scenes in movies,
Spooky spiders scare Sara so she suddenly scoots somewhere safe.
Suddenly, Sara seems quite sensible in the end.

---

EMBEDDED IMAGE ANSWER: Turn the image upside down. Then stare at the stem of the chalice and you will see two faces looking at each other in the white outline across the left and right sides, extending to the full length of the chalice. Keep looking; they will appear. The third image to see is Casper the Friendly Ghost in the black area above the stem. The fourth image is Snoopy from the *Peanuts* cartoon. This can be seen by holding the image to the original position. He is in the black area near the lower edge of the chalice.

Two men were discussing Beatles songs. "I've never understood," one man wondered, "why they say, 'the girl with colitis goes by.'" After a puzzled pause, his friend lit up. "Ah," he said, "it's 'the girl with kaleidoscope eyes.' That's a line from *Lucy in the Sky with Diamonds*." That's also a classic mondegreen.

**WHAT IS A MONDEGREEN?** A mondegreen is a mishearing of oft-used words resulting in a misinterpretation of the lyrics of popular songs and hymns, and the contents of patriotic affirmations, prayers, familiar adages and epigrams, advertising slogans, and the like.

Pop songs yield a bumper crop of mondegreens. **"The girl from Emphysema goes walking"** is a mondegreen for "The girl from Ipanema goes walking." **"The ants are my friends"** is a mondegreen for "The answer, my friends, is blowin' in the wind." **"I've thrown a custard in his face"** is not the national anthem for clowns. It's a mondegreen for "I've grown accustomed to his face." **"Return December, bad dress unknown"** is a mondegreen for "Return to sender, address unknown," and **"Don't cry for me, Marge and Tina"** is a mondegreen for "Don't cry for me, Argentina." To the surprise of many rock and roll enthusiasts, Jimi Hendrix sang, " 'Scuse me while I kiss the sky," not **"'Scuse me while I kiss this guy."** Actually, George Gershwin wrote "Rhapsody in Blue," not **"Rap City in Blue."** **"Clown control to Mao Zedong"** is at least as colorful and imaginative as David Bowie's original lyric: "Ground control to Major Tom." Herman's Hermits sang, "There's a kind of hush all over the world tonight," not **"There's a can of fish all over the world tonight."** But the fish is better. And if Davy Crockett was **"killed in a bar when he was only three,"** who was that at the Alamo?

# JOSE, CAN YOU SEE?

## by Richard Lederer

Contributing editor for the
*Farmers' Almanac*
and a well-known verbalist.

The word "mondegreen" was coined by Sylvia Wright, who wrote a *Harper's* column about them in 1954, when she recounted hearing a Scottish folk ballad, "The Bonny Earl of Murray." She heard the lyric **"Oh, they have slain the Earl of Murray/And Lady Mondegreen."** Wright powerfully identified with Lady Mondegreen, the faithful friend of the Bonny Earl. Lady Mondegreen died for her liege with dignity and tragedy. How romantic!

It was some years later that Wright learned that the

last two lines of the stanza were really "They have slain the Earl of Murray/ And laid him on the green." She named such sweet slips of the ear mondegreens, and thus they have been evermore.

Children are especially prone to misinterpreting the boundaries that separate words in fresh and unconventional ways. Our patriotic songs and statements have been delightfully revised by misspelt youth:

**Jose, can you see by the Donzerly light? Oh, the ramrods we washed, were so gallantly steaming. And the rockets' red glare, the bombs bursting in there, grapefruit through the night, that our flag was still rare.**
\* \* \*
**I pledge the pigeons to the flag of the United States of America, and to the republic for Richard Stans, one naked individual, underground, with liver, tea, injustice for all.**
\* \* \*
**God bless America, land that I love, Stand aside, sir, and guide her, with delight through the night from a bulb. America, America, God's red Chef Boyardee.**

**Miniza seen the glory of the coming of the Lord. He has trampled out the vintage where the great giraffes are stored.**
\* \* \*
And it's **"Oh, beautiful for space ship guys,"** not "Oh, beautiful for spacious skies."

Another territory lush with mondegreens is religion. Many a youngster has recited the famous line from the Twenty-Third Psalm as "Shirley, good Mrs. Murphy will follow me all the days of my life." Many other imaginary characters inhabit the lyrics of hymns and words from the Bible. Battalions of children have grown up singing a song about an ophthalmologically-challenged ursid named **Gladly – "The cross-eyed bear."**

**Our father, Art, in heaven, Harold be thy name. Thy King done come, thy will be done, on earth as it is in heaven. Give us this day our jelly bread, and forgive us our press passes, as we forgive those who press past us. And lead us not into Penn Station, but deliver us some e-mail.**

For religious mondegreens, the fracturing of Christmas carols especially opens up new worlds of meaning and imagination. Try singing along with these new takes on old favorites, revised by children:

**He's making a list, of chicken and rice.**
\* \* \*
**Deck the halls with Buddy Holly.**
\* \* \*
**Good King Wences' car backed out on a piece of Stephen.**
\* \* \*
**We three kings of porridge and tar.**
\* \* \*
**Olive, the other reindeer.**
\* \* \*
**On the first day of Christmas my tulip gave to me.**
\* \* \*
**Later on we'll perspire, as we dream by the fire.**
\* \* \*
**With the jelly toast proclaim.**
\* \* \*
**You'll go down in Listerine.**
\* \* \*
**Where shepherds washed their socks by night.**
\* \* \*
**Sleep in heavenly peas, sleep in heavenly peas.**

*continued*

Noel, Noel, Barney's the
king of Israel.

\* \* \*

Frosty the Snowman is a
ferret elf, I say.

\* \* \*

Get dressed, ye married
gentlemen, get huffing
you this May.

\* \* \*

Chipmunks roasting on
an open fire.

\* \* \*

Oh, what fun it is to ride
with one horse, soap,
and hay.

In the meadow, we can
build a snowman, then
pretend that he is sparse
and brown.

\* \* \*

What a friend we have in
cheeses.

\* \* \*

O come, froggy faithful.

\* \* \*

You'll tell Carol, "Be a
skunk, I require."

\* \* \*

Round John Virgin, mother
and child, Holy Vincent, so
tender and mild.

I nominate Richard Stans,
Art, Harold, good Mrs.
Shirley Murphy, Round
John Virgin, Vincent, a
reindeer named Olive, and
that cross-eyed bear
named Gladly for a Pullet
Surprise. But the ultimate
winner, who received her
prize posthumorously, of
course, must be . . . Lady
Mondegreen!

## SKEETER'S SCIENCE POTPOURRI QUIZ ANSWERS (from page 54)

**1.** D—Aristotle, the son of a Greek herbal physician, had over 2,000 disciples and wrote over 200 treatises; among the most important of the latter to have survived are two books entitled *History of Plants* and *Causes of Plants*.

**2.** B—Raspberries, like blackberries and strawberries, are actually aggregate fruits, not berries at all.

**3.** B—Only the barrel cactus's pulp contains enough obtainable water for humans to rely on in emergency situations. However, all cacti bear fruits and seeds that are edible, albeit only obtainable a few months of the year.

**4.** D—Just six of those ten plants (the cereals—wheat, barley, rye, oats, rice, and corn) feed more than 50% of the world's population—that's over 1 billion tons worth of food a year.

**5.** C—Agave. Many people might think of tequila when the agave plant is mentioned (since tequila is made from agave); however, it is also grown for its fiber (sisal). Agaves are erroneously called "century plants," because it was thought that they only flowered after growing for 100 years. They do, however, only flower once, then wither and die.

**6.** A—Global albedos, measured from beyond the atmosphere, range from high values of 50-60% at the polar regions to lows of 20-30% in the tropical and equatorial latitudes.

**7.** C—Leonardo da Vinci. As perceptive as da Vinci was, even he could not have appreciated the full meaning of his statement, based on the scientific knowledge of his time. Without the cycling of water, the earth's biogeochemical cycles could not exist, ecosystems could not function, and life could not be maintained.

**8.** D—0.035%. Although $CO_2$ is a trace gas in the atmosphere, there has been a 25% increase in atmospheric $CO_2$ since 1850 (arguably resulting in the greenhouse effect), largely as a result of the burning of fossil fuels and deforestation.

**9.** A—Less than 7. Although distilled water is theoretically "pure," with a pH of 7, its real pH always becomes less than 7, because it dissolves the atmospheric carbon dioxide that comes in contact with the water, to form carbonic acid ($H_2CO_3$); the actual pH of a glass of distilled water is usually about 5.7.

**10.** D—None of the above. Technically, no animal is actually "cold-blooded," except when air temperatures around them are cold. Poikilotherms' body temperatures are dependent on their surrounding environment. It is normal for many reptiles to reach body temperatures exceeding 100° F, and some frogs can survive being frozen. Poikilotherms include all animals, except birds and mammals.

# HEALTH AND MEDICAL HINTS

## *From the* 1901 FARMERS' ALMANAC

☐ Never begin a journey until the breakfast has been eaten.

☐ Never omit regular bathing, for unless the skin is in active condition, the cold will close the pores and favor congestion and other diseases.

☐ Very many attacks of sick headache, says the *Journal of Health*, can be prevented, if those who are subject to them are careful about their diet and largely restrict the same to vegetables and fruits easy of digestion. They must forego meat, cheese, pastry, beer, etc.; in fact, neither eat nor drink anything which is stimulating in character, and at all likely to tax the digestive organs.

☐ Most persons suffering from a cold of the chest can be greatly relieved by eating boiled or roasted onions. They will be found to be a most excellent remedy for a cough, and the clogging of the bronchial tubes, which is usually the cause of the cough. If they are eaten freely at the outset of a cold, they will break up what promised, from the severity of the attack, to have been a severe one.

☐ Nose Bleeding—A correspondent of the *Scientific American* says: "The best remedy for bleeding at the nose, as given by Gleason, in one of his lectures, is a vigorous motion of the jaws, as if in the act of mastication. In the case of a child, a wad of paper should be placed in its mouth, and the child instructed to chew it hard. It is the motion of the jaws that stops the flow of blood. This remedy is so very simple, that many will feel inclined to laugh at it, but it has never been known to fail, even in very severe cases."

☐ Cure for Corns—Here is the latest suggestion: Soak a piece of bread in strong vinegar; apply to the corn as a poultice. The effect is, the corn is so softened that it can be easily removed.

**EDITOR'S NOTE:** Remember these hints were written 100 years ago!

# In praise of
# TREES

When we think of the world's natural wonders, the awe-inspiring Grand Canyon or the incredible aurora borealis may come to mind. But trees are remarkable natural wonders that live around us and enrich our lives in countless, invaluable ways. They are sources of inspiration and symbols of steadfastness and strength. Trees beautify our landscapes and clean our air, soil, and water. And they provide us with an amazing variety of fruits, nuts, medicines, and other unique and useful substances . . .

*By* Jean Grigsby

**WE ALL KNOW THAT TREES ARE PLANTS, BUT WHAT MAKES A PLANT A TREE?** Most trees are at least 15 feet tall; live for many years (sometimes hundreds or even thousands of years); have one main trunk protected by bark, and a "crown" of leaves. The shape of the crown differs depending on the type of tree: conifers tend to have pointed, triangular shapes, while broadleaf (deciduous) trees have rounded crowns.

**TREES ARE AMONG THE MOST SUCCESSFUL ORGANISMS ON THE PLANET.** They cover more of the earth's surface than any other kind of organism. There are more than 700 million forested acres in the United States alone.

**TREES ARE THE LARGEST AND LONGEST-LIVED OF ALL ORGANISMS.** While there is some debate over which tree is the largest overall (based on crown, girth, height, and volume), experts agree that the giant sequoias, *Sequoiadendron giganteum*, found in California, are among the most massive trees in the world. They also are among the oldest living things on earth. But the distinction of the oldest tree in the United States goes to a bristlecone pine, *Pinus longaeva* (living in

California), aptly named the Methuselah tree, which is more than 4,600 years old.

**THE NEXT TIME YOU TAKE A BREATH OF FRESH AIR OR A DRINK OF COOL WATER, THANK A TREE.** Trees make the planet livable by regulating the amounts of oxygen and carbon dioxide in the atmosphere. Just as we use oxygen and give off carbon dioxide, trees take in carbon dioxide and then release oxygen. Trees cool the Earth by creating shade and giving off moisture. They act like huge pumps, sucking water up from the soil and then putting it back into the air. The thousands of leaves on one tree may draw more than 10,000 gallons of water from the soil and put it back into the air in a single growing season. Trees also help clean the air, because they retain pollution particulates. (Unfortunately, pollution hurts them just like it hurts humans.)

**TREES ARE SO UBIQUITOUS THAT WE OFTEN TAKE THEM FOR GRANTED.** Yet, we rely heavily on the more than 5,000 different products made from trees. Aside from the obvious fruits, nuts, lumber, and paper, there are a number of by products that may

come as a surprise: rayon fabric is made from chemically treated wood pulp, and the salicylic acid used in aspirin and other medicinals comes from willow bark. In addition, some of our most coveted substances are related to trees: amber is the fossilized sap of prehistoric evergreens; silk is produced by moths that feed on the leaves of mulberry trees; and chocolate is made from the seeds of the cacao tree.

---

**ONE OF THE BEST AND EASIEST WAYS TO MAKE THE WORLD A BETTER PLACE IS TO PLANT A TREE.** Trees are invaluable because they are renewable, natural resources; when they are harvested for use, they are able to be replaced through natural regrowth or the planting of new trees. There are a growing number of organizations dedicated to educating the public about the importance of trees and encouraging people to plant them:
- American Forests at www.americaforests.org or call 202-955-4500
- The National Arbor Day Foundation at www.arborday.org or call 402-474-5655
- The National Tree Trust at www.nationaltreetrust.org or call 202-628-8733

# THE BEES OF WAR

**BY NICK HOWES**

In Rudyard Kipling's *The Second Jungle Book*, Mowgli (the main character) enlists the unwitting aid of the Little People of the Rocks to halt an invasion of the Jungle by a ferocious pack of red dogs called *dholes*. A super-colony of bees, the Little People of the Rocks, live along the river Waingunga, stinging to death any intruders. Mowgli leads the ferocious dogs through their domain, alarming the Little People who swarm and destroy half of the pack.

The concept of using bees to protect and defend was not unique to Kipling. Thousands of years of bee-keeping have led people all around the world to search for a role for bees in wars, as primitive biological weapons. Recognition of their potential existed in Biblical times, as indicated by several passages, such as this from Exodus 23:28: "And I will send hornets before thee, which will drive out the Hivite, the Canaanite, and the Hittite before thee."

One of the earliest historical accounts (first century B.C.) that mentions bees being used against enemies involves the Heptakometes of Asia Minor (present-day Turkey) and Pompey the Great. With the aid of their bees, the Heptakometes temporarily halted an advance by Pompey's soldiers. The Heptakometes knew that when bees gather pollen from such plants as rhododendron or azalea the honey crop produced is loaded with alkaloids which are harmless to bees but toxic to humans. They were able to obtain and leave a cache of poisoned honey in the path of 1,000 advancing Roman soldiers.

During that time, the gains from raiding and looting were part of a soldier's pay, so the Romans naturally seized the honey and consumed it. They were soon deathly ill, and in no shape to resist the attack that followed.

The Roman legions were less subtle in their use of bees. Their attacks were often preceded by the catapulting of portable beehives at enemy positions; when the hives smashed explosively among the enemies, a sudden assault by angry bees occurred. At one point during the many clashes between the Dacians (of modern-day Romania) and the Romans (between 112 B.C. and A.D. 106, when the Romans gained complete control), the Dacians used beehives with effect to, again only temporarily, halt Roman advances into their homeland. In naval battles of the time, bees, housed in earthen hives designed specifically for shipboard use, were catapulted at enemy ships.

## BEES IN THE WALLS

In medieval times, would-be conquerors laid siege to the cities and castles they coveted. However, castles were designed and built by builders who included as many possible defensive features as they could think of. Often, they incorporated bee hives within the walls, an unwelcome surprise for any attackers who might breach a wall at the wrong spot. Straw hives were kept out of the way atop city walls, where they were also at hand during sieges.

There were advantages to using bees that go beyond the mere unreasoning fear many people have of them. Imagine a mounted knight in heavy armor, fully dependent on his horse for any real mobility, sharing his helmet with several maddened bees.

## BEES AT SEA

From a later era comes another story (of questionable truth) about bees and pirates. According to the story, a 17th-century-merchant ship, bound for Cuba and Mexico, sailed from Barcelona carrying bees which had established a hive under the upper deck near the bow. The crew took the presence of the beehive as a good omen, and let it

alone. Their belief seemed justified by fair winds and a quick trip through the Atlantic Ocean chill, which kept the bees quiet.

In the warmer waters near the Caribbean, the bees continued to cooperate and merely sortied from their hive for short distances.

Near the ship's first destination, pirates struck. Damp powder prevented the merchantman's crew from firing their guns, a problem the pirates did not have. The merchantman took several poundings from the pirates' cannons, including one in the ship's bow. The pirate vessel closed and the buccaneers prepared to board at the bow of the merchantman. The vibration of the cannon ball in the bow, followed by the collision of the two hulls, understandably set off the bees. The pirates found themselves under attack from an unanticipated enemy. They cast off and quickly pulled away. Falling to their knees, the merchantman's crew thanked God for their deliverance.

As the crew enjoyed liberty ashore at Santiago de Cuba, the bees gathered pollen from the exotic flowers of Cuba. Convinced of the power of the bees, the sailors were concerned when some of the heavily laden bees fell into the water. So a canvas platform was prepared for the bees to land on before their makeshift hive's entrance. The ship then continued on without incident to its Mexican landfall.

*continued*

## BACK ON LAND, YEARS LATER

During the Civil War at Antietam, attacking Federal troops advancing through a farmyard were routed, not by the heavy gunfire they faced, but by enraged bees from hives shattered by Confederate artillery fire. There's also a well-known case of British troops, in action in German East Africa during WWI, encountering maddened bees, but, as at Antietam, it appears accidental.

During the Vietnam War, Viet Cong guerrillas were masters of improvised weaponry, and before attacking, were known to lob 30 or more nests of hornets and wasps into military outposts . They also set up ingenious booby traps, placing nests, with firecrackers attached, along trails. When an enemy patrol walked past a nest, a patient VC would set off the firecracker.

## FROM WEAPONS TO CAUSING WAR

On a few occasions, bees have been less the weapon than the cause of war or near war. There is a tale in Ireland, that Congal, the king of Ulster, was stung in the eye and blinded by a bee during a visit to the home of Domnall. The supporters of Congal Caech (One-Eye) demanded retribution—the eye of Domnall' s firstborn son.

Domnall quickly ordered the bee hive destroyed, hoping the gesture might satisfy the Ulstermen. It did not. Ulster went to war against Domnall but lost.

## THE "HELPER" BEE

Aside from military uses, there are instances in the historical record where bees helped civilians. For example, a group of nuns in Beyenburg (Beetown in English), Germany, drove off a band of robbers by releasing bees into their convent yard before seeking cover.

Another story tells how a Swiss beekeeper smuggled a cargo of fine Italian honey into Switzerland. He had an Italian beekeeper park a stash of honey right at the border. The Swiss took his own beehives and set them about 1,000 yards away. The bees went straight for the available honey and took it back to their hive, 200 pounds of it.

Today, bees are being examined as possibly a cheap and effective way to clear deadly minefields. Landmines are a cheap weapon in war, but they are usually left in place after the shooting stops. Worldwide, huge tracts of productive land are unusable, too dangerous to clear because of their mines.

Bees may provide the astonishing answer to the problem. At Sandia National Laboratories, New Mexico, and at the University of Montana, researchers hope to make bees into biological mine detectors. They are trying to train the bees to respond to the odor of TNT, the primary landmine component, as if it's food, and then track the bees into minefields with tiny rice-sized radio tags attached to the bees' bodies. Mowgli would be thoroughly confused by the technical aspects of the proposal, but he would need no convincing of the martial value of the Little People of the Rocks.

Nick Howes is a freelance writer located in Nashville, Illinois.

# The Basic BUZZ on BEES

## Did you know...

■ There are 20,000 bee species.

■ Most, such as the squash, leafcutter, mining, and sweat bees, are solitary and don't form colonies.

■ Only 500 species (honeybee, bumblebee, and tropical stingless bee, to name a few) are social and form colonies.

■ Social bees build hives from secreted wax. These bees survive the winter by staying in their hives, sharing body heat, and eating stored honey. Nonsocial bees hibernate.

■ A queen bee can lay up to 1,500 eggs a day. These eggs hatch as mature adults in three weeks.

■ Daily, many worker bees die of overwork. They perform a variety of specialized tasks, such as collecting pollen and nectar for honey production, or removing dead bees from the hive.

■ The average flight speed for a bee is 12 miles an hour.

■ Odors, or pheromones, emitted by bees are an important factor in their communications. For example, an alarm odor is released when the hive is threatened.

■ By a dance pattern, honeybees also communicate the direction and distance of a nectar source.

■ A commercial beehive produces an average of 50 pounds of honey annually.

■ *Apis mellifera*, the Old World honeybee, has numerous geographically based subspecies. One is the imported Italian honeybee, the most common commercial strain in the U.S.

■ Honeybees pollinate more than 30 percent of all fruits and vegetables.

■ Bees attack only when they or their hives are threatened, not while foraging.

■ Stings from 200 bee species can kill a person. For the five percent of the population that is allergic, one sting can mean death.

■ During her mating flight, a new queen mates with six to twelve male drones and returns to the hive to begin laying eggs. All the drones will eventually be forced out of the hive, and then starve.

**–NICK HOWES**

## *Unique* "Thank Yous"

Sometimes it's difficult to find the time to send out thank you cards, especially when there's a large group of people you need to send them to. Here are a few tips that might help save time and money (postage) while also expressing your gratitude:

**Baby Shower**/Wrap cookies in plastic wrap, then tie pink and blue ribbons around the packages. Attach short thank you notes and hand to guests before they leave.

**Bridal Shower**/Bake or purchase heart-shaped cookies, wrap as above but use white ribbon. Attach short thank you notes to the cookies.

**Birthday Party**/Give everyone a balloon as they leave. You can either write "Thank You" on the balloon with a marker, attach a note to the balloon, or physically say "thank you" to all of your guests as you hand each one a balloon.
If any of the above parties are a surprise, the host can have all of these "thank yous" ready ahead of time.

## Penny-pinching plans for retirement.
### How to SAVE for the future (inexpensively).

- Start early with a plan and stick to it.
- Make regular weekly or monthly contributions to a savings or investment plan.
- Educate yourself by attending free financial seminars, and reading and learning through your local library (and the Internet).
- Squirrel away every spare penny and dollar in your investment plan.
- Take advantage of tax breaks, and know your limitations.
- Downsize your lifestyle now for a better tomorrow.
- If you are already a senior or middle-ager, concentrate on accelerating your savings and investments, and make sure you prepare a will.

## Penny-pinching party tips.
### How to cut costs without seeming cheap.

- Make it a BYOD (bring your own drink) or BYOF (bring your own food) event. Potluck dinners can be fun and offer a variety of appealing dishes.
- Pick a theme (ethnic night, country & western theme, barbecue, etc.).

This will help your guests decide what food to bring and also help you decorate.

### Penny-Pinching PLANS
#### From Ian Nicholson
**North America's No. 1 Miser**

- Make your own decorations. Have kids help. Magazine cutouts, crepe paper, and newspaper hats are inexpensive, but add to a party's festivities.
- Entertainment doesn't have to cost a lot. Pull out those board games, or play charades. Fun and inexpensive.

## How can you cut corners during the holidays?

- Start a gift basket/closet early in the year. This way you can pick up bargains and unique items throughout the year.
- Don't limit your holiday shopping to specific venues. Take advantage of craft shows, garage and yard sales, auctions, etc. If you keep the holidays in

mind while visiting these places, you may find most of your gifts at great prices!
- Set limitations on both the number of people you're going to buy for as well as the dollar amount you want to spend per person.
- Homemade gifts are appreciated and often less expensive to give.
- Remember the reason for the season. Sometimes a simple phone call, letter, visit, or gesture is even more appreciated than a gift.

## How can you live cheaply without seeming cheap?

- Ignore others' expectations and forget about keeping up with the mythical Joneses.
- Have a financial goal and a plan to achieve your goal. Don't lose sight of it.
- Stay out of debt. Manage your credit responsibly. Avoid high interest debts and credit cards. Limit yourself to one credit card.
- Understand your needs versus wants.
- Recognize that time is the factor that defeats most plans. People expect to save tomorrow and spend today. Better to earn and save today for a better tomorrow.

Ian Nicholson is the publisher of *The Miser's Gazette* and "North America's Number 1 Miser." For more frugal lifestyle tips, subscribe to *The Miser's Gazette*. *The Miser's Gazette* reveals how tightwads, penny-pinchers and misers do all these things and more. To subscribe, write to : Miser Gazette, P.O. Box 1344, Kanata, Ontario, Canada K2K 1X5, or go to www.misersgazette.com

# EIGHT
## *Wonderful Gifts*
### THAT DON'T COST A CENT.

#### THE GIFT OF LISTENING
But you must really listen. No interrupting, no daydreaming, no
planning your responses, no second-guessing. Just listen.

—

#### THE GIFT OF AFFECTION
Be generous with appropriate hugs, kisses, and pats on the back.
Let these small actions demonstrate the love you have
for your family and close friends.

—

#### THE GIFT OF LAUGHTER
Clip and share cartoons and funny stories. Your gift will say,
"I love to laugh with you."

—

#### THE GIFT OF A WRITTEN NOTE
It can be a simple "Thanks for the help" note or
a full sonnet. A brief, handwritten note may be remembered
for a lifetime, and may even change a life.

—

#### THE GIFT OF A COMPLIMENT
A simple and sincere, "You look great in red," "You did a super job,"
or "That was wonderful," can make someone's day.

—

#### THE GIFT OF A FAVOR
Every day, go out of your way to do something kind.

—

#### THE GIFT OF SOLITUDE
There are times when you want nothing more than to be left alone.
Be sensitive to that same need in others and give the gift of
solitude when it seems needed.

—

#### THE GIFT OF A CHEERFUL DISPOSITION
The easiest way to feel good is to offer a kind word to someone.
Really, just a cheery "Hello," or "How are you?"
can go a long way.

# Take a HIKE!

BY MICHAEL TOUGIAS

**HIKING** is a fun way to get some exercise while observing nature at its best. Here are some tips that will help make your hikes safer and more enjoyable, with or without children.

Thoreau viewed walking as a way to lose oneself: *"What business have I in the woods, if I am thinking of something out of the woods."* He walked often and far afield. *"I think that I cannot preserve my health and spirits, unless I spend four hours a day at least–and it is commonly more than that–sauntering through the woods and over the hills and fields, absolutely free from all worldly engagements."*

A few suggestions ... Maybe you cannot walk four hours a day, but even a weekly walk is good for the body and spirit. (One reason Thoreau could walk so much is because he lived with his parents and had no mortgage!) Here are a few simple things you can do to make your outings more enjoyable:

## CHOOSE YOUR PATH WISELY

If possible, choose a loop walk. This way, you'll end up back at your starting point, without having to retrace your steps. You'll get to see new scenery with each passing mile.

If you don't go on a loop path, get a trail map. It will help you follow marked paths. If a map isn't available, make your own as you go along (with plenty of obvious landmarks). It's also a good idea to talk with local experts, such as park rangers, about trail conditions and the types of terrain you may encounter.

Walks that lead to overlooks or views give you a goal to reach and a destination for resting.

It's not advisable for people to hike alone. Ask a friend who shares your love of the outdoors, or better yet, pick a friend who spends more time indoors than out, and introduce him or her to the joys of walking in the great outdoors.

Getting lost in the woods is no fun. Allow enough time before you set out to get back well before dark.

Even at the smaller parks, it's possible to get lost. Always tell someone where you plan to explore and when you plan to return.

## WHAT TO WEAR

To avoid tick bites, always wear long pants, preferably with the pants tucked into your socks. Try to keep out of fields of tall grass during the warm weather months. And, to be on the safe side, give yourself a "tick check" after every hike by examining yourself all over, especially the scalp, neck, armpits, groin and ankles.

*continued*

Be on the lookout for poison ivy—identified by its three shiny leaves. Again, long pants are recommended.

During cold weather months, layer your clothes so that you can peel off or add items easily. Always bring a hat.

For relatively gentle terrain, a pair of sneakers or walking shoes are fine, but for steep, rocky trails, a good pair of hiking boots provides better traction and more ankle support.

Wearing two pairs of socks will help protect your feet from blisters. For long hikes, the newer fabrics such as polypropylene will whisk away sweat from your skin, unlike cotton which stays wet. Coats with a Gortex (a lightweight and durable fabric) outer shell are a good choice for staying dry.

No matter what the season, it's wise to get the latest weather forecast. If severe weather is expected, consider postponing your hike.

Deer hunting season is in the fall. To be on the safe side, you should wear something orange, even if you're in a no-hunting area.

## WHAT TO BRING

If you are a frequent hiker, keep a small backpack permanently stocked for nature walks. That way, all you'll need to do is fill a water bottle and go.

Items to be included in a permanent or day pack are bug spray, compass, camera, snacks high in carbohydrates (such as a trail mix of peanuts, chocolate and raisins), a lighter, a spare pair of boot or shoe laces, and a first aid kit. Remember to bring extra film for the camera. And, of course, don't forget to bring a drink, preferably water or a sports drink, especially when it's warm outside.

Although there is edible food in the woods, eat only what you carry in, unless you are an expert at identifying edible plants.

## LOCATING HIKING TRAILS

Finding the best trails suited to your taste and abilities has never been easier.

There are all sorts of hiking books available. You can also locate trails by calling the state park service, local conservation commissions, national parks, and outdoor groups such as the Appalachian Mountain Club and the Audubon Society. Trails can also be found on the Internet.

## HIKING WITH CHILDREN

Spending time outdoors with a child is a great way to become closer with one another, and at the same time, teach him or her respect for nature. The key to success is preparation, and even more importantly, the adult's attitude.

Enthusiasm and flexibility can make the difference between a wonderful experience or a potential nightmare. My first outing with my three-year-old son turned into the latter. Brian was fine on the trek to the hilltop, but on the way down he decided he had walked enough, plopping himself down on the trail, refusing to take another step. Guess who carried him down?

I had ignored one of my own basic rules about walking with children, which is not to extend your outdoor objective onto the child. In this case, it was I who really wanted to get to the hilltop, and I did not fully factor in the effect this would have on Brian's little legs (he probably takes three steps to my one). A half-mile walk is about right for a three-year-old, anything more than a mile and you're asking for trouble.

## A LITTLE PREPARATION GOES A LONG WAY

Supplying a snack and a drink is crucial; in fact, it is often the highlight of the trip for the children. A picnic in the woods is a new experience for them, and the energy gained from a nutritious snack (such as raisins) refuels them for more exploration. The same is true of making frequent rest stops. Should the children say they want to head home, do so–remember, the idea is to have them learn to enjoy the outdoors, and that means at their pace.

I've found some of our best walks occur when I "let go" and share in the sense of wonder and discovery with my two children. We sing, skip, and talk to trees. When they see you happy in the natural world, it forms a positive imprint on their young minds, and they are likely to want to repeat the experience.

Pack a field guidebook to identify birds, animals, reptiles and plants. In the springtime, admire the beauty of plants without picking them. Stop and admire the little things, such as a chipmunk hole, toadstools, pine cones and acorns. Binoculars are always a big hit, and allow the child to see much more than a fleeting glimpse of wildlife. There are some sturdy and inexpensive models on the market.

Show the child a map of the area you are exploring, and explain how to interpret the map. Let the youngster pick a trail to explore.

You might want to purchase a small backpack. From the child's viewpoint, this seems to somehow make the trip more of an adventure, as if you are going to explore some far-off place.

Pack a whistle in the backpack and explain that it's to be used (blown at regular intervals) only if the child gets separated from you.

Allowing a playmate to go along on a hike is a good idea. The two children will enjoy climbing rocks and discovering little caves. Talk to them about the wildlife that lives nearby, and encourage them to tell you about their own outdoor experiences. Praise them for their efforts, and show them how to be responsible, by picking up any trash, even if it's not theirs.

Children love ponds and streams, and they make a good "destination" for your walk.

Try to see the world through their eyes and enjoy the simple things that feed their enthusiasm. When you take a rest, tell stories about nature or browse through a field guidebook together.

Remember, the woods are out there for all of us to enjoy. Take some time this fall or spring to explore some of the parks or hiking trails in your area. You might find that hiking is a lot easier and a lot more fun than you ever expected.

*Michael Tougias is author of* Autumn Rambles of New England.

## TRAIL COURTESY
■ Be sure to follow the "carry-in, carry-out" principle when it comes to trash. ■ Do not remove any plant from the woods. ■ Keep to the established trails. ■ Give wildlife a wide berth. ■ Binoculars and a telephoto lens on your camera will allow you to view the wildlife without forcing it to flee.

# Living off the land:
# IS IT FOR YOU?

## BY JUDITH GERBER
*Freelance writer who lives in Southern California*

Does the thought of breaking free from the stress and pressures of modern life, with its traffic, crowds, and accelerated pace, seem irresistible to you? Do you often wish you could go back to a simpler time, when living off the land was the norm?

While many of us long to escape today's busy, complex society, the dream of how to do this is different for each individual. For example, some people fantasize about moving to a small cabin in the woods and living among the trees and animals. For others, the dream is to become a modern homesteader, which includes buying a piece of land, building a home, and becoming totally self-sufficient. **But did you stop to think about what it's like to live off the land? Or question whether or not it really offers a simpler lifestyle?**

To help you decide if this choice is right for you, read the following tips and advice from people who are already living off the land.

## Modern-day "Woodswoman."

Anne LaBastille, modern-day "woodswoman," is a noted nature and environmental author who has published over a dozen books. She is an adjunct professor of natural resources at Cornell University, and an ecological consultant. For the past 30 years, LaBastille has lived in the Adirondacks in a small cabin in the woods. Her cabin is without modern conveniences: she lives by using propane gas lamps and candles for light, and burning wood for heat and cooking. There is no indoor plumbing, simply an outhouse in the woods. At her cabin, LaBastille believes she is totally self-reliant.

She writes using one of five manual typewriters, and says that in order for her to create, it is essential that she live that way. Her life has been devoted to living in harmony with the land, using the least amount of resources possible. Her mission is to write about nature and she considers herself an "ecological evangelist."

*continued*

## Can you ever be totally isolated?

Yet despite this rural existence, she hasn't totally isolated herself from the rest of society. LaBastille believes "you can never get away from society totally, it's part of being a human being." But there is another, more practical, reason why she hasn't been able to completely cut herself off from the modern world—finances.

When she first chose to live a life in the woods, all she needed was a few thousand dollars to get started. Today, however, this has changed. According to LaBastille, a person who wants to live in the wilderness needs at least $9,000-$10,000 each year.

Despite being self-reliant once she's at her cabin, she has to rely on the outside world to get that way. Like all of us, she has to purchase her food and other supplies. Her cabin is so isolated that in order to reach it she must travel more than 2 miles away from "civilization" just to get there. In the winter, this means traveling over snow with a toboggan. Not surprisingly, she can't grow her own food because of harsh winters and because the cabin is surrounded by virgin forest.

In order to make a living and, in recent years, to run her publishing business (she now publishes her own books), she purchased a "winter home" in New York's Champagne Valley. This home is equipped with all the modern conveniences, including telephone, fax, and electricity. She lives at her winter place from October until the ice on the lake near her cabin starts to thaw.

She also reveals that, despite living her isolated existence, she still has to pay taxes and insurance. The State of New York found out that she had a home way out in the woods and began charging her property taxes. And because her cabin is so isolated, she says it's essential that she have a car to get close to it and to get back out. This means she has to have money for auto insurance and maintenance costs. She also must purchase health insurance for herself, and has even had to purchase liability insurance, because of her business.

## From woods to land.

There are other ways to live off the land besides heading to the woods. Another type of people who live off the land are the homesteaders. Traditionally, homesteaders were pioneer families who lived on land that they received free from the government. Today, however, this is not possible since there is no longer any free land available from the government.

## What is homesteading in this modern day?

According to Yonderway.com, a popular homesteading Internet site, homesteading is, "living in the country and being able to grow or make most of your own food, energy, and supplies. This frequently means raising your own crops and livestock, making your own soap, electricity, etc." Although they are not always able to achieve it, today's homesteaders strive to become self-sufficient.

But running a homestead also takes some start-up money. While many homesteaders manage on an average or even below-average income, they did need to have money saved up to start this style of life. For instance, there is a significant outlay of money to purchase the land and the supplies necessary for building a house (most homesteaders find it cheaper and more desirable to build their own homes).

The biggest piece of advice from homesteaders is to think carefully before buying a piece of land, because the land will be the most important aspect of a life as a homesteader. There are a lot of factors that come into play when purchasing land in very rural, remote areas. You will have to research whether or not you can grow food or raise livestock on this piece of property. You might find a great deal on a piece of property, but if it doesn't have electricity, a phone line, water well, or a road, the cost of providing these can add up to thousands of dollars.

These and other factors reiterate the importance of doing homework and finding out as much as possible before purchasing property. When looking for an ideal homestead, you also must address the following concerns.

### Location.

First and foremost, you need to decide where in the country you want to live. While doing this, you'll need to consider whether or not you are going to keep an existing job and try and commute or telecommute, or if you are going to find a new job. Depending on your answer and goal, you may have to stay within a certain distance of your office, or research where the closest place is that you can find a job.

### Cold or hot?

Think about your weather preferences, as well. Do you love or hate snow and ice, extreme heat or wind, and how will this affect any potential livelihood you hope to make from your land?

### Don't forget your health.

Do you have any medical conditions or problems that require a location close to hospitals and doctors?

### Research, research, research.

Once you have found a piece of land that interests you, find out if the land is controlled by an association, what the taxes will be on both the property and the house, what kind of limitations the town or area might have on building your dream home, and what the property boundaries are.

Don't forget to check the cleanliness of the water and the soil type. Does the property flood or become uninhabitable in different weather conditions, such as rain or snow? Are there any streams or creeks that run across it? What is the property's elevation? Is there a road or other public property on the land?

Since a big part of homesteading is food production, if you are planning to grow fruits and vegetables, learn what the growing season is and what you can grow there. By answering these questions up front, you can avoid problems later on.

Another factor to consider is a significant decrease in disposable income, which for some, might be difficult to accept. More than likely, you will be leaving a steady job and going to a lifestyle where you have no

*continued*

consistent outside source of income. Yet there will always be ongoing expenses, such as buying equipment and supplies.

In addition to these concerns, homesteading can be very tough for some people, because it's hard, physical work. However, life as a modern homesteader does benefit from some modern conveniences. Today, there are affordable, independent, home energy systems, and reliable alternative energy sources such as solar and wind power, and steam engines.

Cell phones are another convenience for homesteaders. As reception improves each year, cell phones do not require the expense of having a phone line installed. The same is true for satellite TV dishes that can bring that medium to even the most isolated areas of the country.

Even the Internet has reached the modern homestead. With mail order and Internet companies delivering goods such as food, clothing, parts, and equipment right to your front door, it is even easier to live in the most remote parts of the country.

With all of this in mind, you might ask, "Is life in the woods or as a homesteader really 'simpler'?" According to LaBastille, "Yes, it is simple, you are not living crammed in, with the competition and not keeping up with the Joneses. You can get up and say, 'this is what I am going to do today.' "

But there is hard work that's involved in being independent and self-reliant. She says, "So many people have this fantasy, but it's not true. You have to carry your own water, carry your own wood, and it is hard work. But the trade-off is it keeps you energetic and physically fit, and you live with clean air and clean water."

As for today's homesteaders, according to *Countryside* magazine, "Homesteading is simple in the sense that it's plain, and without pretense—not because it's easy and uncomplicated."

So despite all the challenges, if you still feel the urge to go and live off the land, the following list of resources will help you find more information for planning your big move.

## HELPFUL INTERNET SITES

*Backwoods Home* magazine **www.backwoodshome.com**
*Country Home* magazine **www.countryhomemag.com**
Homesteading/Rural Living Site **www.yonderway.com**
*Rural Living* Web magazine **www.rural-living.com**
*Rural Living* Canada **www.torpw1.netcom.ca/~kenruss/rural.htm**
Homesteaders Ring **www.mcsi.net/ssp/homesteaders**
*Back Home* magazine **www.BackHomeMagazine.com**

## HELPFUL BOOKS AND MAGAZINES

*Readers Digest. Back to Basics : How to Learn and Enjoy Traditional American Skills*,(1987).
Skip Thomsen & Cat Freshwater. *The Modern Homestead Manual*,(1994).
*Countryside and Small Stock Magazine*, (800) 551-5691, (715) 785-7979.
*Backwoods Home* magazine, P.O. Box 40, Montague, CA 96064.
*BackHome* magazine, 119 Third Ave. West, Hendersonville, NC 28792.

# HOME  MADE
## *Made Easy!*

## Hot Chocolate

2 cups instant nonfat dry milk
3/4 cup sugar
1/2 cup unsweetened cocoa
1 tsp. salt
1 cup miniature marshmallows (optional)

Stir all ingredients together and store in a tightly closed jar or container for up to 2 months. To use, put 2 or 3 heaping tablespoons of the mix into a cup filled with either boiling water or hot milk. For a present, place in an empty glass jar, write the directions on a small piece of paper and attach the paper to the lid with ribbon or yarn.

## Doggie Treats

1 pound liver, organs, or other meat
(enough to make 2 cups cooked meat)
2 cups bran
2 cups old-fashioned oatmeal
1/4 cup cooking oil

Place meat in a pot and cover with cold water. Bring to a boil. Immediately lower heat and simmer for 35 minutes. Remove meat from water and let cool. Retain water. Once the meat is completely cool, chop into 1-inch pieces. Grind in a food processor or chop in a blender until it is finely ground. Mix together the ground meat, bran, oatmeal and oil, adding the meat cooking water as necessary to make a thick dough. Be careful not to add too much liquid. Make it wet enough to work with. Shape the dough into desired shapes (bones, or flat circles) and place on an oiled baking sheet. Bake at 250°F for 3 hours. Then turn the oven off, but leave the biscuits in until they cool. This will ensure that they are hard and crunchy. Let the biscuits air-dry for 24 hours and then store in an airtight container. They will keep for at least one month. (Makes a great gift for pet lovers!)

## Make-It-Yourself "Cracker Jacks"

4 cups popped popcorn
1 cup shelled peanuts
1/2 cup molasses
1/4 cup sugar

Note: A candy thermometer is recommended to test the temperature of the syrup that binds the popcorn and nuts together.

Mix popcorn and peanuts together in a large bowl. Cook molasses and sugar together until the mixture reaches a temperature of 235°F on a candy thermometer. If you don't have a thermometer, test the syrup by letting some drop from a spoon into a cup of cold water. If the syrup forms a thread as it drops into the water, it's done. Pour the hot syrup over the popcorn-nut mixture and stir to coat evenly. Cool and break into chunks with a wooden spoon. Store in an airtight container. (Gift idea: place in a clean jelly Mason jar or ornamental paper gift bag.)

**W**hen I was growing up in the 1950s, I can remember my Grandmother's icebox. The "Iceman," who drove a horse-drawn trolley would deliver the large, cut ice blocks. He would use tongs to lift the ice, carry it into her kitchen, and then neatly slide the single ice cake into the ice chamber of her icebox. The average ice chamber was about two feet long, two feet deep, and eighteen inches wide. If I was lucky, the Iceman would give me ice chips to bite on. Today, in the age of refrigerators, freezers, and icemakers, we can have access to ice whenever we want it. Most people either don't know about the process of ice, take it for granted, or have forgotten about the "Ice Harvest."

Prior to 1805, there was no regular commercial traffic in ice in North America. The first supply was provided in the winter of 1805-1806 at Boston, Massachusetts, by Frederick Tudor. The export trade reached its height about this time. Tudor shipped his first cargo to the West Indies in the summer of 1806, where there was a yellow fever epidemic. He became known as the "Ice King," as he carried the fame of Boston ice all around the world. Cargoes were consigned to London, the East Indies, the West Indies, Rio de Janeiro, Calcutta, China, Japan, and Australia.

Domestic and export trade were both of very slow growth. In 1825, the ice consumed in the United States was probably less than fifty thousand tons. During the thirty years following, the consumption of ice increased more rapidly, and by 1855, the estimated amount of ice stored in the U.S. was two million tons, with six or seven million dollars of capital invested.

By the British North America Act of 1867, the dominion of Canada was created. Early records indicate that by 1869, the Alberta Ice Company in Calgary was harvesting fifty thousand tons of ice a year from an artificial lake west of Calgary. The ice was then shipped in specially equipped trains to points in Alberta and southern British Columbia. In 1870, James Fairhead, known as Canada's "Ice King," had incorporated the Spring Water Ice Company in Toronto. He supplied ice to butchers, hotels, and restaurants in the city. By 1890, Fairhead had also set up the Knickerbocker Ice Company on the

**by Gloria Troyer**
*Freelance author located in Geulph, Ontario*

# The Ice

Engraving courtesy of North Wind Picture Archives

shores of Lake Simcoe, at Jacksons Point, Ontario. At that time, there were five large ice companies from the United States that formed an Ice Union, cutting and sending ice from Lake Simcoe to various cities in the eastern United States.

## THE SECOND ICE AGE

The year-round availability of ice inspired many new uses. During war, the American government was a large purchaser for use in hospitals. Brewers, who had to suspend operations during the heat of the summer, were able to brew year-round. Meat could be transported over thousands of miles. And, thanks to the advent of the commercial ice harvest, fish-

eries were able to transport their freshly frozen product to market. The demand for ice creams and cooled drinks rose, and by 1892, nearly the entire population of the USA used ice directly or indirectly.

Many physicians used ice for the alleviation of suffering among the sick. Even before the introduction of the ice trade, many doctors and managers of hospitals had private stores of ice which they used on their patients. The directors of the Pennsylvania Hospital at Philadelphia may be credited with being the pioneer ice dealers of that city. In the early 1800s, they disposed of their surplus stores of ice by selling them to the community.

## MONITORING THE CLEANLINESS

As the industry grew, more attention was given to the sanitary conditions of the sources from where the natural ice was obtained. Laws were written with regards to clean ice. Ice cut on specified polluted waters was prohibited for any use other than cooling purposes. In several states, the ice crop was protected by laws that made it a misdemeanor to destroy or injure ice in the field where it was to be cut. Ice cutting rights were divided into two classes. Ice on navigable waters was under the authority of the national government. "Navigable" being used to denote tide waters, the proprietary rights of owners of the abutting properties were limited to the water line at high tide. On all such waters, navigation being closed, the ice was free and secured by preemption; the first one to stake out a claim was entitled to cut the

*continued*

# Harvest

ice. Rivers, small lakes and navigable streams above tide water were termed public. The rights to ice were subject to contract and sale. Lakes which were fed by springs, and had clean beds; running streams, especially those with a rapid current (which purified their waters very rapidly); exposure to light and air; the influence of oxygen and the motion of the water, all contributed to a higher value for cut ice. The purity of brooks that fed an ice field was carefully preserved; filth was not dumped into them or on their banks. Stables and cesspools were situated where they wouldn't drain into the water. Vegetable refuse and litter which were carried downstream by the current were caught by screens and removed.

## MOTHER NATURE'S INFLUENCE

The weather determined the fate of the ice dealer. Once the water froze at 32° Fahrenheit, the surface assumed a solid form. From that point on, until the crop was stored in the icehouse, the ice dealer devoted all his energy to the care of the ice field. If the ice was formed on top of a running stream, it was necessary for him to monitor any possible pollution or rubbish that may have become embedded in the ice. Motion in the water was also necessary to promote the growth of the ice.

A covering of snow on an ice field was considered to be a great impediment, because it slowed the formation of ice. It was important to remove the snow as early as possible. However, when there was soft ice or warm weather, snow could act as an aid by protecting the ice from the direct heat of the sun and the force of a rain. As soon as the weather would freeze again, the water and snow on top of the ice was known as "snow ice." An inch or two of snow ice lessened any loss because of breakage of the cakes in stowing, and the ice also came out of the icehouse in better

shape. It withstood shipping easier, as it was not as brittle as clear ice.

## THE THICK AND THIN OF IT

Generally speaking, the most desirable thickness for ice was fourteen inches, which was convenient for handling. This thickness varied, of course, due to the season and the average thickness formed at a locality.

Ice harvesting operations could not begin until the ice was at least a foot thick, as it had to support the weight of horses, men, and equipment. When it was time to harvest, the ice field was inspected and mapped out for plowing. All unsound places, air holes, or shallow places where rocks or sandbars neared the surface were marked. A convenient marking method was to bore holes at such places, and plant pieces of brush in the holes. Thin ice that formed where the ice had been removed during cutting was also marked in this manner, to give warning of the danger if walked on.

The ice harvester always took note of the physical advantages of his position. If he could, he would lay out the field so that the current and prevailing winds were in his favor and would assist in floating the ice towards the icehouse. Once the field was looked over and a plan determined, the first task was to lay out baselines, from which the marking and plowing were gauged. Stakes were planted at either end of a baseline, and a heavy cord was drawn taut between them. A hand plow was then passed alongside the line, making a score in the ice from end to end. The groove was three inches deep. This operation was continued until the field was grooved with parallel lines. The field was then scored at right angles to the lines first laid out. A large wooden square, with legs about fifteen feet long, was used to square the ice, and then the field was marked and plowed in both directions.

In 1915, at the Ontario Agricultural

College in Guelph, Ontario, farmers took a course in "Harvesting the Ice Crop" and were encouraged to cooperatively share the expense of tools to be used within their own communities. In order to harvest ice efficiently, a steel scraper was required to remove the snow covering, an ice plow was needed for scoring, a slice bar for breaking off the blocks, pike poles for bearing down on heavy cut ice to prevent it from crashing into or going over the top of the last block, and lots of chain with a heavy pair of ice tongs attached to lift and hoist the ice blocks. A platform was necessary with one end which was let down in the water and the other end raised level with the floor of a sleigh. The ice was removed from the field and then packed into an ice house.

## FROM ICE VAULTS TO ICEHOUSES

Before ice was cut and stored commercially, ice vaults or cellars were used. Vaults or pits, circular at the top, and tapering to a point at the bottom, were scooped out of the ground. The sides and the top were lined thickly with straw, and then filled with tightly packed snow. The doorway was at the top. Brewers, dairymen, butchers, and some physicians had ice vaults or cellars.

The first commercial icehouses were built below the ground, but gradually they emerged into the light and air. Moisture caused by the atmosphere needed proper ventilation to escape. Proper drainage eliminated the moisture that came from the foundation. The size of the icehouse depended on its required needs. In an icehouse where the ice was packed closely, icemen generally allowed about 45 pounds of ice for every cubic foot of space, or 45 cubic feet to the ton. When the ice was loosely packed, they allowed about 40 pounds of ice for every cubic foot of space or about 50 cubic feet to the ton. The larger the icehouse, the less waste in shrinkage.

Wood was the cheapest and best material for building an icehouse. Its porous character was favorable to free evaporation, which was the key to keeping the building dry. Hemlock, spruce, white and yellow pine were preferred. Stone or brick were not used as they retained water vapor and caused sweating which melted the ice. The durability of ice also depended on its density.

Of all the materials used for protection in the walls, on the loft floors and on the ice, sawdust was considered to be the best. Sawdust and dried peat dust were used mostly for filling the walls. Prairie or swamp hay, rye straw, and swamp rushes were often used as loft floor dunnage and also for covering the ice. When good walls were built, it was not advisable to use sawdust over the ice because it soiled it too much. Straw was more liable to retain moisture, but it kept the ice cleaner. The best covering for ice was swamp rushes.

## MODERN ICE MAKING

By 1914, many companies in both Canada and the United States began making plans to manufacture rather than harvest ice. Standard-sized ice blocks were needed for iceboxes. Commercial ice harvesting eventually gave way to the invention of refrigeration, as we know it today. But just recently, I met an ice harvester from New Brunswick, Canada. Recreational ice fishermen use the ice he provides, to keep their drinks cool and their fish fresh. The tradition of ice harvesting, like many other traditions, has survived into the twenty-first century!

# The Planets in 2001

## Brightest Or Best Seen

### ☿ MERCURY

As an evening star, appears in the western sky setting about an hour after the Sun. As a morning star, it appears in the eastern sky rising about an hour before the Sun. There must be a clear, unobstructed horizon on these occasions. Mercury usually appears as a bright "star" with a yellowish or ochre hue.

**Mornings:** February 21 to April 7, June 28 to July 21, October 23 to November 7.

**Evenings:** January 20 to February 3, May 7 to June 4, August 22 to October 5.

**Brightest:** Mercury will be brightest and easiest to spot in the evening sky between May 8 and May 29, and brightest and easiest to spot in the morning sky between October 23 and November 7.

### ♀ VENUS

Always brilliant and shining with a steady, silvery light.

**Mornings:** In the eastern sky at dawn from April 7 to November 13.

**Evenings:** In the western sky at dusk from January 1 to March 21.

**Brightest:** Venus will attain its greatest brilliancy in the evening sky on February 20 and again in the morning sky on May 4. The Moon will pass in front of Venus as seen from North America and Hawaii during the daylight hours of July 17.

### ♂ MARS

Shining like a "star" with a yellowish-orange hue, it can vary considerably in brightness.

**Mornings:** January 1 through June 12.

**Evenings:** June 13 to December 31.

**Brightest:** In 2001 during the month of June, when it will be a brilliant object, shining nearly twice as bright as Sirius (the brightest star in the sky). On June 21, Mars will be closest to Earth for this current apparition: 41,845,000 miles away.

### ♃ JUPITER

Quite brilliant with a silver-white luster.

**Mornings:** July 5 to December 31.

**Evenings:** January 1 to May 23.

**Brightest:** In 2001 during the last half of December.

### ♄ SATURN

Shines like a yellowish-white "star" of moderate brightness. The famous rings are only visible with a telescope.

**Mornings:** June 13 to December 2.

**Evenings:** January 1 to May 6, December 3 to December 31.

**Brightest:** Mid-November to mid-December. The Moon "crosses paths" with Saturn twice in 2001, resulting in the Moon passing in front of Saturn (called an "occultation"). These "Saturn eclipses" are scheduled for November 30 and December 28, the first favoring southern and eastern portions of North America, and occurring during the early evening hours and the other favoring all of North America in the predawn morning hours.

### ⛢ URANUS

**Mornings:** February 25 to August 14.

**Evenings:** January 1 to January 23, August 15 to December 31.

### ♆ NEPTUNE

**Mornings:** February 11 to July 29.

**Evenings:** January 1 to January 9, July 30 to December 31.

### ♇ PLUTO

Will not be visible in 2001.

# THE PLANETS IN 2001

| MORNING STARS | | EVENING STARS | | FAINT OR INVISIBLE | |
|---|---|---|---|---|---|
| MERCURY | FEB 13 to APR 22 | MERCURY | JAN 1 to FEB 12 | MERCURY | Except for brief periods around the dates listed. |
| | JUN 16 to AUG 4 | | APR 23 to JUN 15 | | |
| | OCT 14 to DEC 3 | | AUG 5 to OCT 13 | VENUS | MAR 31 to APR 7 |
| VENUS | MAR 30 to DEC 31 | | DEC 4 to DEC 31 | MARS | NOT IN 2001 |
| MARS | JAN 1 to JUN 12 | VENUS | JAN 1 to MAR 29 | JUPITER | MAY 24 to JUL 4 |
| JUPITER | JUN 14 to DEC 31 | MARS | JUN 13 to DEC 31 | SATURN | MAY 7 to JUN 12 |
| SATURN | MAY 25 to DEC 2 | JUPITER | JAN 1 to JUN 13 | URANUS | JAN 24 to FEB 24 |
| URANUS | FEB 9 to AUG 14 | SATURN | JAN 1 to MAY 24 | NEPTUNE | JAN 10 to FEB 10 |
| NEPTUNE | JAN 26 to JUL 29 | | DEC 3 to DEC 31 | PLUTO | All year |
| | | URANUS | JAN 1 to FEB 8 | | |
| | | | AUG 15 to DEC 31 | | |
| | | NEPTUNE | JAN 1 to JAN 25 | | |
| | | | JUL 30 to DEC 31 | | |

## THE PLANET THAT WASN'T

Within the famous star pattern we call the Big Dipper, we can find the star Mizar, the middle star in the Dipper's handle. Mizar has a fainter companion, about one-fourth as bright, known as Alcor. When Mizar and Alcor are viewed through a telescope, the two appear bright and far apart from each other. But that's not all. Mizar itself is separated into two stars very close together. Back in 1722, a German mathematics professor, J.G. Liebknecht, was examining Mizar with a crude telescope and chanced upon a faint star between Mizar and Alcor.

With some fanfare, he announced that he had discovered a new planet, and named it "Sidus Ludoviciana" or "Ludwig's Star" after his sovereign, the Landgrave Ludwig of Hessen-Darmstadt. But the reaction from other astronomers throughout Europe was universally unfavorable, as they noted that Liebknecht's "new planet" was merely a fixed telescopic star. Nonetheless, to this day, the star still retains the name that was bestowed upon it by Liebknecht when —for a few months anyway—it was thought to be a planet!

# ECLIPSES IN 2001

Eastern Standard Time

## There will be FIVE eclipses in 2001:

# TWO of the SUN and THREE of the MOON.

▶ **January 9**
**Total Eclipse of the Moon.**
This will be the first eclipse of the 21st century. It will be primarily visible from much of Asia, Europe and Africa, where the entire event will be viewable. The visible stages of the eclipse will already be in progress as the Moon rises over eastern portions of South America, mid-Atlantic and northeastern United States, and eastern Canada. The total phase will be observable from the Canadian Maritimes. From Indonesia and Australia, the eclipse will still be in progress as the Moon sets. At its deepest phase, the northern edge of the Moon will be closest to the outer edge of the umbra by 419 miles.

**Circumstances of the Eclipse**
- Moon enters umbra 1:42 p.m.
- Total eclipse begins 2:50 p.m.
- Deepest eclipse 3:21 p.m.
- Total eclipse ends 3:52 p.m.
- Moon leaves umbra 4:59 p.m.
- Magnitude of the eclipse is 1.194.

▶ **June 21**
**Total Eclipse of the Sun.**
The path of totality, from where the disc of the Moon will appear to completely obscure the Sun, will average 103 miles in width and will begin in the south Atlantic Ocean, roughly 250 miles offshore from Mar del Plata, Argentina. The Moon's dark umbral shadow will sweep first northeast, then east over the open ocean, before finally making landfall over the African nation of Angola, between the capital city Luanda and Lobito. The shadow will head eastsoutheast across Zambia (enveloping the capital Lusaka), Zimbabwe and Mozambique. It then will cross the Mozambique Channel and will cut a narrow strip through southern Madagascar before coming to an end in the western Indian Ocean. It will be over the south Atlantic Ocean, approximately 500 miles due west of the central Angolan coast, that the maximum duration of totality–4 minutes 56.6 seconds–will be attained. The associated partial phases will be visible from much of the central and eastern portions of South America, most of the southern and central Atlantic Ocean and the lower three-fourths of Africa.

**Circumstances of the Eclipse**
- Partial eclipse begins 4:33 a.m.
- Central eclipse begins 5:36 a.m.
- Greatest eclipse 7:04 a.m.
- Central eclipse ends 8:32 a.m.
- Partial eclipse ends 9:34 a.m.

▶ **July 5**
**Partial Eclipse of the Moon.**
Primarily visible from eastern Asia, including Indonesia, Australia, New Zealand and the western Pacific Ocean, where the entire eclipse will be visible. The eclipse will already be in progress as the Moon rises over the central and west-central portions of Asia and the eastern third of Africa. From much of the central and eastern Pacific, as well as Hawaii and the Aleutian Islands, the eclipse will still be in progress as the Moon sets. The magnitude of this eclipse is 0.500, which means that at its deepest phase the upper half of the Moon's disc will be immersed in the Earth's umbral shadow.

**Circumstances of the Eclipse**
- Moon enters umbra 9:35 a.m.
- Greatest eclipse 10:55 a.m.
- Moon leaves umbra 12:15 p.m.

# ECLIPSES IN 2001
### Eastern Standard Time

▶ **December 14th**
## Annular Eclipse of the Sun.

The path of annularity, from where the entire silhouette of the Moon's disk will appear against the Sun's brilliant disc (creating an annulus or ring effect), averages 93 miles in width. It begins in the north-central Pacific Ocean, roughly 1,200 miles northeast of Hawaii. Most of the path is, in fact, over water, sweeping southeast, east and finally northeast across the open ocean before finally making landfall over Central America, just before the shadow path comes to an end. The so-called "negative shadow," or anti-umbra passes over northern Costa Rica and southern Nicaragua. The path will come to an end at local sunset in the Caribbean Sea, less than 200 miles south of Jamaica. It will be over the eastern Pacific Ocean, approximately 2,500 miles south-southwest of Los Angeles, that the maximum duration of annularity–3 minutes 53 seconds–will be attained. The associated partial phases will be visible to varying extents over a large portion of the central and eastern Pacific Ocean, much of central and western North America, Central America, and northern and western sections of South America. Generally speaking, for the United States, the eclipse will be visible everywhere except over the northern half of Alaska, extreme northeastern New York state, and much of central and northern New England. In Canada, the eclipse will be visible near and along the Pacific Coast, and for all areas south of a zone extending from roughly Banff to Churchill to Cornwall. Most areas will see less than 30 percent of the Sun's diameter eclipsed by the passing new Moon. The chief exception is Hawaii, where nearly 90 percent coverage will occur soon after sunrise. The times provided are geocentric.

For the exact times and other details concerning your specific area, your newspapers and broadcasts will be full of them. One word of caution–be very, very careful about the precautions for eclipse viewing. **NEVER** look at even a tiny bit of the Sun's disc unless you are using a proper filtration device, like #14 welder's glass or aluminized Mylar plastic to protect your eyes! You'll get all the safety tips from the papers– observe them!

**Circumstances of the Eclipse**
- **Partial eclipse begins 1:03 p.m.**
- **Central eclipse begins 2:08 p.m.**
- **Greatest eclipse 3:52 p.m.**
- **Central eclipse ends 5:36 p.m.**
- **Partial eclipse ends 6:41 p.m.**

▶ **December 30th**
## Penumbral Eclipse of the Moon.

The Moon will pass through the outer portion of the Earth's shadow, the so-called "half-shadow," or penumbra. This shadow is very faint and difficult to perceive unless the Moon's disc is immersed to a degree of at least 70 percent of its diameter within the penumbra, close to the edge of the much darker umbral shadow. This eclipse will be primarily visible from North America, most of the Pacific Ocean and northeast Asia. The eclipse will already be in progress at moonrise for central Asia, Indonesia, Australia and New Zealand, and will still be in progress at moonset for most of South America. The magnitude of this eclipse is 0.919, which means that at, and within about a half-hour of, its deepest phase, even a casual observer should note that the Moon's lower portion appears slightly smudged or tarnished.

**Circumstances of the Eclipse**
- **Moon enters penumbra 3:25 a.m.**
- **Greatest eclipse 5:29 a.m.**
- **Moon leaves penumbra 7:33 a.m.**

# METEORS AND METEOR SHOWERS

Meteors, more commonly referred to as "falling" or "shooting" stars, are metallic or stony particles which become visible when they plunge through our atmosphere. Though 100 million or more strike our atmosphere every 24 hours, those larger than dust particles are usually vaporized long before they can ever get close to the Earth's surface. The average meteor is estimated to weigh 0.0005 ounce.

Meteors may be seen on almost any clear night, though they are more common in the hours after midnight. A single observer, far from bright lights with an unobstructed view of the sky, can usually see about 6 or 7 per hour. When the Earth's orbit intersects a meteor stream, a meteor "shower" is said to be in progress. Occasionally, stupendous meteor displays can fill the sky with celestial fireworks, but these meteor "storms" are rare, occurring at best, only several times per century.

Very bright meteors are termed fireballs. If a solid object reaches the ground, it is called a meteorite. They vary from bits hardly larger than dust particles to chunks weighing tons.

**Best way to view meteors.**

The best way to watch for meteors is to find a place with a clear view of the sky and arrange for deck chairs or some other comfortable rest. Warm clothing and a blanket—even in summer—are advisable. Another factor to consider is bright moonlight, which can considerably cut into the potential number of meteors that might be seen. If a gibbous or full Moon is present during your meteor watch, it will generally obliterate all but the very brightest of meteors.

## Best Dates and Times to View Meteor Showers

The following table lists some of the best-known meteor showers.
If your location observes daylight saving time, add one hour to "best time."
Times given are listed in Eastern Standard Time.

| Name | Maximum Activity | Average Hourly Rate | Best Direction and Time to Watch | Speed and Comments |
| --- | --- | --- | --- | --- |
| Quadrantids | January 3-4 | 60-120 | Northeast 4 to 6 am | Medium |
| Lyrids | April 21-22 | 10-20 | Overhead 2 to 4 am | Swift streaks |
| Eta Aquarids | May 4-5 | 20-40 | Southeast 2 to 4 am | Very swift, long paths |
| Delta Aquarids | July 28-29 | 15-25 | South 1 to 3 am | Slow, long paths |
| Perseids | August 11-13 | 50-100 | Northeast 2 to 4 am | Very swift, rich annual display |
| Orionids | October 21-22 | 15-25 | South 2 to 4 am | Swift streaks |
| South Taurids | November 2-4 | 10-20 | South 1 to 3 am | Very slow, bright |
| North Taurids | November 12-14 | 10-20 | South 12 to 2 am | Slow fireballs |
| Leonids | November 17-18 | 25-50 | S/Southeast 4 to 6 am | Very swift |
| Geminids | December 13-14 | 50-100 | Overhead 1 to 3 am | Medium, white; a rich display |
| Ursids | December 22-23 | 15-25 | North all night | Medium |

# THE MOON

| DATE AND TIME OF FULL MOONS IN 2001—EST | | | |
|---|---|---|---|
| January | 9th | Full Wolf Moon | 3:24 p.m. |
| February | 8th | Full Snow Moon | 2:11 a.m. |
| March | 9th | Full Worm Moon | 12:23 p.m. |
| April | 7th | Full Pink Moon | 10:21 p.m. |
| May | 7th | Full Flower Moon | 8:52 a.m. |
| June | 5th | Full Strawberry Moon | 8:39 p.m. |
| July | 5th | Full Buck Moon | 10:03 a.m. |
| August | 4th | Full Sturgeon Moon | 12:55 a.m. |
| September | 2nd | Full Fruit/Barley Moon | 4:43 p.m. |
| October | 2nd | Full Harvest Moon | 8:48 a.m. |
| November | 1st | Full Hunter's Moon | 12:41 a.m. |
| November | 30th | Full Beaver/Blue Moon | 3:49 p.m. |
| December | 30th | Full Cold Moon | 5:40 a.m. |

## ❧ Planting by the Moon ❧

Many people believe that the Moon plays an important role in gardening. They believe that the phase of the Moon dictates the best time to plant, fertilize, weed and more. For fun we offer the following planting suggestions gathered from various sources.

### ○ FULL MOON

**Dig root crops. They'll keep longer.**

**Plant belowground/root crops (beets, carrots, potatoes or turnips) between the full and new Moon.**

**Cut hay between the full and new Moon; it will dry quicker.**

**Harvest crops between the full and new Moon. They'll keep longer and in better condition.**

### ● NEW MOON

**Plant aboveground crops.**

### ◐ FIRST QUARTER

**Plant corn.**

**Plant flowers between the first quarter and full Moon.**

**Dig sweet potatoes between the first quarter and full Moon.**

### ◑ LAST QUARTER

**Cut timber during the last quarter. It will dry better and not be worm-eaten.**

**Can fruit and vegetables when Moon is decreasing in light (after the full Moon).**

**Fertilize with manure during the third and fourth quarter.**

**Pull out weeds during this phase.**

# EXPLANATION OF THE CALENDAR PAGES

**A**ll events listed on the calendar pages are plotted to an accuracy of approximately one minute, and computed for the sea horizon for the rising and setting of the upper limb of the sun and moon. In addition, allowance has been made for the effects of astronomical refraction. Local conditions, such as the difference between your latitude and those of the calendar pages (35° and 45° north), as well as the character of your local horizon will add uncertainties of up to five minutes.

The times for the rising and setting of the sun and moon are calculated for an observer at 75° west longitude and either 35° or 45° north latitude. However, simple corrections will allow you to obtain sufficient accuracy to all places in the contiguous zones indicated by the headings of the divisions.

**To convert the listed time of an event from civil to standard (clock) time, the following corrections must be made:**

**Daylight Saving Time.** If this is in effect for your region, add one hour to any time obtained from the calendar page.

**Your longitude.** The rise and set times of the sun and moon are given in civil or local mean time (LMT), which differs from ordinary clock time by many minutes at most locations. Our civil time zones are standardized on particular longitudes. Examples in North America are: Eastern–75° west; Central–90° west; Mountain–105° west; Pacific–120° west. If your longitude is very close to one of these, luck is with you and this correction is zero.

**To get standard time add four minutes** to times listed on the calendar page **for each degree of longitude that you are west** of your time zone meridian. Or **subtract four minutes for each degree you are east** of it. Look up your longitude on a map.

*Example: Boston, Massachusetts (longitude 71°) is 4 degrees east of the Eastern time meridian. So, in Boston, subtract 16 minutes to rise and set time obtained from the calendar pages. The result is Eastern Standard Time.*

Find your local correction and commit it to memory; you will use it always. Here are some corrections, in minutes, for selected major cities:

## CORRECTION FROM ZONE TIME TO LOCAL TIME

*(Apply to time found in calendar pages to get clock time)*

| | | | | | | | |
|---|---|---|---|---|---|---|---|
| Atlanta | +38 | Detroit | +32 | Minneapolis | +13 | Rochester, NY | +10 |
| Atlantic City | -01 | Durham | +16 | Nashville | -13 | Salt Lake City | +28 |
| Baltimore | +06 | El Paso | +06 | New Orleans | 00 | San Antonio | +34 |
| Bismarck | +43 | Helena | +28 | New York | -04 | San Diego | -12 |
| Boise | +45 | Houston | +21 | Oklahoma City | +32 | San Francisco | +10 |
| Boston | -16 | Indianapolis | +44 | Pensacola | -11 | Santa Fe | +04 |
| Buffalo | +15 | Jacksonville | +27 | Philadelphia | +01 | Savannah | +24 |
| Chicago | -10 | Kansas City | +18 | Pittsburgh | +20 | Seattle | +10 |
| Cincinnati | +38 | Los Angeles | -07 | Portland, ME | -19 | St. Louis | +01 |
| Cleveland | +27 | Memphis | 00 | Portland, OR | +11 | Tampa | +30 |
| Dallas | +27 | Miami | +21 | Providence | -14 | Tucson | +24 |
| Denver | 00 | Milwaukee | -08 | Richmond | +10 | Washington, D.C. | +08 |

## CHARACTERS, ASPECTS AND ABBREVIATIONS

♄ Saturn – cold, dry
♃ Jupiter – moist, warm
♂ Mars – hot, dry
☉ Sun – fiery, dry
♀ Venus – moist, warm
⊕ Earth
☿ Mercury – warm, dry
☽ Moon – cold, moist
♅ Uranus – hot, dry
♆ Neptune – moist

♇ Pluto
⌢ Moon highest
⌣ Moon lowest
☊ Moon ascending node
☋ Moon descending node
☌ conjunction or near together
☍ opposition or 180° apart
per. – perigee, near to Earth
apo. – apogee, far from Earth

el. – elongation
cl. – close
sta. – stationary
inf. – inferior
mer. – meridian
occ. – occultation
ri. – rises
sup. – superior
E. – East
W. – West

# EXPLANATION OF THE CALENDAR PAGES

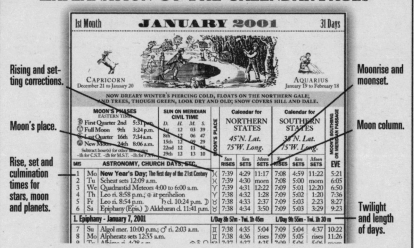

Rising and setting corrections. — Moonrise and moonset.

Moon's place. — Moon column.

Rise, set and culmination times for stars, moon and planets. — Twilight and length of days.

■ **Rising and setting corrections.** Times of rising and setting need correction if your latitude differs from the two divisions. The times of the rising and setting of the sun and moon are given for latitudes 45 and 35 degrees, respectively. To obtain more precision for other latitudes, a more exact time can be obtained by interpolation and extrapolation.

■ **Moon's place.** This indicates the zodiacal constellation that the moon occupies each day at 7:00 a.m. EST. Symbols for each of the twelve zodiacal signs are presented here.

■ **Moonrise and moonset.** Determining moonrise and moonset is similar to sunrise and sunset, except an additional correction factor must be added. This is because the moon's rapid orbital motion alters the lunar rising and setting times slightly if your longitude differs from 75 degrees west.

■ **Rise, set, and culmination times for stars, moon, and planets.** These are found on the wide columns of the calendar pages and are calculated for 35 and 45 degrees north latitude. Morning "a.m." is from midnight to noon and evening "p.m." from noon to midnight. As with the rising and setting times of the sun and moon, use the correction table to convert zone time to local time in order to obtain a greater degree of accuracy. This rule also pertains to culmination or meridian passage ("mer.") time of a given object, for the moon's southing or meridian passage.

■ **Moon column.** Times in the moon rises/sets column are given only for hours of darkness, with the time shown being the first moon event visible on that date. Rising times change to setting times (and vice versa) after sunset on or close to new moon (sets) and full moon (rises). When "morn." appears, no moon rise or set occurs: the next moon event is in the early morning of the following date. The moon rises and sets roughly two minutes later for each time zone west of Eastern Time (0 minutes for Eastern, 2 minutes Central, 4 minutes Mountain and 6 minutes for Pacific).

■ **Twilight and length of days.** Across the calendars and even with the Sunday Liturgical Calendar, you will find the average length of day and length of astronomical twilight beginning Sunday and calculated for 35 and 45 degrees north latitude. To determine the length of day at other locations, use the methods listed earlier to determine sunrise and sunset times for your city. Add 12 hours to the time of sunset, subtract the time of sunrise, and you will have the length of day. *What is twilight?* Twilight is caused by the scattering of sunlight by molecules in the upper troposphere or stratosphere when the Sun is beneath the horizon. Astronomical morning twilight begins and astronomical evening twilight ends when the sun is 18 degrees beneath the observer's horizon. When the sun is more than 18 degrees below the horizon, the portions of the atmosphere illuminated by the sun are so high (50 miles and higher) that the scattered light is not perceptible. No more light is reflected and darkness ensues. The reverse occurs during dawn. Twilight encompasses the entire sky, but the illuminated atmospheric layers are lower and denser in the direction of the sun, and the resulting glow is higher.

# 2001 HEBREW CALENDAR
## YEARS 5761 - 5762
*The Year 5761 is the Fourth of the 304th of 19 years*

| YEAR | NO. | MONTH | DAY | FESTIVAL | CIVIL YEAR |
|------|-----|-------|-----|----------|-----------|
| **5761** | 4/10 | Tebet | 10 | Fast of Tebet | Friday, January 5 |
| | 5/11 | Shebat | 1 | Rosh Chodesh | Thursday, January 25 |
| | | | 15 | Tu B'Shebat | Thursday, February 8 |
| | 6/12 | Adar | *1 | Rosh Chodesh | Saturday, February 24 |
| | | | 13 | Fast of Esther | Thursday, March 8 |
| | | | 14 | Purim (Feast of Lots) | Friday, March 9 |
| | 7/1 | Nisan | 1 | Rosh Chodesh | Sunday, March 25 |
| | | | 15 | First Day of Pesach (Passover) | Sunday, April 8 |
| | | | 22 | Last Day of Pesach | Sunday, April 15 |
| | 8/2 | Iyar | *1 | Rosh Chodesh | Tuesday, April 24 |
| | | | 18 | Lag B'Omer | Friday, May 11 |
| | 9/3 | Sivan | 1 | Rosh Chodesh | Wednesday, May 23 |
| | | | 6 | First Day of Shavuot | Monday, May 28 |
| | 10/4 | Tammuz | *1 | Rosh Chodesh | Friday, June 22 |
| | | | 17 | Fast of Tammuz | Sunday, July 8 |
| | 11/5 | Av | 1 | Rosh Chodesh | Saturday, July 21 |
| | | | 9 | Fast of Av | Sunday, July 29 |
| | 12/6 | Elul | *1 | Rosh Chodesh | Monday, August 20 |
| **5762** | 1/7 | Tishri | 1 | Rosh Hashanah (New Year) | Tuesday, September 18 |
| | | | 3 | Fast of Gedaliah | Thursday, September 20 |
| | | | 10 | Yom Kippur (Day of Atonement) | Thursday, September 27 |
| | | | 15 | First Day of Succot | Tuesday, October 2 |
| | | | 21 | Hoshanah-Rabbah | Monday, October 8 |
| | | | 22 | Shemini Atzereth | Tuesday, October 9 |
| | | | 23 | Simchat Torah | Wednesday, October 10 |
| | 2/8 | Cheshvan | *1 | Rosh Chodesh | Thursday, October 18 |
| | 3/9 | Kislev | 1 | Rosh Chodesh | Friday, November 16 |
| | | | 25 | First Day of Chanukah | Monday, December 10 |
| | 4/10 | Tebet | *1 | Rosh Chodesh | Sunday, December 16 |
| | | | 10 | Fast of Tebet | Tuesday, December 25 |

\* Previous day is also observed as Rosh Chodesh.
Completed with the kind assistance of Rabbi Israel C. Stein, D.D., Congregation Rodeph Sholom, Bridgeport, CT.

# MOVABLE HOLIDAYS AND CHURCH DAYS IN 2001
*Note: Because so many changes are being made by the various churches we are limiting this list to those which are most essential.*

| | | | |
|---|---|---|---|
| Martin L. King, Jr. Birthday ... | Jan. 15 | Eastern Orth. Ascension Day | May 24 |
| Presidents' Day | Feb. 19 | Memorial Day | May 28 |
| Shrove Tuesday | Feb. 27 | Eastern Orth. Pentecost | June 3 |
| Ash Wednesday | Feb. 28 | Father's Day | June 17 |
| Good Friday | Apr. 13 | Labor Day | Sept. 3 |
| Easter Sunday | Apr. 15 | Columbus Day | Oct. 8 |
| Eastern Orth. Easter Sunday .. | Apr. 15 | Election Day | Nov. 6 |
| Mother's Day | May 13 | Thanksgiving Day | Nov. 22 |
| Ascension Day | May 24 | First Sunday in Advent | Dec. 2 |

# CALENDAR FOR 2001

## Ruling Periods of the Twelve Signs of the Zodiac and their Relation to the Body

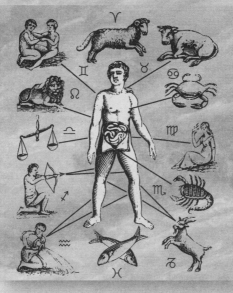

**Ram**
**Aries** ♈
Head & Face
Mar. 20 at 9 a.m.
to Apr. 19 at 8 p.m.

**Twins**
**Gemini** ♊
Arms
May 21 at 8 p.m.
to Jun. 21 at 3 a.m.

**Lion**
**Leo** ♌
Heart
Jul. 22 at 1 p.m.
to Aug. 22 at 9 p.m.

**Balance**
**Libra** ♎
Reins
Sep. 22 at 7 p.m.
to Oct. 23 at 3 a.m.

**Archer**
**Sagittarius** ♐
Thighs
Nov. 22 at 1 a.m.
to Dec. 21 at 2 p.m.

**Waterman**
**Aquarius** ♒
Legs
Jan. 19 at 8 p.m.
to Feb. 18 at 10 a.m.

**Bull**
♉ **Taurus**
Neck
Apr. 19 at 8 p.m.
to May 21 at 8 p.m.

**Crab**
♋ **Cancer**
Breast
Jun. 21 at 3 a.m.
to Jul. 22 at 1 p.m.

**Virgin**
♍ **Virgo**
Bowels
Aug. 22 at 9 p.m.
to Sep. 22 at 7 p.m.

**Scorpion**
♏ **Scorpio**
Secrets
Oct. 23 at 3 a.m.
to Nov. 22 at 1 a.m.

**Goat**
♑ **Capricorn**
Knees
Dec. 21 at 2 p.m.
to Jan. 19 at 8 p.m.

**Fishes**
♓ **Pisces**
Feet
Feb. 18 at 10 a.m.
to Mar. 20 at 9 a.m.

## The Seasons
### EASTERN STANDARD TIME

| Sun enters: | Sign | Long. | Const'n. | |
|---|---|---|---|---|
| | ♑ | 270° | ♐ | Winter begins, Dec. 21, 2000, 8:38 a.m. |
| | ♈ | 0° | ♓ | Spring begins, Mar. 20, 2001, 8:31 a.m. |
| | ♋ | 90° | ♉ | Summer begins, Jun. 21, 2001, 2:38 a.m. |
| | ♎ | 180° | ♏ | Autumn begins, Sep. 22, 2001, 6:05 p.m. |
| | ♑ | 270° | ♐ | Winter begins, Dec. 21, 2001, 2:22 p.m. |

Earth in Perihelion **January 4, 2001  4:00 a.m.** – 91,402,630 miles from the Sun.
Earth in Aphelion **July 4, 2001  9:00 a.m.** – 94,503,470 miles from the Sun.

**ERAS AND CYCLES:** The year **2001** is from **July 4**, the **226th** year of Independence of the United States of America. The Dominical or Sunday Letters G; Epact 5; Golden Number 7; Solar Cycle 22; Roman Indiction 9; Julian Period **6,714** and **January 1**, is the **2,451,911** day since its beginning; Dionysian Period 330; Jewish Lunar Cycle 4.

Selected Church Days, Holidays, Birthdays, Notable Events, Moon's Apogee and Perigee, and the more interesting astronomical events of the year will be found on their proper dates in the wide columns of 12 calendar pages. Unless otherwise stated all figures are in Civil Time. The Moon's place is given in connection with the Lucky and Unlucky Days. Use the Sign as given under Moon's place in the calendar pages for all planting and astrological calculations.

Mail astronomical questions, with stamped, self-addressed envelope, directly to:
**Hart Wright Company, P.O. Box 1609, Lewiston, ME 04241**

# GENERAL WEATHER OUTLOOK
## 2000-2001

### A WARMING TREND?

According to the National Oceanic and Atmospheric Administration, last winter was the warmest one ever recorded in North America. And, almost in confirmation of this warmth, a report issued April 2000, from botanists at the Smithsonian Institution, revealed that many flowering plants in the Washington, D.C., area started blooming about one week earlier than they did thirty years previously. Another document, published in the 1997 journal *Nature*, reported that the growing season north of latitude 45 degrees lengthened by about a week between 1981 and 1991.

While some scientists blame this warming trend on greenhouse gases, others feel that the Earth's weather is influenced chiefly by the antics of the Sun. Their theory suggests that, while variable aspects of the atmosphere, like the jet stream, subtropical high pressure zones, and changing ocean temperatures (the El Niño and La Niña currents) certainly affect our weather, all of those atmospheric conditions are affected by variations in the solar cycle and interrelate with other cycles. Some astronomers are predicting that, before we reach the midpoint of the 21st century, solar activity will quiet down to such low levels we may actually experience a global cooldown.

Based upon all of the new data and reports, many people have asked us if we plan to alter the "secret formula" used for producing our annual weather forecasts. The answer is an unequivocal "no." This complicated formula, devised back in 1818 by our Almanac's first editor, David Young, is based on many astronomical factors, and the observations recorded over a number of years. This year marks the 184th consecutive year that we are applying this formula for the purpose of making long-range weather predictions.

### LAST YEAR'S PREDICTIONS.

Well, as you and the scientists can attest, our forecast of a warming trend for the winter of 1999-2000 came true, with fewer cold snaps and generally warmer than average temperatures. And we were right on the mark in predicting the biggest East Coast snowstorm of the winter season. Our forecast for 12 inches of snow, starting on January 24th, was all but perfect. Unfortunately, earlier in the season, the jet stream threw our predictions a curve ball. While we anticipated an early start for wintry weather, it instead was a warm and virtually snowless beginning to the winter season for many northern locations. It seemed that winter didn't get underway until the middle of January. The antics of La Niña were the likely cause of our weather schedule being thrown off, and we deeply regret the errant behavior of the upper atmosphere!

### GENERAL OUTLOOK FOR THIS YEAR.

Overall, thanks to an active southwest-to-northeast storm track, we are predicting a rainy autumn in 2000 for many locations. The winter of 2000-01 should get off to a late start and turn out to be milder than average, even less severe than this last one. The summer of 2001 will be hot and will be followed (in contrast to 2000) by a fall drought. Hurricanes should pose a threat to the Gulf Coast in mid-July and again at the end of that month. (For more in-depth, regional predictions, see our predictions starting on page 95.)

Happy first year of the 21st century. (We never recognize a century or millennium before its time!)

*Caleb Weatherbee*

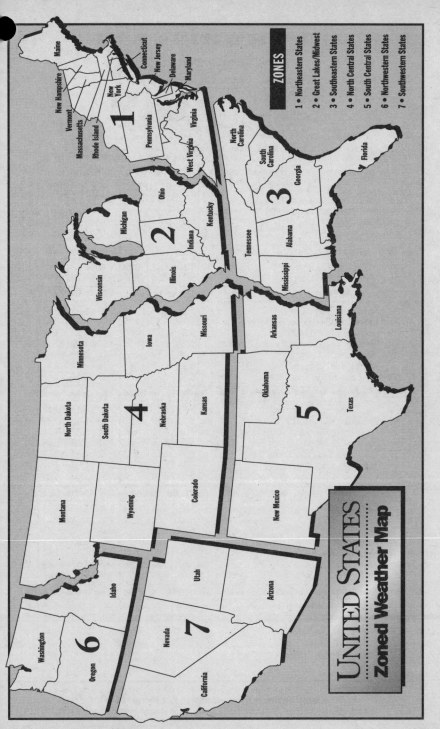

UNITED STATES
Zoned Weather Map

**ZONES**

1 • Northeastern States
2 • Great Lakes/Midwest
3 • Southeastern States
4 • North Central States
5 • South Central States
6 • Northwestern States
7 • Southwestern States

9th Month **SEPTEMBER 2000** 30 Days

♍ VIRGO
August 22 to September 22

♎ LIBRA
September 22 to October 22

**NOW AUTUMN'S GOLDEN STORES BEHOLD, WITH FRUIT EACH TREE IS CROWNED;**
**PEACHES IN SUITS OF RED OR GOLD, EACH TWIG BOWS TOWARD THE GROUND.**

**MOON'S PHASES**
EASTERN STANDARD TIME

| Phase | Date | Time |
|---|---|---|
| ☽ First Quarter | 5th | 11:27 a.m. |
| Full Moon | 13th | 2:36 p.m. |
| ☾ Last Quarter | 20th | 8:28 p.m. |
| New Moon | 27th | 2:53 p.m. |

Subtract hour(s) for other time zones
–1h for C.S.T. –2h for M.S.T. –3h for P.S.T.

**SUN ON MERIDIAN CIVIL TIME**

| D. | H. | M. | S. |
|---|---|---|---|
| 1st | 11 | 59 | 52 |
| 8th | 11 | 57 | 33 |
| 15th | 11 | 55 | 04 |
| 22nd | 11 | 52 | 35 |
| 29th | 11 | 50 | 12 |

Calendar for NORTHERN STATES — *45°N. Lat. 75°W. Long.*
Calendar for SOUTHERN STATES — *35°N. Lat. 75°W. Long.*

| DATE | DAY | ASTRONOMY, CHURCH DAYS, ETC. | MOON'S PLACE | North: Sun RISES | North: Sun SETS | North: Moon SETS | South: Sun RISES | South: Sun SETS | South: Moon SETS | MOON'S SOUTHING OR MERIDIAN PASSAGE EVE |
|---|---|---|---|---|---|---|---|---|---|---|
| 1 | Fr | Albireo mer. 8:45 p.m. | ♎ | 5:22 | 6:38 | 8:39 | 5:33 | 6:27 | 8:47 | 2:52p |
| 2 | Sa | Messier 13 sets 2:31 a.m. | ♎ | 5:24 | 6:36 | 9:07 | 5:34 | 6:26 | 9:20 | 3:40 |
| **36. Twelfth Sunday after Pentecost - September 3, 2000** | | | | **L/Day 13h 09m - Twi. 1h 44m** | | | **L/Day 12h 51m - Twi. 1h 28m** | | | |
| 3 | Su | Scheat mer. 12:13 a.m. | ♏ | 5:25 | 6:34 | 9:36 | 5:34 | 6:25 | 9:55 | 4:27 |
| 4 | Mo | **Labor Day;** Deneb mer. 9:43 p.m. | ♏ | 5:26 | 6:32 | 10:08 | 5:35 | 6:23 | 10:32 | 5:14 |
| 5 | Tu | Sadalmelik mer. 11:03 p.m. | ♐ | 5:27 | 6:31 | 10:45 | 5:36 | 6:22 | 11:12 | 6:02 |
| 6 | We | ♀ sets 7:18 p.m.; Seven Sisters ri. 9:00 p.m. | ♐ | 5:28 | 6:29 | 11:26 | 5:37 | 6:20 | 11:56 | 6:50 |
| 7 | Th | Altair mer. 8:41 p.m. ◡ | ♐ | 5:30 | 6:27 | morn | 5:37 | 6:19 | morn | 7:39 |
| 8 | Fr | Menkar mer. 3:54 a.m.; ☽ apo. 8:00 a.m. ☋ | ♑ | 5:31 | 6:25 | 12:13 | 5:38 | 6:18 | 12:43 | 8:27 |
| 9 | Sa | Mirach mer. 1:58 a.m. | ♑ | 5:32 | 6:23 | 1:05 | 5:39 | 6:16 | 1:43 | 9:15 |
| **37. Thirteenth Sunday after Pentecost - September 10, 2000** | | | | **L/Day 12h 48m - Twi. 1h 42m** | | | **L/Day 12h 35m - Twi. 1h 26m** | | | |
| 10 | Su | Job's Coffin mer. 9:26 p.m. | ♒ | 5:33 | 6:21 | 2:01 | 5:40 | 6:15 | 2:28 | 10:03 |
| 11 | Mo | Fomalhaut mer. 11:32 p.m. | ♒ | 5:34 | 6:19 | 3:01 | 5:40 | 6:13 | 3:24 | 10:49 |
| 12 | Tu | Altair sets 2:57 a.m.; ♂ ri. 3:45 a.m. | ♒ | 5:35 | 6:17 | 4:01 | 5:41 | 6:12 | 4:21 | 11:35 |
| 13 | We | Harvest Full Moon ♄ sta. | ♓ | 5:37 | 6:16 | rises | 5:42 | 6:10 | rises | morn |
| 14 | Th | Holy Cross Day; Aldebaran ri. 10:07 p.m. | ♓ | 5:38 | 6:14 | 7:02 | 5:42 | 6:09 | 7:00 | 12:20 |
| 15 | Fr | Markab mer. 11:23 p.m. | ♈ | 5:39 | 6:12 | 7:28 | 5:43 | 6:08 | 7:31 | 1:05 |
| 16 | Sa | Caph mer. 12:27 a.m. ♂ Regulus cl. a.m. | ♈ | 5:40 | 6:10 | 7:54 | 5:44 | 6:06 | 8:04 | 1:51 |
| **38. Fourteenth Sunday after Pentecost - September 17, 2000** | | | | **L/Day 12h 27m - Twi. 1h 40m** | | | **L/Day 12h 20m - Twi. 1h 25m** | | | |
| 17 | Su | Denebola ri. 5:09 a.m.; ♃ ri. 9:34 p.m. | ♉ | 5:41 | 6:08 | 8:24 | 5:45 | 6:05 | 8:39 | 2:38 |
| 18 | Mo | Enif mer. 9:51 p.m. ♄☽ cl. 9:01 p.m. | ♉ | 5:43 | 6:06 | 8:57 | 5:45 | 6:03 | 9:19 | 3:28 |
| 19 | Tu | Fomalhaut mer. 10:57 p.m. ♀ Spica cl. p.m. | ♊ | 5:44 | 6:04 | 9:37 | 5:46 | 6:02 | 10:03 | 4:21 |
| 20 | We | Ember Day; Pollux ri. 11:59 p.m. | ♊ | 5:45 | 6:02 | 10:25 | 5:47 | 6:00 | 10:55 | 5:16 |
| 21 | Th | Alpheratz mer. 12:07 a.m. ⌒ | ♋ | 5:46 | 6:00 | 11:22 | 5:48 | 5:59 | 11:52 | 6:15 |
| 22 | Fr | Ember Day ☊ | ♋ | 5:47 | 5:58 | morn | 5:48 | 5:57 | morn | 7:14 |
| 23 | Sa | Ember Day; ♄ ri. 8:41 p.m. ☿ Spica cl. p.m. | ♌ | 5:49 | 5:56 | 12:27 | 5:49 | 5:56 | 12:56 | 8:14 |
| **39. Fifteenth Sunday after Pentecost - September 24, 2000** | | | | **L/Day 12h 05m - Twi. 1h 38m** | | | **L/Day 12h 05m - Twi. 1h 24m** | | | |
| 24 | Su | Algol mer. 2:56 a.m.; ☽ per. 3:00 a.m. | ♌ | 5:50 | 5:55 | 1:38 | 5:50 | 5:55 | 2:03 | 9:12 |
| 25 | Mo | Sagitta sets 2:53 a.m. ☽ Regulus cl. 3:10 a.m. | ♍ | 5:51 | 5:53 | 2:53 | 5:51 | 5:53 | 3:12 | 10:08 |
| 26 | Tu | Schedar mer. 12:19 a.m. | ♍ | 5:52 | 5:51 | 4:08 | 5:51 | 5:52 | 4:20 | 11:01 |
| 27 | We | Lyra sets 3:00 a.m. | ♍ | 5:53 | 5:49 | 5:22 | 5:52 | 5:50 | 5:27 | 11:52 |
| 28 | Th | Hydra's Head ri. 1:52 a.m. | ♎ | 5:55 | 5:47 | sets | 5:53 | 5:49 | sets | 12:41p |
| 29 | Fr | Sirius ri. 1:09 a.m. ☽♀ cl. 6:53 a.m. | ♎ | 5:56 | 5:45 | 7:05 | 5:54 | 5:47 | 7:16 | 1:29 |
| 30 | Sa | Rosh Hashanah; ☿ sets 6:29 p.m. ♃ sta. | ♏ | 5:57 | 5:43 | 7:34 | 5:54 | 5:46 | 7:50 | 2:14 |

BIRTHSTONE: Sapphire, symbol of wisdom FLOWER: Aster or Morning Glory

**WEATHER FOLKLORE & LEGEND**

***When spiders weave their webs by noon, fine weather is coming soon.***

# WEATHER FORECAST
## ∽ SEPTEMBER 2000 ∽

ZONE

### ❶ Northeastern States

**1st-3rd.** Wet weather New England; farther south, scattered showers, some thunderstorms. **4th-7th.** Fair, pleasant Labor Day holiday. **8th-11th.** Thunderstorms sweep in from the West, then clearing. **12th-15th.** Fair skies. **16th-19th.** Rain, then turning fair, cooler. **20th-23rd.** Fair skies persist. **24th-27th.** Thunderstorms rumble rapidly across the region, then clearing, cooler. **28th-30th.** Fair skies, then scattered rain showers.

### ❷ Great Lakes and Midwest

**1st-3rd.** Showers, then clearing skies. **4th-7th.** Generally clear, pleasant for Labor Day holiday. **8th-11th.** Thunderstorms, then improving. **12th-15th.** Fair skies. **16th-19th.** Rain, especially Great Lakes, then clearing, cooler. **20th-23rd.** Severe thunderstorms race rapidly toward the Great Lakes region. **24th-27th.** Thunderstorms rumble rapidly through Ohio River Valley, points east, then clearing, colder conditions. **28th-30th.** Squally weather moves in from the West.

### ❸ Southeastern States

**1st-3rd.** Scattered showers, few thunderstorms. **4th-7th.** Hot, oppressively humid for Labor Day holiday. **8th-11th.** Heavy thunderstorms along Gulf Coast with a hurricane threat. **12th-15th.** Fair skies prevail. **16th-19th.** Showers, then clearing. **20th-23rd.** A tropical disturbance brings windy/rainy conditions. **24th-27th.** Squalls sweep across the region from west to east. **28th-30th.** A spell of unsettled weather.

### ❹ North Central States

**1st-3rd.** Showers, then clearing skies. **4th-7th.** Pleasant, Nebraska, Dakotas region, all points east; squalls over Rockies. **8th-11th.** Thunderstorms across Plains States, then clearing. **12th-15th.** Mostly fair, but turning unsettled over Colorado by the 15th. **16th-19th.** Rain, Plains States, points east, then turning fair, cooler. **20th-23rd.** Severe thunderstorms race rapidly east from Rocky Mountain States, across Plains; possible tornadic activity, Kansas. **24th-27th.** Brisk winds, Plains States. **28th-30th.** Unsettled with some wet snow possible over the highest elevations of Montana; squally weather elsewhere.

### ❺ South Central States

**1st-3rd.** Scattered showers, especially Texas, then partial clearing. **4th-7th.** Fair, much of Oklahoma, Texas, points east; squalls over northern New Mexico. **8th-11th.** Heavy thunderstorms, Texas, along Gulf Coast, with a hurricane threat. Elsewhere, thunderstorms, then clearing. **12th-15th.** Mostly fair skies, but turning unsettled over Utah by the 15th. **16th-19th.** Rain, then fair, cooler weather sets in. **20th-23rd.** Dangerous thunderstorms race rapidly east; possible tornadic activity Oklahoma. **24th-27th.** Squalls Texas, move east, then fair, chilly; brisk winds elsewhere. **28th-30th.** Unsettled, especially Texas.

### ❻ Northwestern States

**1st-3rd.** Showers, then clearing. **4th-7th.** Fair weather deteriorates to stormy conditions for Washington, Oregon; turning squally Idaho. **8th-11th.** Fair skies. **12th-15th.** Mostly fair initially, then turning unsettled. **16th-19th.** Pleasant, tranquil weather. **20th-23rd.** Unsettled. **24th-27th.** Gusty winds. **28th-30th.** A return to unsettled weather.

### ❼ Southwestern States

**1st-3rd.** Showers, then improving weather. **4th-7th.** Fair weather deteriorates to unsettled conditions. **8th-11th.** Tranquil weather. **12th-15th.** Mostly fair initially, then unsettled weather spreads east from California coast. **16th-19th.** Pleasant weather. **20th-23rd.** Unsettled again for California coast. **24th-27th.** Quite breezy. **28th-30th.** Unsettled weather returns.

### MEMORABLE WEATHER EVENTS

☛ **SEPTEMBER 24th–30th, 1950 - Blue Sun and Moon**—Appeared for several days over the Northeastern States, caused by forest fires in Alberta, Canada. The sun was reportedly tinted with varying shades of violet, lavender, and blue.

☛ **SEPTEMBER 25th, 1970 - Tragic Santa Ana Winds**—Record temperatures southern California (105°F in Los Angeles; 97°F in San Diego) combined with a 19-month drought to cause widespread firestorms. The worst in California's history.

10th Month **OCTOBER 2000** 31 Days

♎ LIBRA
September 22 to October 22

♏ SCORPIO
October 22 to November 21

**AND NOW THE FROST IS SEEN IN MORN, OVERSPREADING FIELDS WITH WHITE; THE FARMER GATHERS IN HIS CORN, WTH PLEASURE AND DELIGHT.**

**MOON'S PHASES**
EASTERN STANDARD TIME

| | | | |
|---|---|---|---|
| ☽ | First Quarter | 5th | 5:59 a.m. |
| ○ | Full Moon | 13th | 3:53 a.m. |
| ☾ | Last Quarter | 20th | 2:59 a.m. |
| ● | New Moon | 27th | 2:58 a.m. |

Subtract hour(s) for other time zones
–1h for C.S.T. –2h for M.S.T. –3h for P.S.T.

**SUN ON MERIDIAN CIVIL TIME**

| *D.* | *H.* | *M.* | *S.* |
|---|---|---|---|
| 1st | 11 | 49 | 34 |
| 8th | 11 | 47 | 28 |
| 15th | 11 | 45 | 42 |
| 22nd | 11 | 44 | 26 |
| 29th | 11 | 43 | 43 |

Calendar for NORTHERN STATES *45°N. Lat. 75°W. Long.* — Calendar for SOUTHERN STATES *35°N. Lat. 75°W. Long.*

| DATE | DAY | ASTRONOMY, CHURCH DAYS, ETC. | MOON'S PLACE | North Sun RISES | North Sun SETS | North Moon SETS | South Sun RISES | South Sun SETS | South Moon SETS | MOON'S SOUTHING OR MERIDIAN PASSAGE EVE |
|---|---|---|---|---|---|---|---|---|---|---|
| **40. Sixteenth Sunday after Pentecost - October 1, 2000** | | | | L/Day 11h 43m - Twi. 1h 38m | | | L/Day 11h 50m - Twi. 1h 24m | | | |
| 1 | Su | Sirius ri. 1:05 a.m. | ♏ | 5:58 | 5:41 | 8:05 | 5:55 | 5:45 | 8:27 | 3:05p |
| 2 | Mo | Regulus ri. 2:41 a.m. | ♏ | 6:00 | 5:39 | 8:40 | 5:56 | 5:43 | 9:06 | 3:54 |
| 3 | Tu | Messier 31 mer. 11:51 p.m. | ♐ | 6:01 | 5:38 | 9:20 | 5:57 | 5:42 | 9:49 | 4:42 |
| 4 | We | Gemini ri. 10:43 p.m. | ♐ | 6:02 | 5:36 | 10:04 | 5:57 | 5:40 | 10:35 | 5:31 |
| 5 | Th | Denebola ri. 4:00 a.m. ☋ | ♑ | 6:03 | 5:34 | 10:55 | 5:58 | 5:39 | 11:25 | 6:20 |
| 6 | Fr | ☽ apo. 2:00 a.m. ☿ gr. E. el.; ☋ | ♑ | 6:05 | 5:32 | 11:50 | 5:59 | 5:38 | morn | 7:08 |
| 7 | Sa | Capella mer. 4:13 a.m.; ♀ sets 6:47 p.m. | ♑ | 6:06 | 5:30 | morn | 6:00 | 5:36 | 12:18 | 7:56 |
| **41. Seventeenth Sunday after Pentecost - October 8, 2000** | | | | L/Day 11h 21m - Twi. 1h 38m | | | L/Day 11h 34m - Twi. 1h 24m | | | |
| 8 | Su | Fomalhaut mer. 9:51 p.m. | ♒ | 6:07 | 5:28 | 12:48 | 6:01 | 5:35 | 1:13 | 8:43 |
| 9 | Mo | **Columbus Day;** Yom Kippur | ♒ | 6:08 | 5:27 | 1:50 | 6:01 | 5:34 | 2:09 | 9:28 |
| 10 | Tu | Alnilam ri. 10:17 p.m. | ♓ | 6:10 | 5:25 | 2:53 | 6:02 | 5:32 | 3:07 | 10:14 |
| 11 | We | Procyon ri. 12:00 a.m./11:56 p.m. | ♓ | 6:11 | 5:23 | 3:58 | 6:03 | 5:31 | 4:06 | 10:59 |
| 12 | Th | Aquarius mer. 8:57 p.m.; ♂ ri. 3:22 a.m. | ♈ | 6:12 | 5:21 | rises | 6:04 | 5:30 | rises | 11:45 |
| 13 | Fr | Hunter's Moon; Pisces mer. 11:15 p.m. | ♈ | 6:14 | 5:19 | 5:56 | 6:05 | 5:28 | 6:04 | morn |
| 14 | Sa | Succot; Seven Sisters mer. 2:17 a.m. | ♉ | 6:15 | 5:18 | 6:25 | 6:05 | 5:27 | 6:39 | 12:33 |
| **42. Eighteenth Sunday after Pentecost - October 15, 2000** | | | | L/Day 11h 00m - Twi. 1h 38m | | | L/Day 11h 20m - Twi. 1h 24m | | | |
| 15 | Su | Aquila sets 12:49 a.m. ♆ sta. | ♉ | 6:16 | 5:16 | 6:57 | 6:06 | 5:26 | 7:17 | 1:23 |
| 16 | Mo | ☽♄ cl. 1:57 a.m.; ☽♃ Aldebaran cl. 8:00 p.m. | ♊ | 6:17 | 5:14 | 7:36 | 6:07 | 5:24 | 8:01 | 2:16 |
| 17 | Tu | Algol mer. 1:26 p.m. | ♊ | 6:19 | 5:12 | 8:21 | 6:08 | 5:23 | 8:50 | 3:12 |
| 18 | We | Andromeda mer. 11:20 p.m.; ♃ ri. 7:31 p.m. | ♋ | 6:20 | 5:11 | 9:15 | 6:09 | 5:22 | 9:46 | 4:10 |
| 19 | Th | ☽ per. 5:00 p.m. ☊ | ♋ | 6:21 | 5:09 | 10:18 | 6:10 | 5:21 | 10:48 | 5:09 |
| 20 | Fr | Capella mer. 3:20 a.m. | ♌ | 6:23 | 5:07 | 11:27 | 6:11 | 5:19 | 11:53 | 6:08 |
| 21 | Sa | Aries mer. 12:09 a.m.; ☿ combust | ♌ | 6:24 | 5:06 | morn | 6:11 | 5:18 | morn | 7:06 |
| **43. Nineteenth Sunday after Pentecost - October 22, 2000** | | | | L/Day 10h 39m - Twi. 1h 38m | | | L/Day 11h 05m - Twi. 1h 25m | | | |
| 22 | Su | Simchat Torah; Diphda mer. 10:38 p.m. | ♌ | 6:25 | 5:04 | 12:39 | 6:12 | 5:17 | 1:00 | 8:01 |
| 23 | Mo | Altair sets 12:14 a.m. | ♍ | 6:27 | 5:02 | 1:52 | 6:13 | 5:16 | 2:07 | 8:53 |
| 24 | Tu | Lyra sets 1:22 a.m. ☽♂ cl. 3:13 a.m. | ♍ | 6:28 | 5:01 | 3:04 | 6:14 | 5:15 | 3:12 | 9:44 |
| 25 | We | Albireo sets 1:06 a.m.; ♄ ri. 6:31 p.m. | ♎ | 6:29 | 4:59 | 4:15 | 6:15 | 5:14 | 4:17 | 10:32 |
| 26 | Th | Scheat mer. 8:43 p.m. | ♎ | 6:31 | 4:58 | 5:25 | 6:16 | 5:13 | 5:20 | 11:20 |
| 27 | Fr | ♅ sta.; ♀ Antares cl. p.m. | ♏ | 6:32 | 4:56 | sets | 6:17 | 5:11 | 6:23 | 12:08p |
| 28 | Sa | Alphard mer. 1:28 a.m. | ♏ | 6:33 | 4:55 | 6:02 | 6:18 | 5:10 | sets | 12:56 |
| **44. Twentieth Sunday after Pentecost - October 29, 2000** | | | | L/Day 10h 18m - Twi. 1h 40m | | | L/Day 10h 50m - Twi. 1h 25m | | | |
| 29 | Su | Daylight Saving Time ends ☿ inf. ☌ | ♏ | 6:35 | 4:53 | 6:35 | 6:19 | 5:09 | 7:00 | 1:44 |
| 30 | Mo | Arcturus ri. 4:34 a.m. | ♐ | 6:36 | 4:52 | 7:13 | 6:20 | 5:08 | 7:41 | 2:33 |
| 31 | Tu | Halloween; Canes Venatici ri. 1:32 a.m. | ♐ | 6:38 | 4:50 | 7:56 | 6:20 | 5:07 | 8:27 | 3:23 |

BIRTHSTONE: Opal or Tourmaline, symbols of hope FLOWER: Calendula or Cosmos

**WEATHER FOLKLORE & LEGEND**

***A severe autumn denotes a windy summer; a windy winter a rainy spring.***

ZONE

### ❶ *Northeastern States*

**1st-3rd.** Mostly fair. **4th-7th.** Dry, windy weather. **8th-11th.** Strong disturbance sweeps east off the Atlantic Coast: heavy rain Mid-Atlantic States; stormy with gale-force winds (39+ m.p.h.) along New England Coast. Clearing by the 11th. **12th-15th.** Showers reach New York, Pennsylvania, through the rest of the Northeast by the 15th, accompanied by milder air. **16th-19th.** Dry, milder, especially New England. **20th-23rd.** Severe thunderstorms move in from the West, then clearing, unseasonably cold conditions with a widespread frost. **24th-27th.** Fair at first, then turning unsettled by the 27th. **28th-31st.** Trick-or-treaters will enjoy mostly fair weather.

### ❷ *Great Lakes and Midwest*

**1st-3rd.** A spell of fine, dry weather. **4th-7th.** Very unsettled/wet conditions developing. **8th-11th.** Squally Ohio, Indiana, clearing all points east. **12th-15th.** Unsettled again, especially Ohio, Kentucky, then clearing. **16th-19th.** Squalls Great Lakes. **20th-23rd.** Severe thunderstorms roll through Ohio, Indiana, then clearing, unseasonably cold with widespread frost. **24th-27th.** Fair initially, then turning unsettled by the 27th. **28th-31st.** Fair skies for Halloween.

### ❸ *Southeastern States*

**1st-3rd.** Dry, tranquil conditions. **4th-7th.** Gusty winds, mainly fair. **8th-11th.** Heavy rain, thanks to a strong disturbance moving off the Atlantic Coast. **12th-15th.** Chilly rains from Gulf Coast north to the Carolinas. **16th-19th.** Drying out after a week of dull, damp weather. **20th-23rd.** Scattered showers, then clearing, unseasonably cold with an early frost for some localities. **24th-27th.** Light rain. **28th-31st.** Fair skies.

### ❹ *North Central States*

**1st-3rd.** Fair skies. **4th-7th.** Stormy: some wet snow Rockies, flurries Plains. **8th-11th.** Fair, cold. **12th-15th.** Turning unsettled, then clearing. **16th-19th.** Stormy weather spreads first into Colorado, then heavy rain spreads into Central States. **20th-23rd.** Clearing skies, colder. **24th-27th.** Fair skies rapidly change to unsettled conditions. **28th-31st.** Tranquil at first, then turning stormy over Rockies; increasing cloudiness elsewhere.

### ❺ *South Central States*

**1st-3rd.** Fair weather. **4th-7th.** Stormy with some wet snow, flurries over higher terrain areas. **8th-11th.** Mostly fair, cold. **12th-15th.** Turning unsettled, then clearing. **16th-19th.** Heavy rains spread into the region. **20th-23rd.** Rain, thunderstorms Texas, points east, then clearing skies, colder weather. **24th-27th.** Fair skies rapidly change to unsettled conditions; light rain Texas, points east. **28th-31st.** Tranquil, then increasing cloudiness with very unsettled conditions spreading in from New Mexico.

### ❻ *Northwestern States*

**1st-3rd.** Fair, dry. **4th-7th.** Very unsettled weather. **8th-11th.** Fair, chilly. **12th-15th.** Showery. **16th-19th.** Stormy weather sweeps east from Pacific Coast. **20th-23rd.** Clearing skies, turning colder. **24th-27th.** Fair initially, then turning unsettled again. **28th-31st.** Starting off pleasant, then turning stormy, colder for Washington, Oregon, points east.

### ❼ *Southwestern States*

**1st-3rd.** Fair skies, tranquil. **4th-7th.** Windy with a few scattered showers, especially California. **8th-11th.** Turning fair, rather cold. **12th-15th.** Scattered shower activity. **16th-19th.** Windy, rainy; stormy Utah. **20th-23rd.** Clearing skies, colder. **24th-27th.** Fair initially, then turning unsettled again. **28th-31st.** Starting off pleasant, then turning stormy, colder for California, points east.

---

### MEMORABLE WEATHER EVENTS

☞ **OCTOBER 12th, 1962-Columbus Day "Big Blow" in Oregon and Washington**—Winds in excess of 100 m.p.h.; 28.42" barometer; 10 million board feet of timber blown down in forests; extensive structural damage; 48 deaths; $210 million loss. Gusts also felt in British Columbia.

☞ **OCTOBER 30th–31th, 1991-The Halloween Storm**—Unusual because of its intensity (near-hurricane-force winds) and movement (from east to west); affected most shorelines from the Mid-Atlantic States to the Canadian Maritimes with extremely high tides and devastating floods.

**♏ Scorpio**
October 22 to November 21

**♐ Sagittarius**
November 21 to December 21

TIME ON HIS WING FAST HASTES AWAY, AND CHILLS EACH WARM SUCCEED;
TO CAPRICORN SOL HASTES EACH DAY, SO NIGHTS THE DAYS EXCEED.

## MOON'S PHASES
EASTERN STANDARD TIME

| | | | |
|---|---|---|---|
| ☽ First Quarter | 4th | 2:26 a.m. |
| ○ Full Moon | 11th | 4:14 p.m. |
| ☾ Last Quarter | 18th | 10:25 a.m. |
| ● New Moon | 25th | 6:11 p.m. |

Subtract hour(s) for other time zones
–1h for C.S.T.  –2h for M.S.T.  –3h for P.S.T.

### SUN ON MERIDIAN CIVIL TIME

| D. | H. | M. | S. |
|---|---|---|---|
| 1st | 11 | 43 | 36 |
| 8th | 11 | 43 | 47 |
| 15th | 11 | 44 | 39 |
| 22nd | 11 | 46 | 13 |
| 29th | 11 | 48 | 26 |

Calendar for **NORTHERN STATES** 45°N. Lat. 75°W. Long.

Calendar for **SOUTHERN STATES** 35°N. Lat. 75°W. Long.

| DATE | DAY | ASTRONOMY, CHURCH DAYS, ETC. | | Sun RISES | Sun SETS | Moon SETS | Sun RISES | Sun SETS | Moon SETS | EVE |
|---|---|---|---|---|---|---|---|---|---|---|
| 1 | We | All Saints' Day; Pleiades mer. 1:06 a.m. | ♋ | 6:39 | 4:49 | 8:44 | 6:21 | 5:06 | 9:15 | 4:12p |
| 2 | Th | All Souls' Day; ☽ apo. 11:00 p.m. | ♌ | 6:40 | 4:47 | 9:38 | 6:22 | 5:05 | 10:07 | 5:01 |
| 3 | Fr | Vega sets 12:39 a.m. | ♌ | 6:42 | 4:46 | 10:35 | 6:23 | 5:04 | 11:01 | 5:49 |
| 4 | Sa | Cepheus mer. 6:21 p.m. | ♌ | 6:43 | 4:45 | 11:35 | 6:24 | 5:03 | 11:57 | 6:35 |

### 45. Twenty-first Sunday after Pentecost - November 5, 2000
L/Day 9h 59m - Twi. 1h 40m    L/Day 10h 38m - Twi. 1h 27m

| | | | | | | | | | | |
|---|---|---|---|---|---|---|---|---|---|---|
| 5 | Su | Algenib (The Wing) mer. 9:14 p.m. | ♒ | 6:44 | 4:43 | morn | 6:25 | 5:03 | morn | 7:21 |
| 6 | Mo | Hamal mer. 11:00 p.m.; ♀ sets 6:48 p.m. | ♓ | 6:46 | 4:42 | 12:37 | 6:26 | 5:02 | 12:53 | 8:06 |
| 7 | Tu | **Election Day;** Mirfak mer. 12:17 a.m. | ♓ | 6:47 | 4:41 | 1:40 | 6:27 | 5:01 | 1:51 | 8:51 |
| 8 | We | Diphda mer. 9:29 p.m. | ♓ | 6:49 | 4:39 | 2:45 | 6:28 | 5:00 | 2:50 | 9:36 |
| 9 | Th | Alpheratz mer. 8:50 p.m. | ♈ | 6:50 | 4:38 | 3:52 | 6:29 | 4:59 | 3:51 | 10:23 |
| 10 | Fr | Arcturus ri. 3:47 a.m. | ♈ | 6:51 | 4:37 | 5:02 | 6:30 | 4:58 | 4:54 | 11:13 |
| 11 | Sa | **Veterans' Day;** Great Square mer. 10:44 p.m. | ♉ | 6:53 | 4:36 | rises | 6:31 | 4:58 | rises | morn |

### 46. Twenty-second Sunday after Pentecost - November 12, 2000
L/Day 9h 41m - Twi. 1h 42m    L/Day 10h 25m - Twi. 1h 27m

| | | | | | | | | | | |
|---|---|---|---|---|---|---|---|---|---|---|
| 12 | Su | ☽ cl. 7:18 a.m.; ☽♃ cl. 11:37 p.m. | ♉ | 6:54 | 4:35 | 5:31 | 6:32 | 4:57 | 5:54 | 12:05 |
| 13 | Mo | ♂ ri. 2:55 a.m.; ☽ Aldebaran cl. 1:34 a.m. | ♊ | 6:55 | 4:34 | 6:15 | 6:33 | 4:56 | 6:43 | 1:01 |
| 14 | Tu | Spica ri. 4:25 a.m.; ☽ per. 6:00 p.m. | ♊ | 6:57 | 4:33 | 7:07 | 6:34 | 4:55 | 7:38 | 2:01 |
| 15 | We | Bellatrix mer. 1:48 a.m. ☿ gr. W. el.; ♋♌ | 6:58 | 4:32 | 8:09 | 6:35 | 4:55 | 8:39 | 3:02 |
| 16 | Th | Markab mer. 7:19 p.m. | ♌ | 6:59 | 4:31 | 9:17 | 6:36 | 4:54 | 9:45 | 4:03 |
| 17 | Fr | Leonid Meteors 1:00 to 6:00 a.m. | ♌ | 7:01 | 4:30 | 10:29 | 6:37 | 4:54 | 10:52 | 5:02 |
| 18 | Sa | El Nath mer. 1:36 a.m.; ♃ ri. 5:17 a.m. | ♌ | 7:02 | 4:29 | 11:42 | 6:38 | 4:53 | 11:59 | 5:58 |

### 47. Twenty-third Sunday after Pentecost - November 19, 2000
L/Day 9h 25m - Twi. 1h 43m    L/Day 10h 14m - Twi. 1h 28m

| | | | | | | | | | | |
|---|---|---|---|---|---|---|---|---|---|---|
| 19 | Su | Caph mer. 8:12 p.m.    ♄ opp. | ♍ | 7:03 | 4:28 | morn | 6:39 | 4:53 | morn | 6:51 |
| 20 | Mo | Almach mer. 10:02 p.m. | ♍ | 7:05 | 4:27 | 12:54 | 6:40 | 4:52 | 1:04 | 7:41 |
| 21 | Tu | Scheat sets 2:53 a.m. | ♎ | 7:06 | 4:26 | 2:04 | 6:41 | 4:52 | 2:08 | 8:29 |
| 22 | We | Algol mer. 10:58 p.m.; ☿ ri. 5:26 a.m. | ♎ | 7:07 | 4:25 | 3:13 | 6:42 | 4:51 | 3:10 | 9:15 |
| 23 | Th | **Thanksgiving Day** | ♎ | 7:09 | 4:25 | 4:21 | 6:43 | 4:51 | 4:12 | 10:02 |
| 24 | Fr | Capella mer. 1:05 a.m.; ♄ sets 6:26 a.m. | ♏ | 7:10 | 4:24 | 5:28 | 6:44 | 4:50 | 5:12 | 10:49 |
| 25 | Sa | Castor ri. 7:03 p.m. | ♏ | 7:11 | 4:23 | 6:34 | 6:45 | 4:50 | 6:13 | 11:37 |

### 48. Christ the King Sunday - November 26, 2000
L/Day 9h 11m - Twi. 1h 44m    L/Day 10h 05m - Twi. 1h 29m

| | | | | | | | | | | |
|---|---|---|---|---|---|---|---|---|---|---|
| 26 | Su | Aldebaran mer. 12:16 a.m.; ☿ combust | ♐ | 7:12 | 4:23 | sets | 6:45 | 4:50 | sets | 12:25p |
| 27 | Mo | Pollux mer. 3:21 a.m.    ♃♂ | ♐ | 7:14 | 4:22 | 5:49 | 6:46 | 4:49 | 6:20 | 1:15 |
| 28 | Tu | Sirius mer. 2:17 a.m. | ♐ | 7:15 | 4:22 | 6:36 | 6:47 | 4:49 | 7:07 | 2:05 |
| 29 | We | Diphda sets 1:11 a.m. | ♑ | 7:16 | 4:21 | 7:27 | 6:48 | 4:49 | 7:58 | 2:54 |
| 30 | Th | Betelgeuse mer. 1:19 a.m.; ☽ apo. 7:00 p.m. | ♑ | 7:17 | 4:21 | 8:23 | 6:49 | 4:49 | 8:51 | 3:42 |

BIRTHSTONE: Topaz, symbol of fidelity   FLOWER: Chrysanthemum

### WEATHER FOLKLORE & LEGEND
*When the rooster crows on the ground, the rain will fall down;*
*When the rooster crows on the fence, the rain will depart hence.*

# WEATHER FORECAST
## ∞ NOVEMBER 2000 ∞

ZONE

### ❶ Northeastern States
**1st-3rd.** Fair skies. **4th-7th.** Stormy weather Mid-Atlantic States, with an early-season snowfall possible, then clearing, cold. **8th-11th.** Light snow rapidly sweeps into New England from the West, then fair. **12th-15th.** Fair skies persist. **16th-19th.** Squally conditions into Mid-Atlantic States; stormy New England, then clearing, much colder. **20th-23rd.** Fair, then turning wet with rain/wet snow hilly terrain of New England; a cold rain Virginia, Maryland area. **24th-27th.** Mostly fair, cold. **28th-30th.** Generally fair.

### ❷ Great Lakes and Midwest
**1st-3rd.** Sunny to partly cloudy. **4th-7th.** Stormy, especially Ohio River Valley where accumulating snow is possible, then clearing, colder. **8th-11th.** Light snow, Michigan, Ohio, then fair. **12th-15th.** Continued generally fair. **16th-19th.** Squally Kentucky; stormy Great Lakes area, then clearing, much colder. **20th-23rd.** Fair, then turning wet. **24th-27th.** Mostly fair, cold. **28th-30th.** Very unsettled with snow, especially Great Lakes area.

### ❸ Southeastern States
**1st-3rd.** Fair weather. **4th-7th.** Stormy, especially Gulf Coast, then clearing, cold. **8th-11th.** Fair skies give way to rain, then clearing. **12th-15th.** Fair skies. **16th-19th.** Windy, rainy, squally Tennessee, then clearing, much colder; frost reaches down to Gulf Coast. **20th-23rd.** A cold rain for the Gulf Coast, spreading across rest of the Southeast. **24th-27th.** Mostly fair, cold. **28th-30th.** Generally fair skies.

### ❹ North Central States
**1st-3rd.** Stormy weather initially over Colorado, spreads north, east; squalls, Missouri. **4th-7th.** Fair, cold. **8th-11th.** Light snow, Rocky Mountain States, points east. **12th-15th.** Fair, then turning stormy, including the Plains. **16th-19th.** Storms clear Dakotas, Nebraska, all points west; turning colder. **20th-23rd.** Light snow, Rockies, across Plains, then clearing. **24th-27th.** Mostly fair, then a heavy snowfall for Rockies. **28th-30th.** Very unsettled Dakotas, Nebraska, with significant snow; Southwest storms dump additional snow as far east as Missouri.

### ❺ South Central States
**1st-3rd.** Widespread stormy/squally weather. **4th-7th.** Fair, cold weather. **8th-11th.** Light snow New Mexico, points east, then clearing. **12th-15th.** Fair, then stormy; squally New Mexico, Texas. **16th-19th.** Storms clear east; turning colder. **20th-23rd.** Some snow, parts of New Mexico, west Texas, then fair; cold rain Texas, Louisiana coasts. **24th-27th.** Mostly fair, then a significant snowfall for much of New Mexico, northern Texas, Oklahoma. **28th-30th.** Storms out of the Southwest dump additional snow as far east as Arkansas.

### ❻ Northwestern States
**1st-3rd.** Very unsettled conditions. **4th-7th.** Fair, quite chilly. **8th-11th.** Showers Washington, Oregon. **12th-15th.** Fair, then turning stormy. **16th-19th.** Stormy weather moves on to the east, then a trend toward drier, colder weather. **20th-23rd.** Some scattered showers of rain or (higher elevations) snow. **24th-27th.** Fair at first, then becoming stormy with gales (39+ m.p.h.); heavy snow over the mountains. **28th-30th.** Generally fair weather.

### ❼ Southwestern States
**1st-3rd.** Stormy Utah; squalls elsewhere. **4th-7th.** Fair, cold. **8th-11th.** Light snow, Nevada, Utah, much of northern Arizona. **12th-15th.** Fair, then stormy. **16th-19th.** Stormy weather moves east, then drier, colder. **20th-23rd.** Unsettled; some snow again for Nevada, Utah, northern Arizona. **24th-27th.** Fair, then becoming stormy with gales (39+ m.p.h.) along California coast, heavy snow (6" to 12") over the mountains. **28th-30th.** Storms sweep out of the Southwest States, replaced by clearing skies.

---

### MEMORABLE WEATHER EVENTS

☛ **NOVEMBER 11th, 1940-Armistice Day Storm**—Over the Upper Midwest and the Great Lakes; blizzard conditions in Manitoba, Minnesota, Wisconsin, and western Ontario; 49 dead in Minnesota alone; gales on Lake Michigan caused wrecks and the loss of 59 sailors; 17" snowfall in Iowa; barometer at 28.66", Duluth, MN.

# DECEMBER 2000

♐ SAGITTARIUS
November 21 to December 21

♑ CAPRICORN
December 21 to January 19

**COLD BLOWS THE WIND, THE FROZEN RAIN AND FLEECY SNOW DESCEND;
FOR, FREEZING WINTER'S COME AGAIN, AND SO THE YEAR DOES END.**

**MOON'S PHASES**
EASTERN STANDARD TIME

| | | | |
|---|---|---|---|
| ☽ | First Quarter | 3rd | 10:55 p.m. |
| ☺ | Full Moon | 11th | 4:02 a.m. |
| ☾ | Last Quarter | 17th | 7:41 p.m. |
| ● | New Moon | 25th | 12:21 p.m. |

Subtract hour(s) for other time zones
–1h for C.S.T. –2h for M.S.T. –3h for P.S.T.

**SUN ON MERIDIAN CIVIL TIME**

| D. | H. | M. | S. |
|---|---|---|---|
| 1st | 11 | 49 | 10 |
| 8th | 11 | 52 | 03 |
| 15th | 11 | 55 | 18 |
| 22nd | 11 | 58 | 45 |
| 29th | 12 | 02 | 13 |

| DATE | DAY | ASTRONOMY, CHURCH DAYS, ETC. | MOON'S PLACE | Calendar for NORTHERN STATES 45°N. Lat. 75°W. Long. Sun RISES | Sun SETS | Moon SETS | Calendar for SOUTHERN STATES 35°N. Lat. 75°W. Long. Sun RISES | Sun SETS | Moon SETS | MOON'S SOUTHING OR MERIDIAN PASSAGE EVE |
|---|---|---|---|---|---|---|---|---|---|---|
| 1 | Fr | Messier 42 mer. 12:56 a.m. | ♒ | 7:18 | 4:20 | 9:22 | 6:50 | 4:49 | 9:46 | 4:29p |
| 2 | Sa | Seven Sisters mer. 11:00 p.m. | ♒ | 7:19 | 4:20 | 10:22 | 6:51 | 4:48 | 10:42 | 5:15 |
| **49. First Sunday of Advent - December 3, 2000** | | | | **L/Day 8h 59m - Twi. 1h 45m** | | | **L/Day 9h 56m - Twi. 1h 30m** | | | |
| 3 | Su | Canis Minor mer. 2:57 a.m. | ♒ | 7:21 | 4:20 | 11:24 | 6:52 | 4:48 | 11:38 | 5:59 |
| 4 | Mo | Arcturus ri. 2:13 a.m. | ♓ | 7:22 | 4:19 | morn | 6:53 | 4:48 | morn | 6:43 |
| 5 | Tu | Aries sets 4:40 a.m. | ♓ | 7:23 | 4:19 | 12:27 | 6:53 | 4:48 | 12:35 | 7:27 |
| 6 | We | Virgo ri. 2:32 a.m. | ♈ | 7:24 | 4:19 | 1:32 | 6:54 | 4:48 | 1:34 | 8:12 |
| 7 | Th | Algol in Eclipse 7:33 p.m.; ♀ sets 7:36 p.m. | ♈ | 7:25 | 4:19 | 2:39 | 6:55 | 4:48 | 2:34 | 8:59 |
| 8 | Fr | Conception B.V.M.; Corvus ri. 2:06 a.m. | ♉ | 7:26 | 4:19 | 3:49 | 6:56 | 4:48 | 3:37 | 9:50 |
| 9 | Sa | Aldebaran mer. 11:21 p.m. | ♉ | 7:27 | 4:19 | 5:01 | 6:57 | 4:49 | 4:44 | 10:44 |
| **50. Second Sunday of Advent - December 10, 2000** | | | | **L/Day 8h 51m - Twi. 1h 46m** | | | **L/Day 9h 52m - Twi. 1h 31m** | | | |
| 10 | Su | ☽♃ cl. 4:34 a.m.; ☽ Aldebaran cl. 4:20 p.m. | ♊ | 7:28 | 4:19 | rises | 6:57 | 4:49 | rises | 11:43 |
| 11 | Mo | Sickle mer. 4:49 a.m.; ♂ ri. 2:29 a.m. | ♊ | 7:28 | 4:19 | 4:53 | 6:58 | 4:49 | 5:23 | morn |
| 12 | Tu | Alpheratz sets 2:40 a.m.; ☽ per. 5:00 p.m. | ♋ | 7:29 | 4:19 | 5:52 | 6:59 | 4:49 | 6:24 | 12:45 |
| 13 | We | Geminid Meteors ♂ Spica cl. 2:34 a.m.; ⌢☊ | ♋ | 7:30 | 4:19 | 7:00 | 7:00 | 4:49 | 7:30 | 1:49 |
| 14 | Th | Canis Major mer. 1:28 a.m. | ♌ | 7:31 | 4:19 | 8:14 | 7:00 | 4:50 | 8:40 | 2:51 |
| 15 | Fr | Saiph mer. 12:14 a.m.; ☽ Regulus cl. 9:48 p.m. | ♌ | 7:32 | 4:19 | 9:29 | 7:01 | 4:50 | 9:49 | 3:51 |
| 16 | Sa | Castor mer. 1:55 a.m. | ♍ | 7:32 | 4:19 | 10:44 | 7:02 | 4:50 | 10:57 | 4:47 |
| **51. Third Sunday of Advent - December 17, 2000** | | | | **L/Day 8h 47m - Twi. 1h 46m** | | | **L/Day 9h 48m - Twi. 1h 30m** | | | |
| 17 | Su | Capella mer. 11:30 p.m. | ♍ | 7:33 | 4:20 | 11:55 | 7:03 | 4:51 | morn | 5:38 |
| 18 | Mo | Orion's Belt mer. 11:46 p.m.; ♃ sets 5:27 a.m. | ♍ | 7:34 | 4:20 | morn | 7:03 | 4:51 | 12:01 | 6:27 |
| 19 | Tu | Vega sets 9:36 p.m. | ♎ | 7:34 | 4:20 | 1:05 | 7:03 | 4:51 | 1:04 | 7:14 |
| 20 | We | Ember Day ☽♂ cl. 4:11 a.m. | ♎ | 7:35 | 4:21 | 2:12 | 7:04 | 4:52 | 2:05 | 8:00 |
| 21 | Th | Winter Solstice 8:38 a.m. EST | ♏ | 7:35 | 4:21 | 3:19 | 7:04 | 4:52 | 3:05 | 8:46 |
| 22 | Fr | Ember Day; Chanukah; Dubhe mer. 5:00 a.m. | ♏ | 7:36 | 4:22 | 4:24 | 7:05 | 4:53 | 4:05 | 9:33 |
| 23 | Sa | Ember Day; Menkalinan mer. 11:49 p.m. | ♏ | 7:36 | 4:22 | 5:28 | 7:05 | 4:53 | 5:04 | 10:21 |
| **52. Fourth Sunday of Advent - December 24, 2000** | | | | **L/Day 8h 46m - Twi. 1h 47m** | | | **L/Day 9h 48m - Twi. 1h 31m** | | | |
| 24 | Su | Rigel mer. 10:59 p.m.; ♄ sets 4:17 a.m. | ♐ | 7:37 | 4:23 | 6:29 | 7:06 | 4:54 | 6:01 | 11:10 |
| 25 | Mo | **Christmas Day** ☿ sup. ☌ | ♐ | 7:37 | 4:23 | sets | 7:06 | 4:54 | 6:55 | 11:59 |
| 26 | Tu | Crux mer. 6:07 a.m. ◡☋ | ♑ | 7:37 | 4:24 | 5:20 | 7:07 | 4:55 | sets | 12:48p |
| 27 | We | Sirius mer. 12:23 a.m. | ♑ | 7:38 | 4:25 | 6:14 | 7:07 | 4:56 | 6:44 | 1:37 |
| 28 | Th | Regulus mer. 3:42 a.m.; ☽ apo. 10:00 a.m. | ♑ | 7:38 | 4:26 | 7:12 | 7:07 | 4:56 | 7:38 | 2:25 |
| 29 | Fr | Arcturus ri. 12:34 a.m. ☽♀ cl. 8:25 p.m. | ♒ | 7:38 | 4:26 | 8:12 | 7:08 | 4:57 | 8:33 | 3:11 |
| 30 | Sa | Spica ri. 1:26 a.m. | ♒ | 7:38 | 4:27 | 9:13 | 7:08 | 4:58 | 9:29 | 3:55 |
| **53. First Sunday after Christmas - December 31, 2000** | | | | **L/Day 8h 50m - Twi. 1h 46m** | | | **L/Day 9h 50m - Twi. 1h 30m** | | | |
| 31 | Su | New Year's Eve | ♓ | 7:38 | 4:28 | 10:15 | 7:08 | 4:58 | 10:25 | 4:39 |

BIRTHSTONE: Turquoise, Lapis Lazuli or Zircon, symbols of success and prosperity FLOWER: Narcissus or Holly

**WEATHER FOLKLORE & LEGEND**

***If Christmas day on Monday be, a great winter that year you'll see.***

# WEATHER FORECAST
## ∽ DECEMBER 2000 ∽

ZONE

### ❶ Northeastern States
**1st-3rd.** Stormy, with a heavy snowfall from Mid-Atlantic States to New England, then clearing skies. **4th-7th.** Becoming unsettled. **8th-11th.** Cold, dry. **12th-15th.** Another snowstorm, with significant accumulations as far south as Maryland, Virginia, then fair, cold. **16th-19th.** Mostly fair. **20th-23rd.** Light snow from Pennsylvania, New York, to Maine, then fair, very cold. **24th-27th.** Fair skies. **28th-31st.** Stormy through New England; rainy for Mid-Atlantic States, then fair, cold.

### ❷ Great Lakes and Midwest
**1st-3rd.** Skies become generally fair. **4th-7th.** Becoming unsettled. **8th-11th.** Fair, cold, dry. **12th-15th.** A significant snowfall, then fair, cold. **16th-19th.** Light snow, especially Great Lakes area. **20th-23rd.** Changeable skies: mixed sun, clouds with scattered snow showers, flurries. **24th-27th.** White Christmas? heavy snow around Great Lakes area. **28th-31st.** Clearing skies.

### ❸ Southeastern States
**1st-3rd.** Heavy rain, Gulf Coast north, east to Carolinas, then all clearing. **4th-7th.** Chilly rain. **8th-11th.** Cold, dry conditions. **12th-15th.** Showery/thundery conditions, then fair. **16th-19th.** Mainly fair skies. **20th-23rd.** Showery Mississippi, all points east, then clearing, very cold; frosts down to Florida. **24th-27th.** Sunshine giving way to increasingly cloudy skies. **28th-31st.** Rain from Florida, points north, then fair, colder.

### ❹ North Central States
**1st-3rd.** Mostly fair. **4th-7th.** Wet snow, or rain showers, Rockies, Plains States. **8th-11th.** Heavy snow, Colorado (8" to 12"), out over the Plains. **12th-15th.** Clearing skies. **16th-19th.** Mostly fair, then light snow Rockies, points east. **20th-23rd.** Fair, very cold Plains States, points west. **24th-27th.** Heavy snow Rockies, Plains States. **28th-31st.** Mostly fair as the 20th century comes to a close.

### ❺ South Central States
**1st-3rd.** Generally fair skies. **4th-7th.** Unsettled conditions. **8th-11th.** Rainy weather, especially Texas, mixed with or changing to sleet, snow over parts of northern New Mexico. **12th-15th.** Showers/thunder Arkansas, Louisiana, then fair; clearing skies elsewhere. **16th-19th.** Mostly fair, then light snow parts of New Mexico, Texas, Oklahoma; showers farther to the south, east. **20th-23rd.** Showers Louisiana, then clearing, sharply colder weather; fair, very cold Plains States, points west. **24th-27th.** If you're dreamin' of a white Christmas, northern New Mexico might get it; farther south, east, across Texas, the Mississippi Valley, a heavy rain falls. **28th-31st.** As the 20th century comes to a close, fair skies return.

### ❻ Northwestern States
**1st-3rd.** Mostly fair weather. **4th-7th.** Fair, then unsettled Washington, Oregon. **8th-11th.** Fair, milder at first, then stormy weather sweeps in from Pacific. **12th-15th.** Skies slowly clear; drier. **16th-19th.** Mostly fair, then unsettled with showers. **20th-23rd.** Fair, unusually chilly. **24th-27th.** Stormy, especially along coastal plain. **28th-31st.** Turning mostly fair as the 20th century comes to a close.

### ❼ Southwestern States
**1st-3rd.** Generally fair skies. **4th-7th.** Fair skies, then showery from California, all points east. **8th-11th.** Fair, milder at first, then stormy weather sweeps in from the Pacific; heavy rain in the valleys, heavy snow over the mountains. **12th-15th.** Drier, clearer conditions move in. **16th-19th.** Mostly fair, then unsettled with showers; light snows over Nevada, points east. **20th-23rd.** Fair, unseasonably cold. **24th-27th.** Stormy, especially along California coast. **28th-31st.** As we move into the 21st century, fair weather returns.

### MEMORABLE WEATHER EVENTS
☞ **DECEMBER 26th–27th, 1947-New York's Big Snow**—New York City's (NY) deepest snowstorm; 26.4" in Central Park in 24 hours; 32" in suburbs; traffic completely stopped; removal cost $8 million; 27 died.
☞ **December 16th–18th, 1973-Southern New England Ice Storm**—One to three inches of ice fell on CT and adjacent sections of MA and RI.

# 1st Month — JANUARY 2001 — 31 Days

♑ CAPRICORN
December 21 to January 19

♒ AQUARIUS
January 19 to February 18

**NOW DREARY WINTER'S PIERCING COLD, FLOATS ON THE NORTHERN GALE; AND TREES, THOUGH GREEN, LOOK DRY AND OLD; SNOW COVERS HILL AND DALE.**

**MOON'S PHASES**
EASTERN STANDARD TIME

| Phase | Day | Time |
|---|---|---|
| ☽ First Quarter | 2nd | 5:31 p.m. |
| ○ Full Moon | 9th | 3:24 p.m. |
| ☾ Last Quarter | 16th | 7:34 a.m. |
| ● New Moon | 24th | 8:06 a.m. |

Subtract hour(s) for other time zones
–1h for C.S.T. –2h for M.S.T. –3h for P.S.T.

**SUN ON MERIDIAN CIVIL TIME**

| D. | H. | M. | S. |
|---|---|---|---|
| 1st | 12 | 03 | 39 |
| 8th | 12 | 06 | 47 |
| 15th | 12 | 09 | 29 |
| 22nd | 12 | 11 | 38 |
| 29th | 12 | 13 | 10 |

Calendar for NORTHERN STATES — *45°N. Lat. 75°W. Long.*
Calendar for SOUTHERN STATES — *35°N. Lat. 75°W. Long.*

| DATE | DAY | ASTRONOMY, CHURCH DAYS, ETC. | MOON'S PLACE | North: Sun RISES | North: Sun SETS | North: Moon SETS | South: Sun RISES | South: Sun SETS | South: Moon SETS | MOON'S SOUTHING OR MERIDIAN PASSAGE EVE |
|---|---|---|---|---|---|---|---|---|---|---|
| 1 | Mo | **New Year's Day; The first day of the 21st Century** | ♓ | 7:39 | 4:29 | 11:17 | 7:08 | 4:59 | 11:22 | 5:21p |
| 2 | Tu | Scheat sets 12:09 a.m. | ♓ | 7:39 | 4:30 | morn | 7:08 | 5:00 | morn | 6:05 |
| 3 | We | Quadrantid Meteors 4:00 to 6:00 a.m. | ♈ | 7:39 | 4:31 | 12:22 | 7:09 | 5:01 | 12:20 | 6:50 |
| 4 | Th | Leo ri. 8:58 p.m.; ⊕ at perihelion | ♈ | 7:38 | 4:32 | 1:28 | 7:09 | 5:02 | 1:20 | 7:36 |
| 5 | Fr | Leo ri. 8:54 p.m. ☽♄ cl. 10:24 p.m. | ♉ | 7:38 | 4:33 | 2:37 | 7:09 | 5:03 | 2:23 | 8:27 |
| 6 | Sa | Epiphany (Epis.) ☽ Aldebaran cl. 11:41 p.m. | ♉ | 7:38 | 4:34 | 3:50 | 7:09 | 5:03 | 3:29 | 9:23 |
| **1. Epiphany - January 7, 2001** | | | | **L/Day 8h 57m - Twi. 1h 45m** | | | **L/Day 9h 55m - Twi. 1h 30m** | | | |
| 7 | Su | Algol mer. 10:00 p.m.; ♂ ri. 2:03 a.m. | ♊ | 7:38 | 4:35 | 5:04 | 7:09 | 5:04 | 4:37 | 10:22 |
| 8 | Mo | Alpheratz sets 12:55 a.m. | ♊ | 7:38 | 4:36 | rises | 7:09 | 5:05 | rises | 11:26 |
| 9 | Tu | Albireo ri. 4:28 a.m. ⌒☊ | ♋ | 7:37 | 4:37 | 4:35 | 7:09 | 5:06 | 5:06 | morn |
| 10 | We | ♆ combust; ☽ per. 4:00 p.m. | ♋ | 7:37 | 4:38 | 5:48 | 7:09 | 5:07 | 6:16 | 12:30 |
| 11 | Th | Aries mer. 7:07 p.m. | ♌ | 7:37 | 4:40 | 7:06 | 7:09 | 5:08 | 7:29 | 1:34 |
| 12 | Fr | Pleiades mer. 8:16 p.m. | ♌ | 7:36 | 4:41 | 8:24 | 7:08 | 5:09 | 8:40 | 2:34 |
| 13 | Sa | Sirius (Dog Star) mer. 11:13 p.m. | ♍ | 7:36 | 4:42 | 9:40 | 7:08 | 5:10 | 9:49 | 3:30 |
| **2. First Sunday after Epiphany - January 14, 2001** | | | | **L/Day 9h 08m - Twi. 1h 44m** | | | **L/Day 10h 03m - Twi. 1h 29m** | | | |
| 14 | Su | Gemini mer. 11:39 p.m.; ♀ sets 8:50 p.m. | ♍ | 7:35 | 4:43 | 10:53 | 7:08 | 5:11 | 10:55 | 4:22 |
| 15 | Mo | **M.L. King, Jr. Birthday** (obs.) | ♎ | 7:35 | 4:45 | morn | 7:08 | 5:12 | 11:58 | 5:11 |
| 16 | Tu | El Nath mer. 9:02 p.m. | ♎ | 7:34 | 4:46 | 12:03 | 7:07 | 5:13 | morn | 5:58 |
| 17 | We | Pollux mer. 11:54 p.m. ♀ gr. E. el. | ♎ | 7:34 | 4:47 | 1:11 | 7:07 | 5:14 | 1:00 | 6:44 |
| 18 | Th | Beehive mer. 12:52 a.m. | ♏ | 7:33 | 4:48 | 2:17 | 7:07 | 5:15 | 2:00 | 7:31 |
| 19 | Fr | False Cross mer. 12:31 a.m. | ♏ | 7:32 | 4:50 | 3:22 | 7:06 | 5:15 | 2:59 | 8:18 |
| 20 | Sa | ☿ sets 6:17 p.m. | ♐ | 7:31 | 4:51 | 4:24 | 7:06 | 5:17 | 3:56 | 9:06 |
| **3. Second Sunday after Epiphany - January 21, 2001** | | | | **L/Day 9h 21m - Twi. 1h 42m** | | | **L/Day 10h 12m - Twi. 1h 28m** | | | |
| 21 | Su | Regulus mer. 2:08 a.m.; ♃ sets 3:02 a.m. | ♐ | 7:31 | 4:52 | 5:22 | 7:06 | 5:18 | 4:51 | 9:55 |
| 22 | Mo | Virgo ri. 11:26 p.m. ◡☋ | ♐ | 7:30 | 4:54 | 6:15 | 7:05 | 5:18 | 5:43 | 10:44 |
| 23 | Tu | Zubenelgenubi ri. 1:36 a.m. | ♑ | 7:29 | 4:55 | 7:02 | 7:05 | 5:20 | 6:31 | 11:33 |
| 24 | We | ♅ combust; ☽ apo. 2:00 p.m. ♄ sta. | ♑ | 7:28 | 4:56 | sets | 7:04 | 5:21 | sets | 12:21p |
| 25 | Th | Rigel mer. 8:53 p.m. ☽☿ cl. 6:38 p.m.; ♃ sta. | ♒ | 7:27 | 4:58 | 6:04 | 7:04 | 5:22 | 6:27 | 1:08 |
| 26 | Fr | El Nath sets 4:59 a.m. ♆☌☉ | ♒ | 7:26 | 4:59 | 7:05 | 7:03 | 5:23 | 7:23 | 1:53 |
| 27 | Sa | Pollux mer. 11:18 p.m.; Corvus ri. 10:47 p.m. | ♒ | 7:25 | 5:01 | 8:07 | 7:02 | 5:24 | 8:19 | 2:37 |
| **4. Third Sunday after Epiphany - January 28, 2001** | | | | **L/Day 9h 38m - Twi. 1h 40m** | | | **L/Day 10h 23m - Twi. 1h 27m** | | | |
| 28 | Su | Spica ri. 11:29 p.m. ☿ gr. E. el. | ♓ | 7:24 | 5:02 | 9:09 | 7:02 | 5:25 | 9:15 | 3:19 |
| 29 | Mo | Arcturus ri. 10:29 p.m. | ♓ | 7:23 | 5:03 | 10:11 | 7:01 | 5:26 | 10:12 | 4:02 |
| 30 | Tu | ♄ sets 1:48 a.m. | ♈ | 7:22 | 5:05 | 11:16 | 7:00 | 5:27 | 11:10 | 4:45 |
| 31 | We | Castor mer. 10:52 p.m. | ♈ | 7:21 | 5:06 | morn | 7:00 | 5:28 | morn | 5:30 |

BIRTHSTONE: Garnet, symbol of constancy and fidelity FLOWER: Carnation or Snowdrop

**WEATHER FOLKLORE & LEGEND**

***When the snow falls dry, it means to lie; but flakes light and soft bring rain oft.***

ZONE

### ❶ Northeastern States

**1st-3rd.** Fair, then unsettled, with snow spreading in from Great Lakes. Then clearing, cold. **4th-7th.** Windy, colder Mid-Atlantic States to Maine. **8th-11th.** Stormy from Great Lakes area with snow accumulations of 6" to 12". Then fair, colder. **12th-15th.** Mostly fair, cold. **16th-19th.** Wet weather spreads in from the West across New England, then fair, cold. **20th-23rd.** Fair skies. **24th-27th.** Stormy weather spreads eastward; snow falls as far south as Mid-Atlantic region, then clearing, cold. **28th-31st.** Flurries, then clearing skies; showers over Virginia.

### ❷ Great Lakes and Midwest

**1st-3rd.** Snow Great Lakes, then clearing, cold. **4th-7th.** Mostly fair, very cold. **8th-11th.** Stormy weather centered on Great Lakes area: 6" to 12" of snow possible, then fair skies, colder temperatures. **12th-15th.** Fair, cold. **16th-19th.** Wet Michigan, Ohio area, points east, then fair. **20th-23rd.** Sun gives way to increasing cloudiness. **24th-27th.** Stormy Ohio River Valley, points east, then fair, cold. **28th-31st.** Flurries spread across Great Lakes, then clearing skies.

### ❸ Southeastern States

**1st-3rd.** Rain, then fair. **4th-7th.** Mostly fair and cold, with frosts down to the Gulf Coast. **8th-11th.** Cold rains. **12th-15th.** Mostly fair, cold. **16th-19th.** Scattered showers, then clearing. **20th-23rd.** Fair weather. **24th-27th.** Snow Tennessee, parts of North Carolina, then clearing, cold; frosts to Florida. **28th-31st.** Fair skies, then showers, which may threaten Super Bowl XXXV in Tampa.

### ❹ North Central States

**1st-3rd.** Milder, then snow for Rockies, points east, then fair, cold weather. **4th-7th.** Clouding up, turning very unsettled. **8th-11th.** Stormy conditions shift to the east, then fair, much colder weather. **12th-15th.** Snow over Rockies, Plains. **16th-19th.** Becoming fair, cold. **20th-23rd.** Severe storms for Wyoming, points east. **24th-27th.** Fair and cold. **28th-31st.** Flurries across Rockies, then fair skies.

### ❺ South Central States

**1st-3rd.** Milder conditions, then some light snow, then fair, cold. **4th-7th.** Clouds lower and thicken, then stormy conditions; frosty conditions possible for Texas and Louisiana coasts. **8th-11th.** Stormy weather moves out, then clearing skies; much colder. **12th-15th.** Snow. **16th-19th.** Clearing and cold. **20th-23rd.** Squalls for New Mexico, Texas and parts of Oklahoma. **24th-27th.** Some snow for Arkansas, otherwise clearing skies and cold. **28th-31st.** Scattered flurries, then fair weather.

### ❻ Northwestern States

**1st-3rd.** Milder with showery weather. **4th-7th.** Becoming stormy for Oregon and Washington, spreading east. **8th-11th.** Drier and much colder. **12th-15th.** Unsettled conditions spread east from Pacific Coast. **16th-19th.** Gradual clearing. **20th-23rd.** Very unsettled; severe storms for Idaho. **24th-27th.** Cold and dry. **28th-31st.** Showers near and along the coast, mixing with and changing over to flurries farther east.

### ❼ Southwestern States

**1st-3rd.** Milder with showers; snow over higher elevations. **4th-7th.** Unsettled. **8th-11th.** Clearing and turning much colder. **12th-15th.** Unsettled weather sweeps east from the Pacific Coast. **16th-19th.** Showers near and along the coast, snow elsewhere. **20th-23rd.** Squalls for Arizona, Nevada, and Utah. **24th-27th.** Cold; drier. **28th-31st.** Showery weather, chiefly near and along the coast.

### MEMORABLE WEATHER EVENTS

☞ **JANUARY 21st, 1921- The Great Olympic Blowdown**—Winds swept the coastal plain from central Oregon to southern British Columbia. Sustained speeds of up to 85 m.p.h.; damage confined to the coastal strip between the Olympic Mountains and the Pacific Ocean. An estimated eight billion board feet of timber were destroyed.

☞ **JANUARY 15th, 1932 - Los Angeles, CA, Snowstorm**—A steady snow fell and covered the ground; one to two inches deep at the Civic Center.

# FEBRUARY 2001

28 Days

♒ AQUARIUS
January 19 to February 18

♓ PISCES
February 18 to March 20

**ALTHOUGH THE WINTER GREY WITH AGE, YET REIGNS A SOVEREIGN KING;**
**SOL'S PLASTIC RAYS WILL SOON ASSUAGE, AND USHER IN THE SPRING.**

**MOON'S PHASES**
EASTERN STANDARD TIME

| Phase | Date | Time |
|---|---|---|
| ☽ First Quarter | 1st | 9:02 a.m. |
| ○ Full Moon | 8th | 2:11 a.m. |
| ☾ Last Quarter | 14th | 10:23 p.m. |
| ● New Moon | 23rd | 3:21 a.m. |

Subtract hour(s) for other time zones
–1h for C.S.T. –2h for M.S.T. –3h for P.S.T.

**SUN ON MERIDIAN CIVIL TIME**

| *D.* | *H.* | *M.* | *S.* |
|---|---|---|---|
| 1st | 12 | 13 | 38 |
| 8th | 12 | 14 | 12 |
| 15th | 12 | 14 | 08 |
| 22nd | 12 | 13 | 30 |

| | | | | Calendar for NORTHERN STATES *45°N. Lat. 75°W. Long.* | | | Calendar for SOUTHERN STATES *35°N. Lat. 75°W. Long.* | | | MOON'S SOUTHING OR MERIDIAN PASSAGE |
|---|---|---|---|---|---|---|---|---|---|---|
| DATE | DAY | ASTRONOMY, CHURCH DAYS, ETC. | MOON'S PLACE | *Sun* RISES | *Sun* SETS | *Moon* SETS | *Sun* RISES | *Sun* SETS | *Moon* SETS | EVE |
| 1 | Th | Cancer mer. 11:53 p.m. | ♉ | 7:20 | 5:08 | 12:22 | 6:59 | 5:29 | 12:09 | 6:17p |
| 2 | Fr | Purification, Groundhog & Candlemas Day | ♉ | 7:19 | 5:09 | 1:30 | 6:58 | 5:30 | 1:12 | 7:08 |
| 3 | Sa | Cor Caroli mer. 4:04 a.m. | ♊ | 7:17 | 5:11 | 2:41 | 6:57 | 5:31 | 2:17 | 8:04 |
| **5. Fourth Sunday after Epiphany - February 4, 2001** | | | | **L/Day 9h 56m - Twi. 1h 40m** | | | **L/Day 10h 36m - Twi. 1h 26m** | | | |
| 4 | Su | Rigel mer. 8:15 p.m.; ☿ combust | ♊ | 7:16 | 5:12 | 3:52 | 6:56 | 5:32 | 3:23 | 9:04 |
| 5 | Mo | Pollux mer. 10:43 p.m. ⌒☊ | ♋ | 7:15 | 5:13 | 5:01 | 6:56 | 5:33 | 4:29 | 10:06 |
| 6 | Tu | ♂ ri. 1:30 a.m.; Job's Coffin ri. 4:52 a.m. | ♋ | 7:14 | 5:15 | rises | 6:55 | 5:34 | rises | 11:10 |
| 7 | We | Deneb ri. 1:35 a.m.; ☽ per. 5:00 p.m. | ♌ | 7:12 | 5:16 | 4:34 | 6:54 | 5:35 | 5:00 | morn |
| 8 | Th | Boy Scouts Day ☽ Regulus cl. 6:12 p.m. | ♌ | 7:11 | 5:18 | 5:54 | 6:53 | 5:36 | 6:14 | 12:13 |
| 9 | Fr | Seven Sisters mer. 6:29 p.m. ♅☌☉ | ♍ | 7:10 | 5:19 | 7:14 | 6:52 | 5:37 | 7:26 | 1:12 |
| 10 | Sa | Dubhe mer. 1:45 a.m. | ♍ | 7:08 | 5:21 | 8:29 | 6:51 | 5:38 | 8:36 | 2:08 |
| **6. Fifth Sunday after Epiphany - February 11, 2001** | | | | **L/Day 10h 15m - Twi. 1h 39m** | | | **L/Day 10h 49m - Twi. 1h 25m** | | | |
| 11 | Su | Kids mer. 8:00 p.m.; Praesepe mer. 11:14 p.m. | ♍ | 7:07 | 5:22 | 9:45 | 6:50 | 5:39 | 9:42 | 3:00 |
| 12 | Mo | Alphard mer. 11:54 p.m.; ♄ at quadrature | ♎ | 7:05 | 5:23 | 10:57 | 6:49 | 5:40 | 10:48 | 3:50 |
| 13 | Tu | Orion's Belt sets 2:04 a.m. ☿ inf. ☌ | ♎ | 7:04 | 5:25 | morn | 6:48 | 5:41 | 11:51 | 4:38 |
| 14 | We | St. Valentine's Day; ♀ sets 9:12 p.m. | ♏ | 7:02 | 5:26 | 12:06 | 6:47 | 5:42 | morn | 5:26 |
| 15 | Th | Sagitta ri. 3:08 a.m. ☽♂ cl. 6:08 a.m. | ♏ | 7:01 | 5:28 | 1:13 | 6:46 | 5:43 | 12:51 | 6:14 |
| 16 | Fr | Sirius mer. 8:57 p.m. | ♐ | 6:59 | 5:29 | 2:16 | 6:45 | 5:44 | 1:50 | 7:03 |
| 17 | Sa | False Cross mer. 10:33 p.m. | ♐ | 6:58 | 5:31 | 3:16 | 6:44 | 5:45 | 2:46 | 7:52 |
| **7. Sixth Sunday after Epiphany - February 18, 2001** | | | | **L/Day 10h 36m - Twi. 1h 38m** | | | **L/Day 11h 02m - Twi. 1h 24m** | | | |
| 18 | Su | Regulus mer. 12:15 a.m. ◡☋ | ♐ | 6:56 | 5:32 | 4:11 | 6:43 | 5:45 | 3:39 | 8:41 |
| 19 | Mo | **Presidents' Day** | ♑ | 6:55 | 5:33 | 5:00 | 6:42 | 5:46 | 4:29 | 9:30 |
| 20 | Tu | ♀ at gr. brilliancy; ☽ apo. 5:00 a.m. | ♑ | 6:53 | 5:35 | 5:43 | 6:40 | 5:47 | 5:13 | 10:18 |
| 21 | We | Alioth mer 2:52 a.m.; ♃ sets 1:06 a.m. | ♒ | 6:51 | 5:36 | 6:20 | 6:39 | 5:48 | 5:54 | 11:05 |
| 22 | Th | El Nath mer. 7:14 p.m.; ♂ at quadrature | ♒ | 6:50 | 5:38 | 6:51 | 6:38 | 5:49 | 6:30 | 11:51 |
| 23 | Fr | Vega ri. 11:29 p.m. | ♒ | 6:48 | 5:39 | sets | 6:37 | 5:50 | sets | 12:35p |
| 24 | Sa | Libra ri. 11:42 p.m. | ♓ | 6:46 | 5:40 | 7:02 | 6:36 | 5:51 | 7:10 | 1:18 |
| **8. Seventh Sunday after Epiphany - February 25, 2001** | | | | **L/Day 10h 57m - Twi. 1h 38m** | | | **L/Day 11h 18m - Twi. 1h 24m** | | | |
| 25 | Su | Denebola mer. 1:28 a.m. | ♓ | 6:45 | 5:42 | 8:05 | 6:34 | 5:52 | 8:07 | 2:01 |
| 26 | Mo | Pollux mer. 9:20 p.m.; ♄ sets 12:06 a.m. | ♈ | 6:43 | 5:43 | 9:08 | 6:33 | 5:53 | 9:04 | 2:44 |
| 27 | Tu | Shrove Tuesday; Mardi Gras | ♈ | 6:41 | 5:44 | 10:14 | 6:32 | 5:54 | 10:03 | 3:28 |
| 28 | We | Ash Wednesday | ♉ | 6:40 | 5:46 | 11:20 | 6:31 | 5:55 | 11:04 | 4:14 |

BIRTHSTONE: Amethyst, symbol of sincerity FLOWER: Violet or Primrose

## WEATHER FOLKLORE & LEGEND

***If Candlemas Day is fair and bright, winter will take another fight;***
***If Candlemas Day brings storm and rain, winter is gone and will not come again.***

ZONE

### ❶ Northeastern States

**1st-3rd.** Fair and cold. **4th-7th.** Stormy with heavy snow (12 inches or more), then fair, colder. Some snow extends as far south as Maryland, Virginia area, then fair and cold. **8th-11th.** Dry, albeit very cold weather. **12th-15th.** Some snow New York, Massachusetts area to Maine, then clearing. **16th-19th.** Fair from New England down to Mid-Atlantic States. **20th-23rd.** Stormy with heavy snow (6" to 12"), then fair. **24th-28th.** Light snow spreads in from the West, then turning fair by the 28th.

### ❷ Great Lakes and Midwest

**1st-3rd.** Fair, cold weather. **4th-7th.** Stormy weather; heavy snow for Great Lakes area, with 12 or more inches possible, then clearing and colder. Lighter snow to the south toward Kentucky. **8th-11th.** Snow spreads eastward into Michigan, Illinois. **12th-15th.** Mostly fair, cold. **16th-19th.** Stormy weather. **20th-23rd.** Fair, cold. **24th-28th.** Light snow, then turning fair by month's end.

### ❸ Southeastern States

**1st-3rd.** Fair and cold; frosts penetrate to Florida. **4th-7th.** Snow Tennessee Valley and parts of the Carolinas. Cold rain farther south, then fair, cold. **8th-11th.** Fair skies; possible frosts for Georgia and Florida. **12th-15th.** Rainy, then clearing, cold weather. **16th-19th.** Pleasant weather. **20th-23rd.** Cold winds and rain, then fair and cold. **24th-28th.** Showery, windy from Gulf Coast to the Carolinas, then fair skies.

### ❹ North Central States

**1st-3rd.** Becoming stormy Rocky Mountain States to Dakotas, Nebraska area. **4th-7th.** Snow for Kansas to all points east, then fair and cold weather. Fair, cold from the Rockies and points west. **8th-11th.** Fair, then turning unsettled, with snow spreading east across the Plains. **12th-15th.** Fair and cold. **16th-19th.** Stormy weather spreads in from the West. **20th-23rd.** Fair weather spreads west-to-east from Rockies to Missouri. **24th-28th.** Light snow spreads rapidly from Colorado, east across the Plains. Skies clear by the 28th.

### ❺ South Central States

**1st-3rd.** Widespread storminess. **4th-7th.** Snow for Oklahoma and all points east, then fair and cold weather. Fair and cold from the Rockies and points west. **8th-11th.** Fair, then turning unsettled, with light snow spreading across the Southern Plains from the West to Texas. **12th-15th.** Showers linger along the Texas Gulf Coast, otherwise fair and cold. **16th-19th.** Stormy weather rapidly spreads as far east as Louisiana. **20th-23rd.** Fair weather spreads west-to-east from Rockies to Oklahoma. **24th-28th.** Showers and windy for New Mexico, Texas and Oklahoma Panhandle, shifting east, then fair skies. Showery for Texas and Louisiana coasts; hopefully clear and dry by Mardi Gras time.

### ❻ Northwestern States

**1st-3rd.** Unsettled conditions. **4th-7th.** Fair, quite chilly. **8th-11th.** Fair, then turning wet and unsettled. **12th-15th.** Fair, but cold. **16th-19th.** Stormy weather moves in from Pacific. **20th-23rd.** Fair weather returns. **24th-28th.** Quick changes: showers & gusty winds, then clearing.

### ❼ Southwestern States

**1st-3rd.** Stormy for California and the South Plateau. **4th-7th.** Fair and rather cold. **8th-11th.** Fair, then unsettled conditions. **12th-15th.** Cold in California and on South Plateau. **16th-19th.** Stormy, especially over Arizona. **20th-23rd.** Fair Pacific Coast through Nevada, Utah and points east. **24th-28th.** Light snow for Utah and points east. Showers, windy for California and points east. All areas clear by month's end.

---

**MEMORABLE WEATHER EVENTS**

☞ **FEBRUARY 9th, 1934 - Peak of Severe Cold Wave**—February 1934 marked the longest period of sustained cold in the region from Michigan to the North Atlantic Coast, including Ontario, Quebec and the Maritime Provinces. The lowest temperatures occurred on February 9, when Vanderbilt, MI, dropped to -51°F and Stillwater Reservoir, NY, reached -52°F.

3rd Month **MARCH 2001** 31 Days

♓ PISCES
February 18 to March 20

♈ ARIES
March 20 to April 19

**NOW SPRING HAS COME, THE BIRDS REJOICE, AND CHAUNT THE CHEERFUL LAY; THE FARMER WITH EXULTING JOYS, PREPARES FOR APRIL'S DAY.**

**MOON'S PHASES**
EASTERN STANDARD TIME

| | | |
|---|---|---|
| ☽ First Quarter | 2nd | 9:03 p.m. |
| Full Moon | 9th | 12:23 p.m. |
| ☾ Last Quarter | 16th | 3:45 p.m. |
| New Moon | 24th | 8:21 p.m. |

Subtract hour(s) for other time zones
–1h for C.S.T. –2h for M.S.T. –3h for P.S.T.

**SUN ON MERIDIAN CIVIL TIME**

| *D.* | *H.* | *M.* | *S.* |
|---|---|---|---|
| 1st | 12 | 12 | 21 |
| 8th | 12 | 10 | 47 |
| 15th | 12 | 08 | 54 |
| 22nd | 12 | 06 | 52 |
| 29th | 12 | 04 | 45 |

Calendar for NORTHERN STATES *45°N. Lat. 75°W. Long.* — Calendar for SOUTHERN STATES *35°N. Lat. 75°W. Long.*

| DATE | DAY | ASTRONOMY, CHURCH DAYS, ETC. | MOON'S PLACE | N. Sun RISES | N. Sun SETS | N. Moon SETS | S. Sun RISES | S. Sun SETS | S. Moon SETS | MOON'S SOUTHING OR MERIDIAN PASSAGE EVE |
|---|---|---|---|---|---|---|---|---|---|---|
| 1 | Th | St. David; Pleiades sets 12:41 a.m. | ♉ | 6:38 | 5:47 | morn | 6:29 | 5:56 | morn | 5:02p |
| 2 | Fr | Regulus mer. 11:24 p.m. ☽♃ cl. 12:36 a.m. | ♊ | 6:36 | 5:49 | 12:29 | 6:28 | 5:56 | 12:06 | 5:55 |
| 3 | Sa | Aquila ri. 2:34 a.m. | ♊ | 6:34 | 5:50 | 1:38 | 6:27 | 5:57 | 1:10 | 6:51 |
| **9. First Sunday of Lent - March 4, 2001** | | | | **L/Day 11h 19m - Twi. 1h 37m** | | | **L/Day 11h 32m - Twi. 1h 24m** | | | |
| 4 | Su | Alkaid mer. 2:58 a.m. ⌒ | ♊ | 6:32 | 5:51 | 2:45 | 6:26 | 5:58 | 2:14 | 7:50 |
| 5 | Mo | Bellatrix sets 12:56 a.m. ☊ | ♋ | 6:31 | 5:53 | 3:48 | 6:24 | 5:59 | 3:16 | 8:51 |
| 6 | Tu | Gemini mer. 8:14 p.m. | ♋ | 6:29 | 5:54 | 4:43 | 6:23 | 6:00 | 4:14 | 9:53 |
| 7 | We | Ember Day; Fast of Esther; ♂ ri. 12:49 a.m. | ♌ | 6:27 | 5:55 | 5:30 | 6:22 | 6:01 | 5:05 | 10:52 |
| 8 | Th | ☽ per. 4:00 a.m. ☽ Regulus cl. 5:44 a.m. | ♌ | 6:25 | 5:57 | rises | 6:20 | 6:02 | rises | 11:47 |
| 9 | Fr | Ember Day; Purim; Capella sets 4:17 a.m. | ♍ | 6:23 | 5:58 | 6:02 | 6:19 | 6:03 | 6:11 | morn |
| 10 | Sa | Ember Day ☿♅ very cl. 5:25 a.m. | ♍ | 6:22 | 5:59 | 7:19 | 6:18 | 6:03 | 7:20 | 12:44 |
| **10. Second Sunday of Lent - March 11, 2001** | | | | **L/Day 11h 41m - Twi. 1h 38m** | | | **L/Day 11h 48m - Twi. 1h 25m** | | | |
| 11 | Su | Denebola mer. 12:33 a.m. ☿ gr. W. el. | ♎ | 6:20 | 6:01 | 8:34 | 6:16 | 6:04 | 8:28 | 1:32 |
| 12 | Mo | Girl Scouts Day; ☿ ri. 5:16 a.m. | ♎ | 6:18 | 6:02 | 9:47 | 6:15 | 6:05 | 9:34 | 2:26 |
| 13 | Tu | Spica mer. 1:57 a.m.; Sagitta ri. 1:22 a.m. | ♏ | 6:16 | 6:03 | 10:57 | 6:13 | 6:06 | 10:38 | 3:16 |
| 14 | We | Pegasus ri. 3:45 a.m.; ♀ sets 8:08 p.m. | ♏ | 6:14 | 6:04 | morn | 6:12 | 6:07 | 11:39 | 4:06 |
| 15 | Th | Ides of March; Gienah mer. 12:44 a.m. | ♏ | 6:12 | 6:06 | 12:04 | 6:11 | 6:08 | morn | 4:55 |
| 16 | Fr | Canis Minor sets 2:23 a.m. | ♐ | 6:11 | 6:07 | 1:07 | 6:09 | 6:08 | 12:38 | 5:45 |
| 17 | Sa | St. Patrick's Day ♇ sta. ☋ | ♐ | 6:09 | 6:08 | 2:05 | 6:08 | 6:09 | 1:34 | 6:35 |
| **11. Third Sunday of Lent - March 18, 2001** | | | | **L/Day 12h 03m - Twi. 1h 39m** | | | **L/Day 12h 04m - Twi. 1h 25m** | | | |
| 18 | Su | Castor sets 4:01 a.m. ⌣ | ♑ | 6:07 | 6:10 | 2:57 | 6:06 | 6:10 | 2:25 | 7:25 |
| 19 | Mo | Spica mer. 1:59 a.m.; Lynx mer. 10:00 p.m. | ♑ | 6:05 | 6:11 | 3:42 | 6:05 | 6:11 | 3:11 | 8:14 |
| 20 | Tu | ☽ apo. 6:00 p.m. | ♑ | 6:03 | 6:12 | 4:21 | 6:04 | 6:12 | 3:53 | 9:01 |
| 21 | We | ♃ sets 11:33 p.m. ♀ combust | ♒ | 6:01 | 6:14 | 4:54 | 6:02 | 6:12 | 4:30 | 9:47 |
| 22 | Th | Milk Maid's Dipper ri. 2:29 a.m. | ♒ | 5:59 | 6:15 | 5:23 | 6:01 | 6:13 | 5:04 | 10:32 |
| 23 | Fr | Antares ri. 12:00 a.m. /11:56 p.m. | ♓ | 5:57 | 6:16 | 5:48 | 5:59 | 6:14 | 5:36 | 11:16 |
| 24 | Sa | Pollux mer. 7:35 p.m. | ♓ | 5:56 | 6:17 | sets | 5:58 | 6:15 | sets | 11:59 |
| **12. Fourth Sunday of Lent - March 25, 2001** | | | | **L/Day 12h 25m - Twi. 1h 41m** | | | **L/Day 12h 19m - Twi. 1h 26m** | | | |
| 25 | Su | Annunciation Day; Libra mer. 2:54 a.m. | ♈ | 5:54 | 6:19 | 7:00 | 5:57 | 6:16 | 6:58 | 12:42p |
| 26 | Mo | Orion's Belt sets 11:15 p.m. | ♈ | 5:52 | 6:20 | 8:06 | 5:55 | 6:16 | 7:57 | 1:26 |
| 27 | Tu | Kochab mer. 2:31 a.m. | ♈ | 5:50 | 6:21 | 9:13 | 5:54 | 6:17 | 8:58 | 2:12 |
| 28 | We | Cor Caroli mer. 12:32 a.m. ☽♄ cl. 10:18 p.m. | ♉ | 5:48 | 6:22 | 10:22 | 5:52 | 6:18 | 10:00 | 3:00 |
| 29 | Th | ☽ Aldebaran cl. 11:03 p.m.; ♀ inf. ☌ | ♉ | 5:46 | 6:24 | 11:31 | 5:51 | 6:19 | 11:04 | 3:51 |
| 30 | Fr | Algol sets 11:47 p.m.; ♄ sets 10:13 p.m. | ♊ | 5:44 | 6:25 | morn | 5:50 | 6:20 | morn | 4:45 |
| 31 | Sa | Altair ri. 12:42 a.m.; Sirius sets 11:14 p.m. ⌒ | ♊ | 5:42 | 6:26 | 12:38 | 5:48 | 6:20 | 12:08 | 5:43 |

BIRTHSTONE: Aquamarine, symbol of truthfulness FLOWER: Jonquil or Daffodil

**WEATHER FOLKLORE & LEGEND**

***Fish bite the least, when wind is in the east.***

# WEATHER FORECAST
## ∽ MARCH 2001 ∽

### ZONE

### ❶ Northeastern States
**1st-3rd.** Fair but windy. **4th-7th.** Stormy over New England, snowy over higher terrain areas, then fair skies. Rainy for Virginia, Maryland, then fair. A wintry mix elsewhere. **8th-11th.** Some rain for New England. **12th-15th.** Showers clear in Mid-Atlantic States, otherwise mostly fair. **16th-19th.** Stormy weather sweeps in from the West to New England; heavy rain for Mid-Atlantic States. **20th-23rd.** Fair skies. **24th-27th.** Showers for Mid-Atlantic States, then fair. Rain spreads from West over New England, then fair. **28th-31st.** Pleasant weather for entire region.

### ❷ Great Lakes and Midwest
**1st-3rd.** Stormy. **4th-7th.** Turning cold and dry. **8th-11th.** Showers spread in from the West. **12th-15th.** Mixed clouds and Sun. **16th-19th.** Stormy conditions. **20th-23rd.** Fair Great Lakes and points east. **24th-27th.** Rain for Illinois, Michigan area and points east, then fair. **28th-31st.** Becoming stormy for Great Lakes.

### ❸ Southeastern States
**1st-3rd.** Pleasant weather. **4th-7th.** Rainy and rather cold for Mississippi and all points east. **8th-11th.** Scattered showers. **12th-15th.** Turning mostly fair. **16th-19th.** Rain and showers; heaviest activity Tennessee, western sections of the Carolinas, and northern sections of Mississippi, Alabama and Georgia. **20th-23rd.** Sunny skies. **24th-27th.** Showers Gulf States, north and east to the Carolinas, then fair. **28th-31st.** Fair skies.

### ❹ North Central States
**1st-3rd.** Stormy conditions. **4th-7th.** Cold and dry. **8th-11th.** Showers Rockies and points east. **12th-15th.** Stormy weather spreads east from the Rockies. **16th-19th.** Stormy over the Plains; clearing, cold farther west. **20th-23rd.** Fair at first, then turning unsettled for Rockies and points east. **24th-27th.** Pleasant spring weather. **28th-31st.** Rain Colorado and east across the Plains.

### ❺ South Central States
**1st-3rd.** Stormy conditions; blustery weather from Southern Rockies east to Arkansas, Louisiana. **4th-7th.** Cold, dry weather. **8th-11th.** Showers over Rockies and points east. Showery for New Mexico, then fair. **12th-15th.** Stormy weather spreads east into the Rockies. **16th-19th.** Stormy over the Plains; heavy rain for Texas, points east. Clearing, cold conditions for Rockies and points west. **20th-23rd.** Fair at first, then turning unsettled from Rockies to points east. Threatening skies over the Southern Plains. **24th-27th.** Showers for Texas and Louisiana coasts, then fair. Elsewhere, pleasant, tranquil weather. **28th-31st.** Showers for New Mexico, Texas.

### ❻ Northwestern States
**1st-3rd.** Unsettled conditions. **4th-7th.** Dry and chilly. **8th-11th.** Showery. **12th-15th.** Turning stormy. **16th-19th.** Clearing skies. **20th-23rd.** Increasingly cloudy skies; scattered showers. **24th-27th.** Fair and rather pleasant. **28th-31st.** Storminess moves in from the Pacific.

### ❼ Southwestern States
**1st-3rd.** Very unsettled. **4th-7th.** Clearing and chilly. **8th-11th.** Showers for Arizona, then fair. **12th-15th.** Turning stormy for the Pacific Coast and points east. **16th-19th.** Gradual clearing. **20th-23rd.** Fair at first, then threatening skies over California and points east. **24th-27th.** Fair and pleasant. **28th-31st.** Turning stormy; rain for Utah and points east.

---

### MEMORABLE WEATHER EVENTS

☛ **MARCH 11th, 1962 - Iowa's Record Snow** —". . . one of the most paralyzing snowstorms in decades"; 48" on ground at Inwood, Iowa, after the storm.

☛ **MARCH 13th–14th, 1993 - The Blizzard of '93**—Described by the National Weather Service as "one of the worst storms of the century"; the onslaught left 13" of snow in Birmingham, AL, and 36" in Syracuse, NY. Dozens of tornadoes were reported in the South.

4th Month

# APRIL 2001

30 Days

♈ ARIES
March 20 to April 19

♉ TAURUS
April 19 to May 21

**HAIL, APRIL WITH HER SMILING FACE HAS COME TO CHEER THE PLAIN;
THE GRASS IS SEEN TO START APACE, AS DOES THE NEEDFUL GRAIN.**

| MOON'S PHASES EASTERN STANDARD TIME | | |
|---|---|---|
| ☽ First Quarter | 1st | 5:49 a.m. |
| ○ Full Moon | 7th | 10:21 p.m. |
| ☾ Last Quarter | 15th | 10:31 a.m. |
| ● New Moon | 23rd | 10:25 a.m. |
| ☽ First Quarter | 30th | 12:07 p.m. |

| SUN ON MERIDIAN CIVIL TIME D. | H. | M. | S. |
|---|---|---|---|
| 1st | 12 | 03 | 51 |
| 8th | 12 | 01 | 50 |
| 15th | 12 | 00 | 00 |
| 22nd | 11 | 58 | 29 |
| 29th | 11 | 57 | 19 |

| DATE | DAY | ASTRONOMY, CHURCH DAYS, ETC. | MOON'S PLACE | Calendar for NORTHERN STATES 45°N. Lat. 75°W. Long. Sun RISES | Sun SETS | Moon SETS | Calendar for SOUTHERN STATES 35°N. Lat. 75°W. Long. Sun RISES | Sun SETS | Moon SETS | MOON'S SOUTHING OR MERIDIAN PASSAGE EVE |
|---|---|---|---|---|---|---|---|---|---|---|
| **13. Fifth Sunday of Lent - April 1, 2001** | | | | **L/Day 12h 47m - Twi. 1h 43m** | | | **L/Day 12h 34m - Twi. 1h 27m** | | | |
| 1 | Su | April Fools' Day; DST begins 2:00 a.m. ☊ | ♋ | 5:41 | 6:28 | 1:42 | 5:47 | 6:21 | 1:09 | 6:42p |
| 2 | Mo | Spica mer. 12:42 a.m. | ♋ | 5:39 | 6:29 | 2:38 | 5:45 | 6:22 | 2:07 | 7:41 |
| 3 | Tu | Arcturus mer. 1:28 a.m. | ♌ | 5:37 | 6:30 | 3:26 | 5:44 | 6:23 | 2:58 | 8:39 |
| 4 | We | Denebola mer. 10:54 p.m. | ♌ | 5:35 | 6:31 | 4:07 | 5:43 | 6:24 | 3:45 | 9:36 |
| 5 | Th | ☽ per. 5:00 a.m. | ♍ | 5:33 | 6:33 | 4:41 | 5:41 | 6:24 | 4:26 | 10:30 |
| 6 | Fr | Regulus mer. 9:09 p.m. | ♍ | 5:31 | 6:34 | rises | 5:40 | 6:25 | rises | 11:22 |
| 7 | Sa | Albireo ri. 10:34 p.m.; ♂ ri. 11:49 p.m. | ♎ | 5:29 | 6:35 | 6:08 | 5:39 | 6:26 | 6:06 | morn |
| **14. Passion/Palm Sunday - April 8, 2001** | | | | **L/Day 13h 08m - Twi. 1h 46m** | | | **L/Day 12h 50m - Twi. 1h 28m** | | | |
| 8 | Su | First Day of Passover; ☿ combust | ♎ | 5:28 | 6:36 | 7:23 | 5:37 | 6:27 | 7:13 | 12:13 |
| 9 | Mo | Dubhe mer. 9:49 p.m.; ♀ ri. 4:27 a.m. | ♎ | 5:26 | 6:38 | 8:35 | 5:36 | 6:28 | 8:19 | 1:03 |
| 10 | Tu | Virgo mer. 12:20 a.m. | ♏ | 5:24 | 6:39 | 9:46 | 5:35 | 6:28 | 9:23 | 1:53 |
| 11 | We | Aldebaran sets 10:14 p.m. | ♏ | 5:22 | 6:40 | 10:53 | 5:33 | 6:29 | 10:25 | 2:44 |
| 12 | Th | Holy Thursday ☽♂ cl. 11:36 p.m. | ♐ | 5:20 | 6:41 | 11:55 | 5:32 | 6:30 | 11:23 | 3:35 |
| 13 | Fr | Good Friday; Rasalhague ri. 9:26 p.m. | ♐ | 5:19 | 6:43 | morn | 5:31 | 6:31 | morn | 4:26 |
| 14 | Sa | Megrez mer. 10:41 p.m. ∪☋ | ♐ | 5:17 | 6:44 | 12:58 | 5:29 | 6:32 | 12:18 | 5:17 |
| **15. Easter Sunday - April 15, 2001** | | | | **L/Day 13h 30m - Twi. 1h 49m** | | | **L/Day 13h 04m - Twi. 1h 30m** | | | |
| 15 | Su | Greek Orthodox Easter | ♑ | 5:15 | 6:45 | 1:39 | 5:28 | 6:32 | 1:07 | 6:07 |
| 16 | Mo | Castor sets 2:06 a.m. | ♑ | 5:13 | 6:46 | 2:20 | 5:27 | 6:33 | 1:49 | 6:56 |
| 17 | Tu | Sickle mer. 8:30 p.m.; ☽ apo. 1:00 a.m. | ♒ | 5:12 | 6:48 | 2:55 | 5:25 | 6:34 | 2:30 | 7:42 |
| 18 | We | Praesepe mer. 7:00 p.m. | ♒ | 5:10 | 6:49 | 3:25 | 5:24 | 6:35 | 3:05 | 8:27 |
| 19 | Th | Great Orion Nebula sets 9:26 p.m. | ♒ | 5:08 | 6:50 | 3:52 | 5:23 | 6:36 | 3:37 | 9:11 |
| 20 | Fr | Crux (Southern Cross) mer. 10:30 p.m. | ♓ | 5:07 | 6:52 | 4:16 | 5:22 | 6:36 | 4:07 | 9:54 |
| 21 | Sa | Zubenelgenubi mer. 12:52 a.m. | ♓ | 5:05 | 6:53 | 4:39 | 5:21 | 6:37 | 4:36 | 10:38 |
| **16. Second Sunday of Easter - April 22, 2001** | | | | **L/Day 13h 51m - Twi. 1h 54m** | | | **L/Day 13h 19m - Twi. 1h 33m** | | | |
| 22 | Su | Ophiuchus mer. 3:32 a.m. | ♈ | 5:03 | 6:54 | 5:02 | 5:19 | 6:38 | 5:05 | 11:21 |
| 23 | Mo | St. George; "Cat's Eye" ri. 11:56 p.m. ☿ sup. ☌ | ♈ | 5:02 | 6:55 | sets | 5:18 | 6:39 | sets | 12:07p |
| 24 | Tu | Nunki mer. 4:44 a.m. | ♉ | 5:00 | 6:57 | 8:11 | 5:17 | 6:40 | 7:52 | 12:55 |
| 25 | We | Altair ri. 11:00 p.m. | ♉ | 4:58 | 6:58 | 9:22 | 5:16 | 6:40 | 8:56 | 1:46 |
| 26 | Th | Cor Caroli mer. 10:34 p.m. | ♊ | 4:57 | 6:59 | 10:31 | 5:15 | 6:41 | 10:01 | 2:41 |
| 27 | Fr | Aquarius ri. 2:45 a.m. | ♊ | 4:55 | 7:00 | 11:37 | 5:14 | 6:42 | 11:05 | 3:38 |
| 28 | Sa | ♄ sets 8:36 p.m. ∩☊ | ♋ | 4:54 | 7:02 | morn | 5:12 | 6:43 | morn | 4:37 |
| **17. Third Sunday of Easter - April 29, 2001** | | | | **L/Day 14h 13m - Twi. 1h 59m** | | | **L/Day 13h 33m - Twi. 1h 35m** | | | |
| 29 | Su | Denebola mer. 9:29 p.m | ♋ | 4:52 | 7:03 | 12:36 | 5:11 | 6:44 | 12:04 | 5:36 |
| 30 | Mo | Spica mer. 10:48 p.m.; Sirius sets 9:17 p.m. | ♌ | 4:51 | 7:04 | 1:26 | 5:10 | 6:45 | 12:57 | 6:34 |

BIRTHSTONE: Diamond, symbol of innocence FLOWER: Sweet Pea or Daisy

**WEATHER FOLKLORE & LEGEND**

***If it thunders on All Fools' Day, 'twill bring good crops of corn and hay.***

ZONE

### ❶ Northeastern States

**1st-3rd.** Don't forget to push clocks forward one hour on the 1st as we start daylight saving time. Squalls throughout the region, then fair, cold. **4th-7th.** Wet through New England. **8th-11th.** Clearing, then fair skies. **12th-15th.** Squally weather. **16th-19th.** Clearing and unseasonably chilly. **20th-23rd.** Showers spread across New York from the West, through the rest of the region, then fair. **24th-27th.** Pleasant. **28th-30th.** Heavy rain, especially for New England, then fair.

### ❷ Great Lakes and Midwest

**1st-3rd.** Don't forget to push clocks forward one hour on the 1st as we start daylight saving time. Fair, windy. **4th-7th.** Wet Ohio River Valley. **8th-11th.** Mostly fair weather. **12th-15th.** Squally conditions. **16th-19th.** Pleasant early spring weather. **20th-23rd.** Showers spread rapidly east across the Great Lakes, then fair weather. **24th-27th.** Squally weather moves toward the Great Lakes from the West. **28th-30th.** Heavy rain Ohio River Valley, then clear and dry.

### ❸ Southeastern States

**1st-3rd.** Don't forget to push clocks forward one hour on the 1st as we start daylight saving time. Stormy, then fair. **4th-7th.** Scattered showers. **8th-11th.** Fair weather. **12th-15th.** Thunderstorms. **16th-19th.** Fair skies return. **20th-23rd.** Rain along Gulf Coast north and east to Carolinas, then clearing. **24th-27th.** Pleasant conditions. **28th-30th.** Thunderstorms for the Gulf Coast and across the rest of the region, then clearing.

### ❹ North Central States

**1st-3rd.** Don't forget to push clocks forward one hour on the 1st as we start daylight saving time. Fair skies and windy. **4th-7th.** Pleasant initially, then showers over Colorado east through the Plains States. **8th-11th.** Mostly fair skies, then turning stormy from the West through the Rockies. **12th-15th.** Stormy over the Plains. **16th-19th.** Pleasant, then turning wet for the Rockies and Plains States. **20th-23rd.** Mostly fair weather. **24th-27th.** Stormy for Rocky Mountain States, through Dakotas, Nebraska, and points east. **28th-30th.** Fair skies.

### ❺ South Central States

**1st-3rd.** Don't forget to push clocks forward one hour on the 1st as we start daylight saving time. Fair and windy weather. **4th-7th.** Pleasant initially, then showers spread east into the Plains. **8th-11th.** Mostly fair skies, then turning stormy from the West through the Rockies. **12th-15th.** Stormy over the Plains; showery and windy for Texas, Oklahoma. **16th-19th.** Pleasant, then turning wet for the Rockies and Plains States; threatening skies over New Mexico. **20th-23rd.** Rain for Texas and Louisiana Gulf Coasts, then clearing; mostly fair weather elsewhere. **24th-27th.** Stormy for Rocky Mountain States, through Texas to Louisiana, Arkansas area. **28th-30th.** Fair skies.

### ❻ Northwestern States

**1st-3rd.** Don't forget to push clocks forward one hour on the 1st as we start daylight saving time. Fair skies, gusty winds. **4th-7th.** Fair, then scattered showers. **8th-11th.** Mostly fair initially, then turning stormy in Washington and Oregon and points east. **12th-15th.** Slow clearing. **16th-19th.** Pleasant, then unsettled with showers for the coastal plain. **20th-23rd.** Mostly fair skies. **24th-27th.** Squally for the Pacific Coast. **28th-30th.** Fair skies return.

### ❼ Southwestern States

**1st-3rd.** Except in Arizona, don't forget to push clocks forward one hour on the 1st as we start daylight saving time. Pleasant conditions. **4th-7th.** Pleasant, then showers in Utah. Squally for Nevada, then pleasant again. **8th-11th.** Mostly fair, then showers over the South Plateau. **12th-15th.** Gradual clearing skies. **16th-19th.** Scattered showers, especially near the Pacific Coast. **20th-23rd.** Fair skies. **24th-27th.** Squally for the Pacific Coast; gusty winds elsewhere. **28th-30th.** Fair weather.

---

### MEMORABLE WEATHER EVENTS

☞ **APRIL 19th–23rd, 1997- Devastating Floods for the Upper Plains—** Thanks chiefly to a winter that saw three times the normal snowfall, a rapid early spring snowmelt caused a catastrophic flood along the Red River of the North, leading to the emergency evacuation of 50,000 people in Grand Forks, ND.

| 5th Month | MAY 2001 | 31 Days |
|---|---|---|

♉ TAURUS
April 19 to May 21

♊ GEMINI
May 21 to June 21

**WITH VERDURE THE WIDE EARTH'S OVERSPREAD, AND TREES ADORNED WITH BLOOMS; THE PATHS IN MAY BOW SWEET TO TREAD, MID FORESTS OF PERFUME.**

**MOON'S PHASES**
EASTERN STANDARD TIME

| | | |
|---|---|---|
| 🌕 Full Moon | 7th | 8:52 a.m. |
| 🌗 Last Quarter | 15th | 5:10 a.m. |
| 🌑 New Moon | 22nd | 9:46 p.m. |
| 🌓 First Quarter | 29th | 5:09 p.m. |

Subtract hour(s) for other time zones
–1h for C.S.T. –2h for M.S.T. –3h for P.S.T.

**SUN ON MERIDIAN CIVIL TIME**

| D. | H. | M. | S. |
|---|---|---|---|
| 1st | 11 | 57 | 04 |
| 8th | 11 | 56 | 26 |
| 15th | 11 | 56 | 17 |
| 22nd | 11 | 56 | 37 |
| 29th | 11 | 57 | 21 |

| DATE | DAY | ASTRONOMY, CHURCH DAYS, ETC. | MOON'S PLACE | Calendar for NORTHERN STATES 45°N. Lat. 75°W. Long. Sun RISES | Sun SETS | Moon SETS | Calendar for SOUTHERN STATES 35°N. Lat. 75°W. Long. Sun RISES | Sun SETS | Moon SETS | MOON'S SOUTHING OR MERIDIAN PASSAGE EVE |
|---|---|---|---|---|---|---|---|---|---|---|
| 1 | Tu | ☽ per. 11:00 p.m. ☽ Regulus cl. 10:00 p.m. | ♌ | 4:49 | 7:05 | 2:08 | 5:09 | 6:45 | 1:44 | 7:29p |
| 2 | We | Antares ri. 9:19 p.m. | ♍ | 4:48 | 7:07 | 2:43 | 5:08 | 6:46 | 2:25 | 8:23 |
| 3 | Th | Coma Berenices mer. 10:00 p.m. | ♍ | 4:46 | 7:08 | 3:14 | 5:07 | 6:47 | 3:02 | 9:14 |
| 4 | Fr | Pollux sets 12:45 a.m. ♀ at greatest brilliancy | ♍ | 4:45 | 7:09 | 3:41 | 5:06 | 6:48 | 3:37 | 10:03 |
| 5 | Sa | Libra mer. 12:13 a.m. | ♎ | 4:43 | 7:10 | 4:07 | 5:05 | 6:49 | 4:10 | 10:53 |
| **18. Fourth Sunday of Easter - May 6, 2001** | | | | **L/Day 14h 29m - Twi. 2h 06m** | | | **L/Day 13h 45m - Twi. 1h 37m** | | | |
| 6 | Su | Canes Venatici mer. 9:55 p.m. ☿♄cl. 8:07 p.m. | ♎ | 4:42 | 7:11 | rises | 5:04 | 6:49 | rises | 11:42 |
| 7 | Mo | Canis Minor sets 10:55 p.m.; ♄ combust | ♏ | 4:41 | 7:13 | 7:26 | 5:03 | 6:50 | 7:06 | morn |
| 8 | Tu | V.E. Day; ♂ ri. 10:19 p.m. | ♏ | 4:39 | 7:14 | 8:35 | 5:02 | 6:51 | 8:09 | 12:32 |
| 9 | We | Delphinus ri. 10:43 p.m. | ♐ | 4:38 | 7:15 | 9:40 | 5:01 | 6:52 | 9:10 | 1:23 |
| 10 | Th | Alphard sets 11:46 p.m. ♆ sta. | ♐ | 4:37 | 7:16 | 10:40 | 5:00 | 6:53 | 10:07 | 2:15 |
| 11 | Fr | Denebola mer. 8:28 p.m. ♂ sta. ☋ | ♐ | 4:36 | 7:17 | 11:32 | 5:00 | 6:53 | 10:59 | 3:07 |
| 12 | Sa | Crux mer. 9:04 p.m. ◡ | ♑ | 4:34 | 7:19 | morn | 4:59 | 6:54 | 11:46 | 3:59 |
| **19. Fifth Sunday of Easter - May 13, 2001** | | | | **L/Day 14h 45m - Twi. 2h 11m** | | | **L/Day 13h 57m - Twi. 1h 40m** | | | |
| 13 | Su | ♂ rivals Sirius in brightness through Aug. 2 | ♑ | 4:33 | 7:20 | 12:17 | 4:58 | 6:55 | morn | 4:48 |
| 14 | Mo | ♀ ri. 2:58 a.m.; ☽ apo. 8:00 p.m. | ♒ | 4:32 | 7:21 | 12:55 | 4:57 | 6:56 | 12:27 | 5:36 |
| 15 | Tu | Zubeneschamali mer. 11:40 p.m. | ♒ | 4:31 | 7:22 | 1:27 | 4:56 | 6:57 | 1:04 | 6:22 |
| 16 | We | Alioth mer. 9:20 p.m. | ♒ | 4:30 | 7:23 | 1:55 | 4:56 | 6:57 | 1:37 | 7:06 |
| 17 | Th | Corona Borealis mer. 11:50 p.m. | ♓ | 4:29 | 7:24 | 2:19 | 4:55 | 6:58 | 2:07 | 7:49 |
| 18 | Fr | Albireo mer. 3:45 a.m. | ♓ | 4:28 | 7:26 | 2:42 | 4:54 | 6:59 | 2:36 | 8:32 |
| 19 | Sa | Armed Forces Day; Sagittarius mer. 3:17 a.m. | ♈ | 4:27 | 7:27 | 3:05 | 4:54 | 7:00 | 3:05 | 9:15 |
| **20. Sixth Sunday of Easter - May 20, 2001** | | | | **L/Day 15h 02m - Twi. 2h 17m** | | | **L/Day 14h 07m - Twi. 1h 42m** | | | |
| 20 | Su | Rogation Sunday; ☿ El Nath cl. 8:08 p.m. | ♈ | 4:26 | 7:28 | 3:28 | 4:53 | 7:00 | 3:35 | 9:59 |
| 21 | Mo | Fomalhaut ri. 2:51 a.m.; ♃ sets 8:32 p.m. | ♉ | 4:25 | 7:29 | 3:54 | 4:52 | 7:01 | 4:06 | 10:46 |
| 22 | Tu | National Maritime Day ☿ gr. E. el. | ♉ | 4:24 | 7:30 | sets | 4:52 | 7:02 | sets | 11:37 |
| 23 | We | Pegasus ri. 11:05 p.m. | ♊ | 4:23 | 7:31 | 8:17 | 4:51 | 7:03 | 7:49 | 12:31p |
| 24 | Th | Ascension Day; ♃ combust | ♊ | 4:22 | 7:32 | 9:27 | 4:51 | 7:03 | 8:55 | 1:29 |
| 25 | Fr | Messier 13 mer. 12:29 a.m. ♄☌☉ ⌒♌ | ♋ | 4:21 | 7:33 | 10:30 | 4:50 | 7:04 | 9:57 | 2:29 |
| 26 | Sa | Andromeda Galaxy ri. 11:07 p.m. | ♋ | 4:20 | 7:34 | 11:25 | 4:50 | 7:05 | 10:54 | 3:30 |
| **21. Seventh Sunday of Easter - May 27, 2001** | | | | **L/Day 15h 15m - Twi. 2h 23m** | | | **L/Day 14h 16m - Twi. 1h 44m** | | | |
| 27 | Su | Asteroid Pallas at opp.; ☽ per. 2:00 a.m. | ♌ | 4:20 | 7:35 | morn | 4:49 | 7:05 | 11:43 | 4:29 |
| 28 | Mo | **Memorial Day;** Algol ri. 1:39 a.m. | ♌ | 4:19 | 7:36 | 12:10 | 4:49 | 7:06 | morn | 5:26 |
| 29 | Tu | ⛢ sta.; ☽ Regulus cl. 12:22 a.m. | ♌ | 4:18 | 7:37 | 12:47 | 4:48 | 7:07 | 12:27 | 6:20 |
| 30 | We | Regulus sets 12:20 a.m. | ♍ | 4:18 | 7:38 | 1:18 | 4:48 | 7:07 | 1:05 | 7:11 |
| 31 | Th | Eltanin mer. 1:20 a.m. | ♍ | 4:17 | 7:39 | 1:46 | 4:48 | 7:08 | 1:39 | 8:00 |

BIRTHSTONE: Emerald, symbol of happiness FLOWER: Lily of the Valley or Hawthorn

**WEATHER FOLKLORE & LEGEND**

***When clouds appear like rocks and towers, the Earth's refreshed with frequent showers.***

# WEATHER FORECAST
## ∽ MAY 2001 ∽

ZONE

### ❶ Northeastern States

**1st-3rd.** Dry and pleasant. **4th-7th.** Showers, then clearing. **8th-11th.** Fair skies. **12th-15th.** Showery and windy for Mid-Atlantic States north to Maine, then fair and unseasonably chilly. **16th-19th.** Fair, then showers spread in from the West, then clearing. Improving weather for the Preakness at Pimlico. **20th-23rd.** Fair skies. **24th-27th.** Stormy weather spreads in from the West. **28th-31st.** Becoming unsettled.

### ❷ Great Lakes and Midwest

**1st-3rd.** Showers, chiefly for Great Lakes. **4th-7th.** Pleasant weather, but unsettled conditions to the south could possibly make for thundery conditions on Derby Day in Louisville. **8th-11th.** Squally conditions spread into the Ohio River Valley from the West. **12th-15th.** Fair for Michigan, Illinois and Wisconsin. **16th-19th.** Quick changing weather: fair, then showers, then a return to fair weather. **20th-23rd.** Sunshine gives way to increasingly cloudy skies. **24th-27th.** Stormy for Illinois, Michigan area, spreading east. Showers and thunderstorms could threaten the Indy 500. **28th-31st.** Light showers spread east to the Great Lakes.

### ❸ Southeastern States

**1st-3rd.** Fair and dry. **4th-7th.** Scattered thunderstorms from Gulf States north and east to the Carolinas, then fair. **8th-11th.** Fair skies give way to a buildup of clouds. **12th-15th.** Thunderstorms, then fair skies. **16th-19th.** Showers for most of the region. **20th-23rd.** Fair skies. **24th-27th.** Scattered showers and thunderstorms. **28th-31st.** More scattered showers.

### ❹ North Central States

**1st-3rd.** Wet Rockies and Plains States. **4th-7th.** Pleasant weather. **8th-11th.** Thunderstorms: some possibly severe. **12th-15th.** Fair skies. **16th-19th.** Unsettled conditions. **20th-23rd.** Stormy weather spreads east from Colorado. **24th-27th.** Mostly fair. **28th-31st.** Light showers spreading east.

### ❺ South Central States

**1st-3rd.** Wet Rockies and Plains States. **4th-7th.** Scattered thunderstorms linger along Texas, Louisiana Gulf Coasts, then clearing. Fair, pleasant weather elsewhere. **8th-11th.** Dangerous thunderstorms. Showery, windy for New Mexico and Texas. Potent thunderstorms for Arkansas and Louisiana area. **12th-15th.** Fair skies. **16th-19th.** Unsettled conditions. **20th-23rd.** Very unsettled weather spreads eastward. Showery/windy conditions for the Southern Plains. Heavy rain for Texas and Oklahoma. **24th-27th.** Mostly fair. **28th-31st.** Showers spread east. Some rain in Texas.

### ❻ Northwestern States

**1st-3rd.** Showers for Washington, Oregon. **4th-7th.** Pleasant, tranquil conditions. **8th-11th.** Scattered showers. **12th-15th.** Fair weather. **16th-19th.** Clouds, some rain. **20th-23rd.** Turning stormy. **24th-27th.** Mostly fair skies. **28th-31st.** A few passing showers.

### ❼ Southwestern States

**1st-3rd.** Threatening skies. **4th-7th.** Fair, dry and pleasant. **8th-11th.** Scattered showers and possible thunderstorms. **12th-15th.** Fair weather returns. **16th-19th.** Unsettled with some rain. Dust storms for South Plateau. **20th-23rd.** Turning stormy from the Pacific Coast to Utah. **24th-27th.** Mostly fair. **28th-31st.** Light showers; threatening skies for California and along South Plateau.

---

### MEMORABLE WEATHER EVENTS

☞ **MAY 7th, 1912 - Rain in Bagdad, California**—The first measurable precipitation for this San Bernardino County community since August 17, 1909—a total of 993 consecutive days!

☞ **MAY 18th, 1980 - Washington's Mount Saint Helens Erupted**—Smoke plume rose to 80,000 feet; ash fell heavily to northeast; cloud reached East Coast in 3 days; circled world in 19 days.

6th Month

# JUNE 2001

30 Days

♊ GEMINI
May 21 to June 21

♋ CANCER
June 21 to July 22

SOL'S HEATING RAYS EACH MIST RETRACTS, THAT HOVERS OVER THE PLAIN;
THE CLOUDS OVERHEAD GROW THICK AND BLACK, IN TORRENTS POURS THE RAIN.

**MOON'S PHASES**
EASTERN STANDARD TIME

| Phase | Date | Time |
|---|---|---|
| Full Moon | 5th | 8:39 p.m. |
| Last Quarter | 13th | 10:28 p.m. |
| New Moon | 21st | 6:57 a.m. |
| First Quarter | 27th | 10:19 p.m. |

Subtract hour(s) for other time zones
–1h for C.S.T. –2h for M.S.T. –3h for P.S.T.

**SUN ON MERIDIAN CIVIL TIME**

| D. | H. | M. | S. |
|---|---|---|---|
| 1st | 11 | 57 | 47 |
| 8th | 11 | 58 | 59 |
| 15th | 12 | 00 | 25 |
| 22nd | 12 | 01 | 57 |
| 29th | 12 | 03 | 25 |

| | | | | Calendar for NORTHERN STATES 45°N. Lat. 75°W. Long. | | | Calendar for SOUTHERN STATES 35°N. Lat. 75°W. Long. | | | MOON'S SOUTHING OR MERIDIAN PASSAGE |
|---|---|---|---|---|---|---|---|---|---|---|
| DATE | DAY | ASTRONOMY, CHURCH DAYS, ETC. | MOON'S PLACE | Sun RISES | Sun SETS | Moon SETS | Sun RISES | Sun SETS | Moon SETS | EVE |
| 1 | Fr | Aquarius ri. 12:28 a.m. | ♎ | 4:17 | 7:39 | 2:12 | 4:47 | 7:09 | 2:12 | 8:48p |
| 2 | Sa | Aries ri. 2:36 a.m. | ♎ | 4:16 | 7:40 | 2:37 | 4:47 | 7:09 | 2:44 | 9:36 |
| **22. Pentecost Sunday - June 3, 2001** | | | | **L/Day 15h 25m - Twi. 2h 28m** | | | **L/Day 14h 23m - Twi. 1h 46m** | | | |
| 3 | Su | Greek Orth. Pentecost ♇☍ | ♏ | 4:16 | 7:41 | 3:04 | 4:47 | 7:10 | 3:17 | 10:25 |
| 4 | Mo | Graffias mer. 11:10 p.m. | ♏ | 4:15 | 7:42 | rises | 4:47 | 7:10 | rises | 11:15 |
| 5 | Tu | Enif ri. 10:08 p.m.; ☿ combust | ♏ | 4:15 | 7:43 | 7:26 | 4:46 | 7:11 | 6:58 | morn |
| 6 | We | Ember Day ☽☌♂ cl. 8:13 p.m. | ♐ | 4:14 | 7:43 | 8:28 | 4:46 | 7:12 | 7:56 | 12:06 |
| 7 | Th | Corona Borealis mer. 10:27 p.m. ☋ | ♐ | 4:14 | 7:44 | 9:24 | 4:46 | 7:12 | 8:51 | 12:58 |
| 8 | Fr | Ember Day ♀ gr. W. el. ◡ | ♑ | 4:14 | 7:45 | 10:13 | 4:46 | 7:13 | 9:40 | 1:50 |
| 9 | Sa | Ember Day; "Teapot" mer. 1:55 a.m. | ♑ | 4:13 | 7:45 | 10:53 | 4:46 | 7:13 | 10:24 | 2:40 |
| **23. Trinity Sunday - June 10, 2001** | | | | **L/Day 15h 33m - Twi. 2h 32m** | | | **L/Day 14h 28m - Twi. 1h 47m** | | | |
| 10 | Su | Corvus sets 12:02 a.m./11:58 p.m. | ♑ | 4:13 | 7:46 | 11:28 | 4:46 | 7:14 | 11:03 | 3:29 |
| 11 | Mo | Ophiuchus mer. 12:15 a.m.; ☽ apo. 3:00 p.m. | ♒ | 4:13 | 7:47 | 11:57 | 4:46 | 7:14 | 11:37 | 4:16 |
| 12 | Tu | Andromeda Galaxy ri. 10:00 p.m. | ♒ | 4:13 | 7:47 | morn | 4:46 | 7:14 | morn | 5:01 |
| 13 | We | Job's Coffin mer. 3:10 a.m. ♂☍ | ♓ | 4:13 | 7:48 | 12:22 | 4:46 | 7:15 | 12:08 | 5:44 |
| 14 | Th | Flag Day; ♀ ri. 2:14 a.m. ♃☌☉ | ♓ | 4:13 | 7:48 | 12:46 | 4:46 | 7:15 | 12:37 | 6:26 |
| 15 | Fr | Eltanin mer. 12:21 a.m. | ♓ | 4:13 | 7:49 | 1:08 | 4:46 | 7:16 | 1:05 | 7:08 |
| 16 | Sa | Spica mer. 7:43 p.m. | ♈ | 4:13 | 7:49 | 1:30 | 4:46 | 7:16 | 1:34 | 7:51 |
| **24. Corpus Christi Sunday - June 17, 2001** | | | | **L/Day 15h 36m - Twi. 2h 33m** | | | **L/Day 14h 30m - Twi. 1h 48m** | | | |
| 17 | Su | Father's Day; Denebola sets 12:59 a.m. | ♈ | 4:13 | 7:49 | 1:54 | 4:46 | 7:16 | 2:04 | 8:37 |
| 18 | Mo | Fomalhaut ri. 1:08 a.m. | ♉ | 4:13 | 7:50 | 2:21 | 4:46 | 7:17 | 2:37 | 9:25 |
| 19 | Tu | Summer Triangle mer. 1:40 a.m. | ♉ | 4:13 | 7:50 | 2:52 | 4:46 | 7:17 | 3:14 | 10:17 |
| 20 | We | Algenib ri. 11:29 p.m. | ♊ | 4:13 | 7:50 | 3:30 | 4:46 | 7:17 | 3:58 | 11:14 |
| 21 | Th | Summer Solstice 2:38 a.m. EST ☊ | ♊ | 4:13 | 7:50 | sets | 4:47 | 7:17 | sets | 12:14p |
| 22 | Fr | Shaula mer. 11:27 p.m. ◠ | ♋ | 4:14 | 7:51 | 9:16 | 4:47 | 7:18 | 8:44 | 1:17 |
| 23 | Sa | Dschubba sets 2:35 a.m.; ☽ per. 12:00 p.m. | ♋ | 4:14 | 7:51 | 10:06 | 4:47 | 7:18 | 9:38 | 2:19 |
| **25. Third Sunday after Pentecost - June 24, 2001** | | | | **L/Day 15h 37m - Twi. 2h 32m** | | | **L/Day 14h 31m - Twi. 1h 47m** | | | |
| 24 | Su | St. John the Baptist; Nunki mer. 12:44 a.m. | ♌ | 4:14 | 7:51 | 10:46 | 4:47 | 7:18 | 10:25 | 3:19 |
| 25 | Mo | Vega mer. 12:22 a.m. | ♌ | 4:15 | 7:51 | 11:22 | 4:48 | 7:18 | 11:06 | 4:15 |
| 26 | Tu | Altair mer. 1:32 a.m.; ♄ ri. 2:57 a.m. | ♍ | 4:15 | 7:51 | 11:51 | 4:48 | 7:18 | 11:42 | 5:08 |
| 27 | We | Deneb mer. 2:19 a.m. | ♍ | 4:15 | 7:51 | morn | 4:48 | 7:18 | morn | 5:58 |
| 28 | Th | Sagittarius mer. 12:29 a.m. | ♎ | 4:16 | 7:51 | 12:17 | 4:49 | 7:18 | 12:15 | 6:46 |
| 29 | Fr | Algol ri. 11:27 p.m. | ♎ | 4:16 | 7:51 | 12:42 | 4:49 | 7:18 | 12:47 | 7:34 |
| 30 | Sa | Spica sets 12:15 a.m. | ♏ | 4:17 | 7:51 | 1:08 | 4:49 | 7:18 | 1:19 | 8:22 |

BIRTHSTONE: Pearl, Moonstone or Alexandrite, symbols of health and long life
FLOWER: Rose or Honeysuckle

**WEATHER FOLKLORE & LEGEND**

***Gray evening sky, not one day dry.***

ZONE

## ❶ *Northeastern States*

**1st-3rd.** Clearing, then pleasant but rather windy. **4th-7th.** Fair skies. **8th-11th.** Squalls spread east to Mid-Atlantic States, then fair. Stormy for most of New England, then clearing. **12th-15th.** Showers, then clearing. **16th-19th.** Pleasant conditions. **20th-23rd.** Heavy rain for Pennsylvania, New York area up to Maine, then fair. Hurricane threat for the Atlantic Coast. **24th-27th.** Fair, then thunderstorms through New England. Scattered thunderstorms for Maryland, Virginia. **28th-30th.** Fair and cool with northerly winds.

## ❷ *Great Lakes and Midwest*

**1st-3rd.** Mostly fair. **4th-7th.** Hot, then thunderstorms for the Ohio River Valley. **8th-11th.** Squalls for Kentucky, then clearing. Fair skies elsewhere. **12th-15th.** Showers sweep into Great Lakes section from the West, then fair. **16th-19th.** Fair skies, then dangerous thunderstorms. **20th-23rd.** Thunderstorms shift east out of region, then clearing skies. **24th-27th.** Fair, then thunderstorms, chiefly over Great Lakes. **28th-30th.** Fair and dry.

## ❸ *Southeastern States*

**1st-3rd.** Mixed sun and clouds. **4th-7th.** Potential tornado weather for parts of Tennessee, Mississippi, Alabama and all of Georgia. Thunderstorms along the Gulf Coast. **8th-11th.** Squalls Tennessee eastward through the Carolinas, then fair. **12th-15th.** A band of heavy thunderstorms cross the Southeast, then slowly clearing. **16th-19th.** Hot and sultry. **20th-23rd.** Thunderstorms for the Tennessee River Valley; squalls for the Gulf States. Hurricane threat for the Atlantic Coast. **24th-27th.** Scattered thunderstorms. **28th-30th.** Fair skies.

## ❹ *North Central States*

**1st-3rd.** Mostly fair and warm. **4th-7th.** Squally from Colorado east through Plains. **8th-11th.** Fair skies and warm. **12th-15th.** Showers sweep into Nebraska, Dakotas area and points east. **16th-19th.** Fair skies followed by dangerous thunderstorms over the Rockies and Plains States. **20th-23rd.** Showers, thunderstorms end, then clearing skies. **24th-27th.** Fair skies initially, then becoming unsettled, with showers developing over the Plains. **28th-30th.** Hot weather over the Rockies and Plains.

## ❺ *South Central States*

**1st-3rd.** Mostly fair and warm. **4th-7th.** Squally conditions; potential tornado weather for Arkansas. Thunderstorms along the Texas and Louisiana Gulf Coasts. **8th-11th.** Sunshine, dry and warm. **12th-15th.** Threatening skies over the Southern Plains. **16th-19th.** Squalls race east to Texas. **20th-23rd.** Thunderstorms for Arkansas. Squalls along Texas and Louisiana Gulf Coasts. **24th-27th.** Fair skies initially, then becoming unsettled; dust storms New Mexico. Scattered thunderstorms for Texas and points east. **28th-30th.** Hot conditions prevail.

## ❻ *Northwestern States*

**1st-3rd.** Fair skies. **4th-7th.** Gales (39+ m.p.h.) along the coast. **8th-11th.** Fair and warm. **12th-15th.** Wet weather. **16th-19th.** Clouds develop, then showers. **20th-23rd.** Clearing and drier. **24th-27th.** Wet in Washington and Oregon. **28th-30th.** Very warm-to-hot and dry.

## ❼ *Southwestern States*

**1st-3rd.** Sunshine and quite warm. **4th-7th.** Gusty winds near and along the coast. Squalls for Utah and points east. **8th-11th.** Fair, warm. **12th-15th.** Wet, showery. **16th-19th.** Squalls race east from South Plateau to Texas. **20th-23rd.** Skies clear, sunshine. **24th-27th.** Fair initially, then unsettled. Dust storms for Arizona. **28th-30th.** Dry and hot.

---

### MEMORABLE WEATHER EVENTS

☛ **JUNE 14th, 1903 - The Heppner (OR) Disaster**—Caused by a cloudburst in the hills that sent a flood down Willow Creek in northern Oregon; one-third of the town was swept away; 236 killed; $100 million damage.

☛ **JUNE 22nd, 1972 - Hurricane Agnes**—The most costly weather disaster in the United States to that date: dropped 12" of rain across Pennsylvania and New York.

☛ **Late June through Early August 1993-Great Midwest Floods**—Continual bouts of heavy rain lead to record flooding: all of Iowa and parts of eight other states designated disaster areas; 8 million acres flooded, 12 million acres were too wet to grow crops; 50 dead, 70,000 homeless.

7th Month **JULY 2001** 31 Days

♋ CANCER
June 21 to July 22

♌ LEO
July 22 to August 22

THE MOWER WALKS WITH SCYTHE IN HAND, TO YONDER FIELD AWAY;
THE GRASS HE PROSTRATES OVER THE LAND; HOW SWEET THE NEW MADE HAY.

**MOON'S PHASES**
EASTERN STANDARD TIME

| | | |
|---|---|---|
| Full Moon | 5th | 10:03 a.m. |
| Last Quarter | 13th | 1:45 p.m. |
| New Moon | 20th | 2:44 p.m. |
| First Quarter | 27th | 5:08 a.m. |

Subtract hour(s) for other time zones
–1h for C.S.T. –2h for M.S.T. –3h for P.S.T.

**SUN ON MERIDIAN CIVIL TIME**

| D. | H. | M. | S. |
|---|---|---|---|
| 1st | 12 | 03 | 49 |
| 8th | 12 | 05 | 01 |
| 15th | 12 | 05 | 55 |
| 22nd | 12 | 06 | 25 |
| 29th | 12 | 06 | 26 |

Calendar for NORTHERN STATES *45°N. Lat. 75°W. Long.* — Calendar for SOUTHERN STATES *35°N. Lat. 75°W. Long.*

| DATE | DAY | ASTRONOMY, CHURCH DAYS, ETC. | MOON'S PLACE | North Sun RISES | North Sun SETS | North Moon SETS | South Sun RISES | South Sun SETS | South Moon SETS | MOON'S SOUTHING OR MERIDIAN PASSAGE EVE |
|---|---|---|---|---|---|---|---|---|---|---|
| **26. Fourth Sunday after Pentecost - July 1, 2001** | | | | L/Day 15h 34m - Twi. 2h 28m | | | L/Day 14h 28m - Twi. 1h 46m | | | |
| 1 | Su | Algol ri. 11:19 p.m. | ♏ | 4:17 | 7:51 | 1:35 | 4:50 | 7:18 | 1:53 | 9:10p |
| 2 | Mo | Algenib ri. 10:42 p.m. | ♏ | 4:18 | 7:50 | 2:06 | 4:50 | 7:18 | 2:29 | 10:00 |
| 3 | Tu | "Dog Days" begin; Altair mer. 1:05 a.m. | ♐ | 4:19 | 7:50 | 2:41 | 4:51 | 7:18 | 3:09 | 10:51 |
| 4 | We | **Independence Day;** ⊕ at aphelion ☋ | ♐ | 4:19 | 7:50 | rises | 4:51 | 7:18 | rises | 11:43 |
| 5 | Th | Rasalhague mer. 10:37 p.m. ◡ | ♑ | 4:20 | 7:50 | 8:08 | 4:52 | 7:18 | 7:35 | morn |
| 6 | Fr | Antares sets 1:56 a.m.; ♃ ri. 3:30 a.m. | ♑ | 4:21 | 7:49 | 8:48 | 4:52 | 7:18 | 8:08 | 12:34 |
| 7 | Sa | Libra sets 1:11 a.m.; Asteroid Ceres ☍ | ♑ | 4:21 | 7:49 | 9:28 | 4:53 | 7:17 | 9:01 | 1:24 |
| **27. Fifth Sunday after Pentecost - July 8, 2001** | | | | L/Day 15h 26m - Twi. 2h 23m | | | L/Day 14h 24m - Twi. 1h 44m | | | |
| 8 | Su | Fast of Tammuz; ♂ sets 2:09 a.m. | ♒ | 4:22 | 7:48 | 9:59 | 4:53 | 7:17 | 9:37 | 2:11 |
| 9 | Mo | ☽ apo. 6:00 a.m. ☿ gr. W. el. | ♒ | 4:23 | 7:48 | 10:26 | 4:54 | 7:17 | 10:09 | 2:57 |
| 10 | Tu | Albireo mer. 12:17 a.m. | ♓ | 4:24 | 7:47 | 10:49 | 4:55 | 7:17 | 10:38 | 3:40 |
| 11 | We | Spica sets 11:29 p.m. | ♓ | 4:24 | 7:47 | 11:12 | 4:55 | 7:16 | 11:06 | 4:22 |
| 12 | Th | Capricornus mer. 1:38 a.m. | ♓ | 4:25 | 7:46 | 11:33 | 4:56 | 7:16 | 11:34 | 5:04 |
| 13 | Fr | Betelgeuse ri. 4:05 a.m. ☿♃ cl. 3:54 a.m. | ♈ | 4:26 | 7:46 | 11:56 | 4:56 | 7:15 | morn | 5:46 |
| 14 | Sa | ♀ ri. 1:54 a.m.; ☿ ri. 3:21 a.m. | ♈ | 4:27 | 7:45 | morn | 4:57 | 7:15 | 12:03 | 6:29 |
| **28. Sixth Sunday after Pentecost - July 15, 2001** | | | | L/Day 15h 16m - Twi. 2h 17m | | | L/Day 14h 17m - Twi. 1h 42m | | | |
| 15 | Su | St. Swithin's Day ♀♄ very cl. 3:10 a.m. | ♉ | 4:28 | 7:44 | 12:20 | 4:58 | 7:15 | 12:33 | 7:14 |
| 16 | Mo | Draco's head mer. 10:08 p.m. | ♉ | 4:29 | 7:44 | 12:48 | 4:58 | 7:14 | 1:08 | 8:04 |
| 17 | Tu | ☽ Aldebaran cl. 4:38 a.m. | ♊ | 4:30 | 7:43 | 1:22 | 4:59 | 7:14 | 1:47 | 8:57 |
| 18 | We | Seven Sisters ri. 12:38 a.m. | ♊ | 4:31 | 7:42 | 2:04 | 5:00 | 7:13 | 2:34 | 9:55 |
| 19 | Th | Sagitta mer. 12:09 a.m. ♂ sta. ⌒☊ | ♋ | 4:32 | 7:41 | 2:57 | 5:00 | 7:13 | 3:30 | 10:57 |
| 20 | Fr | Zubeneschamali sets 12:55 a.m. | ♋ | 4:33 | 7:40 | sets | 5:01 | 7:12 | sets | 12:00p |
| 21 | Sa | Dschubba sets 12:45 a.m.; ☽ per. 4:00 a.m. | ♌ | 4:34 | 7:39 | 8:42 | 5:02 | 7:11 | 8:16 | 1:03 |
| **29. Seventh Sunday after Pentecost - July 22, 2001** | | | | L/Day 15h 03m - Twi. 2h 11m | | | L/Day 14h 09m - Twi. 1h 39m | | | |
| 22 | Su | Milk Maid's Dipper mer. 10:50 p.m. | ♌ | 4:35 | 7:38 | 9:20 | 5:02 | 7:11 | 9:01 | 2:03 |
| 23 | Mo | Great Square of Pegasus mer. 2:58 a.m. | ♍ | 4:36 | 7:37 | 9:52 | 5:03 | 7:10 | 9:40 | 2:59 |
| 24 | Tu | Sabik sets 2:09 a.m. | ♍ | 4:37 | 7:36 | 10:20 | 5:04 | 7:10 | 10:15 | 3:52 |
| 25 | We | Shaula sets 12:48 a.m. | ♎ | 4:38 | 7:35 | 10:46 | 5:05 | 7:09 | 10:49 | 4:42 |
| 26 | Th | Altair mer. 11:30 p.m.; Rigel ri. 3:30 a.m. | ♎ | 4:39 | 7:34 | 11:12 | 5:05 | 7:08 | 11:21 | 5:31 |
| 27 | Fr | Job's Coffin mer. 12:17 a.m. | ♎ | 4:40 | 7:33 | 11:39 | 5:06 | 7:07 | 11:55 | 6:19 |
| 28 | Sa | Cepheus mer. 12:56 a.m.; ♄ ri. 1:04 a.m. | ♏ | 4:41 | 7:32 | morn | 5:07 | 7:07 | morn | 7:08 |
| **30. Eighth Sunday after Pentecost - July 29, 2001** | | | | L/Day 14h 49m - Twi. 2h 05m | | | L/Day 13h 59m - Twi. 1h 37m | | | |
| 29 | Su | Fast of Av; Hercules sets 3:38 a.m. ♆☍ | ♏ | 4:42 | 7:31 | 12:09 | 5:07 | 7:06 | 12:30 | 7:58 |
| 30 | Mo | Deneb mer. 12:09 a.m. | ♐ | 4:43 | 7:30 | 12:42 | 5:08 | 7:05 | 1:09 | 8:48 |
| 31 | Tu | Vega mer. 9:57 p.m. | ♐ | 4:45 | 7:28 | 1:21 | 5:09 | 7:04 | 1:52 | 9:39 |

BIRTHSTONE: Ruby, symbol of contentment FLOWER: Larkspur or Water Lily

**WEATHER FOLKLORE & LEGEND**

***St. Swithin's Day if ye do rain, for forty days it will remain.***

# WEATHER FORECAST
## ∽ JULY 2001 ∽

ZONE

### ❶ Northeastern States
**1st-3rd.** Hot and sultry. **4th-7th.** Stormy through Mid-Atlantic States and points northward, then fair. **8th-11th.** Hot weather, then scattered showers and thunderstorms. **12th-15th.** Hot and dry. **16th-19th.** Thunderstorms, then clearing. **20th-23rd.** Fair and hot. **24th-27th.** Some showers New York, Massachusetts to Maine, then fair, pleasant. **28th-31st.** Fair, pleasant weather.

### ❷ Great Lakes and Midwest
**1st-3rd.** Thunderstorms. **4th-7th.** Stormy across Ohio River Valley for the holiday, then fair. **8th-11th.** Hot and dry initially, but giving way to showers and thunderstorms. **12th-15th.** Fair and hot. **16th-19th.** Thunderstorms over Ohio River Valley, then skies clear. **20th-23rd.** Fair at first, then scattered thunderstorms for the Great Lakes area. **24th-27th.** Clearing skies; drier. **28th-31st.** Stormy weather develops, especially Ohio, Indiana area.

### ❸ Southeastern States
**1st-3rd.** Hot and sticky. **4th-7th.** Thunderstorms bubble up along the Gulf Coast northward to the Carolinas, then fair. **8th-11th.** Rain for the Gulf Coast and across the rest of the Southeast. **12th-15th.** Hot and dry weather. **16th-19th.** Hurricane threat to the Gulf Coast. **20th-23rd.** Widespread hot weather. **24th-27th.** Thunderstorms along the Gulf Coast. **28th-31st.** Another hurricane threat for the Gulf Coast.

### ❹ North Central States
**1st-3rd.** Thunderstorms for Plains States. Possible tornado weather much of Kansas, eastern Nebraska, Missouri and Iowa. **4th-7th.** A hot and dry holiday. **8th-11th.** Becoming unsettled in Rockies. Scattered thunderstorms elsewhere. **12th-15th.** Hot, then turning stormy with some heavy rain for the Rocky Mountain States to Dakotas, Nebraska section. **16th-19th.** Fair skies. **20th-23rd.** Unsettled conditions with scattered showers. Hot weather for Missouri and parts of Kansas. **24th-27th.** Mainly fair and dry. **28th-31st.** Squally for the Rockies.

### ❺ South Central States
**1st-3rd.** Thunderstorms for Plains States. Possible tornado weather for Texas, Oklahoma and western Arkansas. **4th-7th.** Hot and dry for Independence Day holiday. **8th-11th.** Becoming unsettled in Rockies. Wet in Texas, scattered thunderstorms elsewhere. **12th-15th.** Hot, then turning very unsettled; rain Texas, Louisiana Gulf Coasts. **16th-19th.** Hurricane threat for Texas, Louisiana Gulf Coasts. Elsewhere, fair weather returns. **20th-23rd.** Unsettled conditions with scattered showers. Hot temperatures. **24th-27th.** Thunderstorms for the Texas and Louisiana Gulf Coasts. Elsewhere, mainly fair and dry. **28th-31st.** Squally for the Rockies. Gusty thunderstorms for New Mexico, Texas and parts of Oklahoma. Another hurricane threat for Texas and Louisiana Gulf Coasts.

### ❻ Northwestern States
**1st-3rd.** Stormy conditions. **4th-7th.** Warm-to-hot and dry. **8th-11th.** Scattered showers. **12th-15th.** Warm-to-hot, with a few more possible showers. **16th-19th.** Fair skies. **20th-23rd.** Unsettled with scattered showers. **24th-27th.** Mainly dry and fair. **28th-31st.** Gusty winds along the coast.

### ❼ Southwestern States
**1st-3rd.** Stormy, especially over Utah. **4th-7th.** Hot weather. **8th-11th.** Hot, with widely scattered showers and thunderstorms. **12th-15th.** Continued hot, risk of a few more showers. **16th-19th.** Fair weather. **20th-23rd.** Scattered showers. **24th-27th.** Mainly fair. **28th-31st.** Gusty breezes along the Pacific Coast. Gusty thunderstorms for Nevada, Utah and parts of Arizona.

---

### MEMORABLE WEATHER EVENTS

☛ **JULY 13th, 1977- New York City, NY, Blackout**—Lightning strike on power line near Indian Point, NY, triggered massive 25-hour power blackout.

☛ **JULY 12th–17th, 1995 - Deadly Heat Wave for Midwest and Northeast**—800 people died, 536 in Chicago alone, where an all-time record high of 106°F was attained on July 13th.

8th Month **AUGUST 2001** 31 Days

♌ LEO
July 22 to August 22

♍ VIRGO
August 22 to September 22

THE GATHERING CLOUDS BESPREAD THE SKY, AND GENTLE SHOWERS DESCEND;
THE RIPENING FRUITS WE JUST DESCRY, AS SUMMER IS AT END.

**MOON'S PHASES**
EASTERN STANDARD TIME

| | | |
|---|---|---|
| Full Moon | 4th | 12:55 a.m. |
| Last Quarter | 12th | 2:53 a.m. |
| New Moon | 18th | 9:55 p.m. |
| First Quarter | 25th | 2:54 p.m. |

Subtract hour(s) for other time zones
–1h for C.S.T. –2h for M.S.T. –3h for P.S.T.

**SUN ON MERIDIAN**
**CIVIL TIME**

| D. | H. | M. | S. |
|---|---|---|---|
| 1st | 12 | 06 | 17 |
| 8th | 12 | 05 | 35 |
| 15th | 12 | 04 | 26 |
| 22nd | 12 | 02 | 51 |
| 29th | 12 | 00 | 53 |

| DATE | DAY | ASTRONOMY, CHURCH DAYS, ETC. | MOON'S PLACE | Calendar for NORTHERN STATES 45°N. Lat. 75°W. Long. Sun RISES | Sun SETS | Moon SETS | Calendar for SOUTHERN STATES 35°N. Lat. 75°W. Long. Sun RISES | Sun SETS | Moon SETS | MOON'S SOUTHING OR MERIDIAN PASSAGE EVE |
|---|---|---|---|---|---|---|---|---|---|---|
| 1 | We | Vega mer. 9:53 p.m. ◡☋ | ♐ | 4:46 | 7:27 | 2:06 | 5:10 | 7:03 | 2:39 | 10:30p |
| 2 | Th | Altair mer. 11:02 p.m. | ♑ | 4:47 | 7:26 | rises | 5:10 | 7:02 | rises | 11:19 |
| 3 | Fr | Deneb mer. 11:49 p.m. | ♑ | 4:48 | 7:25 | 7:28 | 5:11 | 7:01 | 7:00 | morn |
| 4 | Sa | Antares mer. 7:37 p.m. | ♒ | 4:49 | 7:23 | 8:01 | 5:12 | 7:01 | 7:37 | 12:08 |
| **31. Ninth Sunday after Pentecost - August 5, 2001** | | | | **L/Day 14h 32m - Twi. 1h 59m** | | | **L/Day 13h 47m - Twi. 1h 35m** | | | |
| 5 | Su | ☽ apo. 4:00 p.m. ☿ sup. ☌ | ♒ | 4:50 | 7:22 | 8:29 | 5:13 | 7:00 | 8:10 | 12:54 |
| 6 | Mo | Job's Coffin mer. 11:38 p.m. | ♒ | 4:51 | 7:21 | 8:53 | 5:13 | 6:59 | 8:41 | 1:38 |
| 7 | Tu | Aquarius mer. 1:20 a.m. | ♓ | 4:53 | 7:19 | 9:16 | 5:14 | 6:58 | 9:09 | 2:20 |
| 8 | We | Lyra mer. 9:38 p.m.; Aries ri. 10:05 p.m. | ♓ | 4:54 | 7:18 | 9:37 | 5:15 | 6:57 | 9:36 | 3:02 |
| 9 | Th | ♂ sets 12:11 a.m.; Nunki sets 2:08 a.m. | ♈ | 4:55 | 7:16 | 9:59 | 5:16 | 6:56 | 10:04 | 3:43 |
| 10 | Fr | Deneb Kaitos ri. 10:24 p.m. | ♈ | 4:56 | 7:15 | 10:22 | 5:16 | 6:54 | 10:33 | 4:25 |
| 11 | Sa | "Dog Days" end; Markab mer. 1:45 a.m. | ♉ | 4:57 | 7:13 | 10:48 | 5:17 | 6:53 | 11:05 | 5:08 |
| **32. Tenth Sunday after Pentecost - August 12, 2001** | | | | **L/Day 14h 13m - Twi. 1h 54m** | | | **L/Day 13h 34m - Twi. 1h 32m** | | | |
| 12 | Su | Kaus Australis sets 12:44 a.m. | ♉ | 4:59 | 7:12 | 11:18 | 5:18 | 6:52 | 11:41 | 5:55 |
| 13 | Mo | Caph mer. 2:43 a.m. ☿ Regulus cl. 7:19 p.m. | ♉ | 5:00 | 7:10 | 11:55 | 5:19 | 6:51 | morn | 6:45 |
| 14 | Tu | V.J. Day ☽♄ cl. 12:05 p.m. | ♊ | 5:01 | 7:09 | morn | 5:20 | 6:50 | 12:23 | 7:39 |
| 15 | We | Assumption B.V.M.; ♀ ri. 2:17 a.m. ♌ | ♊ | 5:02 | 7:07 | 12:41 | 5:20 | 6:49 | 1:13 | 8:38 |
| 16 | Th | Menkar ri. 11:09 p.m.; Taurus ri. 11:43 p.m. ⌒ | ♋ | 5:03 | 7:06 | 1:38 | 5:21 | 6:48 | 2:12 | 9:40 |
| 17 | Fr | Piscis Austrinus mer. 1:14 a.m. | ♋ | 5:04 | 7:04 | 2:47 | 5:22 | 6:47 | 3:19 | 10:43 |
| 18 | Sa | Messier 31 mer. 2:55 a.m. | ♌ | 5:06 | 7:02 | sets | 5:23 | 6:45 | sets | 11:44 |
| **33. Eleventh Sunday after Pentecost - August 19, 2001** | | | | **L/Day 13h 54m - Twi. 1h 50m** | | | **L/Day 13h 21m - Twi. 1h 30m** | | | |
| 19 | Su | ☽ per. 1:00 a.m. ☽☿ cl. 7:26 p.m. | ♌ | 5:07 | 7:01 | 7:48 | 5:23 | 6:44 | 7:33 | 12:43p |
| 20 | Mo | Sagitta mer. 10:00 p.m. | ♍ | 5:08 | 6:59 | 8:18 | 5:24 | 6:43 | 8:11 | 1:39 |
| 21 | Tu | Scheat mer. 1:04 a.m.; ♃ ri. 1:11 a.m. | ♍ | 5:09 | 6:57 | 8:46 | 5:25 | 6:42 | 8:46 | 2:32 |
| 22 | We | Capella ri. 9:15 p.m. | ♎ | 5:10 | 6:56 | 9:13 | 5:26 | 6:40 | 9:20 | 3:23 |
| 23 | Th | Sirius ri. 3:32 a.m. ♇ sta. | ♎ | 5:12 | 6:54 | 9:40 | 5:26 | 6:39 | 9:54 | 4:13 |
| 24 | Fr | Pleiades ri. 10:00 p.m. | ♏ | 5:13 | 6:52 | 10:09 | 5:27 | 6:38 | 10:30 | 5:03 |
| 25 | Sa | Ophiuchus sets 2:06 a.m. | ♏ | 5:14 | 6:50 | 10:42 | 5:28 | 6:37 | 11:08 | 5:54 |
| **34. Twelfth Sunday after Pentecost - August 26, 2001** | | | | **L/Day 13h 34m - Twi. 1h 44m** | | | **L/Day 13h 06m - Twi. 1h 28m** | | | |
| 26 | Su | Capricornus mer. 10:37 p.m. | ♏ | 5:15 | 6:49 | 11:20 | 5:29 | 6:35 | 11:50 | 6:44 |
| 27 | Mo | Pollux ri. 1:32 a.m. | ♐ | 5:16 | 6:47 | morn | 5:29 | 6:34 | morn | 7:35 |
| 28 | Tu | Betelgeuse ri. 1:04 a.m. ◡☋ | ♐ | 5:18 | 6:45 | 12:03 | 5:30 | 6:33 | 12:36 | 8:26 |
| 29 | We | Albireo mer. 9:03 p.m. | ♑ | 5:19 | 6:43 | 12:52 | 5:31 | 6:31 | 1:26 | 9:16 |
| 30 | Th | Alderamin mer. 10:40 p.m. | ♑ | 5:20 | 6:42 | 1:47 | 5:31 | 6:30 | 2:19 | 10:05 |
| 31 | Fr | Cancer ri. 2:46 a.m. | ♑ | 5:21 | 6:40 | 2:45 | 5:32 | 6:29 | 3:14 | 10:51 |

BIRTHSTONE: Sardonyx or Peridot, symbols of happiness FLOWER: Poppy or Gladiolus

**WEATHER FOLKLORE & LEGEND**

***When the stars begin to huddle, the earth will soon become a puddle.***

# WEATHER FORECAST
## ∽ AUGUST 2001 ∽

**ZONE**

### ❶ *Northeastern States*

**1st-3rd.** Thunderstorms through Pennsylvania, New York area to Maine, then fair. Thunderstorms also for the Mid-Atlantic States, then clearing. **4th-7th.** Fair skies, then showery. **8th-11th.** Fair weather. **12th-15th.** Stormy weather spreads across entire region. **16th-19th.** Mostly fair skies. **20th-23rd.** Becoming unsettled, then pleasant conditions. **24th-27th.** Pleasant weather continues; some increase in cloud cover though. **28th-31st.** Thunderstorms from Mid-Atlantic States through New England, then fair.

### ❷ *Great Lakes and Midwest*

**1st-3rd.** Fair and hot. **4th-7th.** Fair weather gives way to some showers. **8th-11th.** Fair weather returns. **12th-15th.** Stormy for Michigan, Illinois section and points east. **16th-19th.** Hot and dry, then showers. **20th-23rd.** Becoming unsettled Michigan, Ohio area and points east, then fair and tranquil. **24th-27th.** Hot weather, then stormy for the Great Lakes area. **28th-31st.** Mainly fair and dry.

### ❸ *Southeastern States*

**1st-3rd.** Thunderstorms for the Carolinas, then clearing. Mainly dry down to the Gulf Coast. Warm-to-hot temperatures. **4th-7th.** Sultry, then scattered showers. **8th-11th.** Fair skies. **12th-15th.** Thunderstorms prevail across the Gulf Coast and most of the region. **16th-19th.** Mostly fair skies. **20th-23rd.** Scattered thunderstorms. **24th-27th.** Heavy rain across Mississippi, Alabama, and Georgia. Scattered showers elsewhere. **28th-31st.** Heavy thunderstorms, then clearing.

### ❹ *North Central States*

**1st-3rd.** Fair and hot. **4th-7th.** Hot and dry, then turning unsettled. **8th-11th.** Severe squalls through the Rockies and big thunderstorms over the Plains States. **12th-15th.** Pleasant conditions. **16th-19th.** Initially hot and dry, then showers. **20th-23rd.** Hot weather. **24th-27th.** Stormy for Rocky Mountain States into Dakotas, Nebraska area. **28th-31st.** Mostly fair skies.

### ❺ *South Central States*

**1st-3rd.** Fair skies and hot temperatures. **4th-7th.** Hot and dry, then conditions turn unsettled. **8th-11th.** Stay alert for severe squalls and big thunderstorms. **12th-15th.** Tranquil conditions. **16th-19th.** Initially hot and dry, then showers. Dust storms for New Mexico. **20th-23rd.** Hot weather prevails. **24th-27th.** Very unsettled weather; heavy rain from Texas and all points east. **28th-31st.** Mainly fair skies.

### ❻ *Northwestern States*

**1st-3rd.** Fair skies. Warm-to-hot weather. **4th-7th.** Continued warm-to-hot and dry, then turning unsettled. **8th-11th.** Unsettled conditions continue. **12th-15th.** Pleasant and dry weather. **16th-19th.** Warm-to-hot and dry. **20th-23rd.** Little overall change. **24th-27th.** Stormy weather. **28th-31st.** Fair and dry.

### ❼ *Southwestern States*

**1st-3rd.** Mainly fair, dry and hot. **4th-7th.** Hot, dry weather initially, then turning unsettled. **8th-11th.** Clearing skies over California. Monsoonal showers over the South Plateau. **12th-15th.** Pleasant conditions. **16th-19th.** Hot conditions; dust storms for Arizona. **20th-23rd.** Hot and dry. **24th-27th.** Stormy, especially over the South Plateau. **28th-31st.** Mainly fair skies.

---

### MEMORABLE WEATHER EVENTS

☛ **AUGUST 17th, 1969- Hurricane Camille**—Made landfall on Mississippi coast, "severest ever to strike populated area in the US"; winds of 200 miles per hour; ranked a 5 on the 1–5 Saffir-Simpson scale; tide 24 feet; caused 144 deaths and nearly $1.3 billion in damage; later floods in Virginia drowned 113 more people.

☛ **August 4th, 1980 - Streak of Extreme Heat Ended at Dallas/Fort Worth, Texas**—A string of 42 consecutive days with a maximum temperature of at least 100°F ended; summer mean temperature was 89°F. Temperature peaked at 113°F during the streak.

# 9th Month SEPTEMBER 2001 30 Days

♍ VIRGO
August 22 to September 22

♎ LIBRA
September 22 to October 23

**NOW AUTUMN'S GOLDEN STORES BEHOLD, WITH FRUIT EACH TREE IS CROWNED;**
**PEACHES IN SUITS OF RED OR GOLD, EACH TWIG BOWS TOWARD THE GROUND.**

**MOON'S PHASES**
EASTERN STANDARD TIME

| Phase | Date | Time |
|---|---|---|
| Full Moon | 2nd | 4:43 p.m. |
| Last Quarter | 10th | 1:59 p.m. |
| New Moon | 17th | 5:27 a.m. |
| First Quarter | 24th | 4:30 a.m. |

Subtract hour(s) for other time zones
–1h for C.S.T. –2h for M.S.T. –3h for P.S.T.

**SUN ON MERIDIAN CIVIL TIME**

| D. | H. | M. | S. |
|---|---|---|---|
| 1st | 11 | 59 | 57 |
| 8th | 11 | 57 | 38 |
| 15th | 11 | 55 | 10 |
| 22nd | 11 | 52 | 42 |
| 29th | 11 | 50 | 18 |

Calendar for NORTHERN STATES 45°N. Lat. 75°W. Long. — Calendar for SOUTHERN STATES 35°N. Lat. 75°W. Long.

| DATE | DAY | ASTRONOMY, CHURCH DAYS, ETC. | MOON'S PLACE | Northern Sun RISES | Northern Sun SETS | Northern Moon RISES | Southern Sun RISES | Southern Sun SETS | Southern Moon RISES | MOON'S SOUTHING OR MERIDIAN PASSAGE EVE |
|---|---|---|---|---|---|---|---|---|---|---|
| 1 | Sa | Cassiopeia mer. 2:42 a.m.; ☽ apo. 6:00 p.m. | ♒ | 5:22 | 6:38 | 6:33 | 5:33 | 6:27 | 6:12 | 11:36p |
| **35. Thirteenth Sunday after Pentecost - September 2, 2001** | | | | **L/Day 13h 12m - Twi. 1h 43m** | | | **L/Day 12h 52m - Twi. 1h 27m** | | | |
| 2 | Su | Gr. Globular Cluster in Hercules sets 2:31 a.m. | ♒ | 5:24 | 6:36 | 6:58 | 5:34 | 6:26 | 6:43 | morn |
| 3 | Mo | **Labor Day;** Regulus ri. 4:33 a.m. | ♓ | 5:25 | 6:34 | 7:21 | 5:34 | 6:25 | 7:12 | 12:19 |
| 4 | Tu | Antares sets 9:56 p.m. | ♓ | 5:26 | 6:32 | 7:43 | 5:35 | 6:23 | 7:40 | 1:01 |
| 5 | We | Lyra sets 4:33 a.m. | ♈ | 5:27 | 6:31 | 8:04 | 5:36 | 6:22 | 8:07 | 1:42 |
| 6 | Th | Cepheus mer. 10:13 p.m. ♄ at quadrature | ♈ | 5:28 | 6:29 | 8:26 | 5:37 | 6:20 | 8:35 | 2:24 |
| 7 | Fr | Piscis Austrinus mer. 11:47 p.m. | ♈ | 5:30 | 6:27 | 8:52 | 5:37 | 6:19 | 9:06 | 3:07 |
| 8 | Sa | Cetus mer. 3:08 a.m.; ♂ sets 11:09 p.m. | ♉ | 5:31 | 6:25 | 9:18 | 5:38 | 6:18 | 9:39 | 3:51 |
| **36. Fourteenth Sunday after Pentecost - September 9, 2001** | | | | **L/Day 12h 51m - Twi. 1h 41m** | | | **L/Day 12h 37m - Twi. 1h 26m** | | | |
| 9 | Su | Algol mer. 4:00 a.m. ☽ Aldebaran cl. 10:22 p.m. | ♉ | 5:32 | 6:23 | 9:51 | 5:39 | 6:16 | 10:18 | 4:39 |
| 10 | Mo | Delphinus mer. 9:26 p.m. | ♊ | 5:33 | 6:21 | 10:32 | 5:40 | 6:15 | 11:03 | 5:30 |
| 11 | Tu | Altair sets 3:01 a.m. ☊ | ♊ | 5:34 | 6:19 | 11:23 | 5:40 | 6:13 | 11:57 | 6:26 |
| 12 | We | Albireo mer. 8:02 p.m. ⌒ | ♋ | 5:35 | 6:17 | morn | 5:41 | 6:12 | morn | 7:24 |
| 13 | Th | Enif mer. 10:10 p.m. | ♋ | 5:37 | 6:16 | 12:25 | 5:42 | 6:10 | 12:58 | 8:25 |
| 14 | Fr | Milk Maid's Dipper sets 11:43 p.m. | ♌ | 5:38 | 6:14 | 1:36 | 5:42 | 6:09 | 2:06 | 9:25 |
| 15 | Sa | Sadalmelik mer. 10:25 p.m. ☽♀ cl. 3:15 a.m. | ♌ | 5:39 | 6:12 | 2:55 | 5:43 | 6:08 | 3:18 | 10:25 |
| **37. Fifteenth Sunday after Pentecost - September 16, 2001** | | | | **L/Day 12h 30m - Twi. 1h 39m** | | | **L/Day 12h 22m - Twi. 1h 25m** | | | |
| 16 | Su | Cancer ri. 1:43 a.m.; ☽ per. 11:00 a.m. | ♍ | 5:40 | 6:10 | 4:16 | 5:44 | 6:06 | 4:32 | 11:22 |
| 17 | Mo | Denebola ri. 5:09 a.m. | ♍ | 5:41 | 6:08 | sets | 5:45 | 6:05 | sets | 12:17p |
| 18 | Tu | Rosh Hashanah ☿ gr. E. el. | ♎ | 5:43 | 6:06 | 7:11 | 5:45 | 6:03 | 7:14 | 1:09 |
| 19 | We | Ember Day; Fomalhaut mer. 10:57 p.m. | ♎ | 5:44 | 6:04 | 7:38 | 5:46 | 6:02 | 7:49 | 2:01 |
| 20 | Th | Libra sets 8:12 p.m.; Pollux ri. 11:59 p.m. | ♏ | 5:45 | 6:02 | 8:07 | 5:47 | 6:00 | 8:25 | 2:53 |
| 21 | Fr | Ember Day; ♃ ri. 11:31 p.m. | ♏ | 5:46 | 6:00 | 8:39 | 5:48 | 5:59 | 9:03 | 3:45 |
| 22 | Sa | Ember Day; Betelgeuse ri. 11:22 p.m. | ♏ | 5:47 | 5:58 | 9:16 | 5:48 | 5:57 | 9:45 | 4:37 |
| **38. Sixteenth Sunday after Pentecost - September 23, 2001** | | | | **L/Day 12h 07m - Twi. 1h 38m** | | | **L/Day 12h 07m - Twi. 1h 24m** | | | |
| 23 | Su | Adhara ri. 2:36 a.m. | ♐ | 5:49 | 5:56 | 9:58 | 5:49 | 5:56 | 10:30 | 5:29 |
| 24 | Mo | Mirfak mer. 3:14 a.m. ☽♂ cl. 7:59 p.m. ◡☋ | ♐ | 5:50 | 5:55 | 10:46 | 5:50 | 5:55 | 11:20 | 6:21 |
| 25 | Tu | ☿ sets 6:32 p.m. | ♑ | 5:51 | 5:53 | 11:39 | 5:51 | 5:53 | morn | 7:12 |
| 26 | We | Aldebaran mer. 4:14 a.m. ♄ sta. | ♑ | 5:52 | 5:51 | morn | 5:51 | 5:52 | 12:12 | 8:01 |
| 27 | Th | Yom Kippur; Lyra sets 3:00 a.m. | ♑ | 5:53 | 5:49 | 12:37 | 5:52 | 5:50 | 1:07 | 8:49 |
| 28 | Fr | ♄ ri. 9:11 p.m. | ♒ | 5:55 | 5:47 | 1:38 | 5:53 | 5:49 | 2:03 | 9:34 |
| 29 | Sa | Hydra's Head ri. 1:48 a.m.; ☽ apo. 1:00 a.m. | ♒ | 5:56 | 5:45 | 2:39 | 5:54 | 5:47 | 2:59 | 10:17 |
| **39. Seventeenth Sunday after Pentecost - September 30, 2001** | | | | **L/Day 11h 46m - Twi. 1h 37m** | | | **L/Day 11h 52m - Twi. 1h 24m** | | | |
| 30 | Su | Fomalhaut mer. 10:18 p.m. | ♓ | 5:57 | 5:43 | 3:41 | 5:54 | 5:46 | 3:56 | 11:00 |

BIRTHSTONE: Sapphire, symbol of wisdom FLOWER: Aster or Morning Glory

**WEATHER FOLKLORE & LEGEND**

***When spiders weave their webs by noon, fine weather is coming soon.***

ZONE

## ❶ Northeastern States

**1st-3rd.** Fair, then scattered showers for Pennsylvania, New York area and most of the region. **4th-7th.** Pleasantly dry and fair. **8th-11th.** Squally weather, followed by clearing skies. **12th-15th.** Tranquil conditions. **16th-19th.** Showery weather, followed by clearing and cool weather. **20th-23rd.** Fair skies for New England. **24th-27th.** Stormy for Virginia, Maryland. Heavy squalls New York, Pennsylvania, then fair. **28th-30th.** Becoming unsettled Pennsylvania into the rest of Northeast.

## ❷ Great Lakes and Midwest

**1st-3rd.** Changeable skies. **4th-7th.** Fair and pleasant. **8th-11th.** Thundery, then clearing skies. **12th-15th.** Dry and fair. **16th-19th.** Scattered showers Great Lakes and points east, then skies clear and it turns cool. **20th-23rd.** Stormy weather spreads into Michigan, Ohio area. **24th-27th.** Clearing skies and turning unseasonably chilly. **28th-30th.** Showers for Great Lakes. Unsettled for Ohio.

## ❸ Southeastern States

**1st-3rd.** A few showers. **4th-7th.** Tranquil conditions. **8th-11th.** Stormy weather. **12th-15th.** Fair and dry. **16th-19th.** Squally conditions along Gulf Coast. Rainy skies Tennessee east to the Atlantic Coast. **20th-23rd.** Stormy for Gulf Coast east through Florida. Warm and dry for Georgia and points north. **24th-27th.** Stormy for Carolinas and points north. **28th-30th.** Showery.

## ❹ North Central States

**1st-3rd.** Showery and windy for the Rockies and across the Plains. **4th-7th.** Pleasant initially, then turning squally for Rocky Mountain States to Nebraska, Dakotas area. **8th-11th.** Mostly fair. **12th-15th.** Fair initially, then showers over the Plains. **16th-19th.** Cooler temperatures; a few showers. **20th-23rd.** Stormy weather spreads east over Rockies and Plains. **24th-27th.** Fair and unseasonably chilly. **28th-30th.** Some light rain, wet snow over the highest elevations of Montana, Wyoming.

## ❺ South Central States

**1st-3rd.** Threatening skies for New Mexico, Texas and Oklahoma. **4th-7th.** Pleasant initially, then turning thundery. **8th-11th.** Mostly fair weather, then stormy for Texas and points east. **12th-15th.** Fair initially, then showers fall over New Mexico. **16th-19th.** Squally conditions for Texas and points east along the Gulf Coast. Rainy for Arkansas. **20th-23rd.** More stormy weather spreads east over Texas and Gulf Coast. **24th-27th.** Fair and unseasonably chilly. **28th-30th.** Threatening skies for the Southern Rockies.

## ❻ Northwestern States

**1st-3rd.** Unsettled. **4th-7th.** Pleasant, then stormy. **8th-11th.** Mostly fair skies. **12th-15th.** Fair, then showery. **16th-19th.** Dry and cooler. **20th-23rd.** Turning stormy near and along the Pacific Coast and all points east. **24th-27th.** Fair and rather chilly. **28th-30th.** Some clouds and a few passing showers.

## ❼ Southwestern States

**1st-3rd.** Unsettled weather. **4th-7th.** Tranquil conditions, then turning stormy. **8th-11th.** Fair and dry. **12th-15th.** Showers for California and points east. **16th-19th.** Cool and dry. **20th-23rd.** Gusty winds for California and over South Plateau. **24th-27th.** Fair and quite chilly. **28th-30th.** Changeable skies, with a few showers possible.

### MEMORABLE WEATHER EVENTS

☞ **SEPTEMBER 8th, 1900-The Great Hurricane Wave at Galveston, Texas —** A severe hurricane tide inundated this island city with up to 15 feet of water; over 6,000 perished; 3,600 houses were destroyed; damage estimated at $30 million.

☞ **AUGUST 24th–25th, 1992 - Hurricane Andrew—**Among the worst of natural disasters ever to strike the U.S. The city of Homestead, FL, and the Homestead Air Force Base were virtually leveled by winds of 165 m.p.h. In Florida, the storm claimed 30 lives, destroyed or damaged 85,000 homes, and left 250,000 people homeless.

# 10th Month **OCTOBER 2001** 31 Days

♎ LIBRA
September 22 to October 23

♏ SCORPIO
October 23 to November 22

**AND NOW THE FROST IS SEEN IN MORN, OVERSPREADING FIELDS WITH WHITE;
THE FARMER GATHERS IN HIS CORN, WTH PLEASURE AND DELIGHT.**

**MOON'S PHASES**
EASTERN STANDARD TIME

| | | | |
|---|---|---|---|
| ○ | Full Moon | 2nd | 8:48 a.m. |
| ☾ | Last Quarter | 9th | 11:19 p.m. |
| ● | New Moon | 16th | 2:23 p.m. |
| ☽ | First Quarter | 23rd | 9:58 p.m. |

Subtract hour(s) for other time zones
–1h for C.S.T. –2h for M.S.T. –3h for P.S.T.

**SUN ON MERIDIAN CIVIL TIME**

| D. | H. | M. | S. |
|---|---|---|---|
| 1st | 11 | 49 | 39 |
| 8th | 11 | 47 | 32 |
| 15th | 11 | 45 | 47 |
| 22nd | 11 | 44 | 30 |
| 29th | 11 | 43 | 45 |

Calendar for NORTHERN STATES — *45°N. Lat. 75°W. Long.*
Calendar for SOUTHERN STATES — *35°N. Lat. 75°W. Long.*

| DATE | DAY | ASTRONOMY, CHURCH DAYS, ETC. | MOON'S PLACE | Northern: Sun RISES | Northern: Sun SETS | Northern: Moon RISES | Southern: Sun RISES | Southern: Sun SETS | Southern: Moon RISES | MOON'S SOUTHIING OR MERIDIAN PASSAGE EVE |
|---|---|---|---|---|---|---|---|---|---|---|
| 1 | Mo | Alpheratz mer. 11:23 p.m. | ♓ | 5:58 | 5:41 | rises | 5:55 | 5:45 | rises | 11:41p |
| 2 | Tu | Succot; Harvest Full Moon | ♓ | 6:00 | 5:39 | 6:09 | 5:56 | 5:43 | 6:10 | morn |
| 3 | We | Aldebaran mer. 3:46 a.m. | ♈ | 6:01 | 5:38 | 6:31 | 5:57 | 5:42 | 6:38 | 12:23 |
| 4 | Th | Alderamin mer. 8:23 p.m. | ♈ | 6:02 | 5:36 | 6:54 | 5:57 | 5:40 | 7:08 | 1:05 |
| 5 | Fr | Denebola ri. 4:00 a.m. | ♉ | 6:03 | 5:34 | 7:21 | 5:58 | 5:39 | 7:40 | 1:51 |
| 6 | Sa | Algenib mer. 11:09 p.m.; ☿ combust | ♉ | 6:05 | 5:32 | 7:52 | 5:59 | 5:38 | 8:17 | 2:37 |
| **40. Eighteenth Sunday after Pentecost - October 7, 2001** | | | | **L/Day 11h 24m - Twi. 1h 38m** | | | **L/Day 11h 36m - Twi. 1h 24m** | | | |
| 7 | Su | ♃ at quadrature; ☽ Aldebaran cl. 3:03 a.m. | ♊ | 6:06 | 5:30 | 8:30 | 6:00 | 5:36 | 9:00 | 3:27 |
| 8 | Mo | **Columbus Day;** ♂ sets 10:35 p.m. ☊ | ♊ | 6:07 | 5:28 | 9:16 | 6:01 | 5:35 | 9:49 | 4:20 |
| 9 | Tu | Mirach mer. 11:57 p.m. ☽♃ cl. 10:29 p.m. ⌒ | ♋ | 6:08 | 5:27 | 10:12 | 6:01 | 5:34 | 10:46 | 5:16 |
| 10 | We | Simchat Torah; Hyades mer. 2:52 a.m. | ♋ | 6:10 | 5:25 | 11:18 | 6:02 | 5:32 | 11:50 | 6:14 |
| 11 | Th | Scheat mer. 9:40 p.m. | ♌ | 6:11 | 5:23 | morn | 6:03 | 5:31 | morn | 7:13 |
| 12 | Fr | Aquarius mer. 8:57 p.m.; ♂ at perihelion | ♌ | 6:12 | 5:21 | 12:32 | 6:04 | 5:30 | 12:58 | 8:11 |
| 13 | Sa | Pisces mer. 11:15 p.m. ☽ Regulus cl. 2:01 a.m. | ♍ | 6:14 | 5:19 | 1:49 | 6:05 | 5:28 | 2:09 | 9:07 |
| **41. Nineteenth Sunday after Pentecost - October 14, 2001** | | | | **L/Day 11h 03m - Twi. 1h 38m** | | | **L/Day 11h 22m - Twi. 1h 25m** | | | |
| 14 | Su | ♂ at quadrature; ☽ per. 6:00 p.m. ☿ inf. ☌ | ♍ | 6:15 | 5:18 | 3:09 | 6:05 | 5:27 | 3:21 | 10:01 |
| 15 | Mo | Arcturus ri. 5:27 p.m.; ☽♀ cl. 4:21 a.m. | ♍ | 6:16 | 5:16 | 4:28 | 6:06 | 5:26 | 4:32 | 10:54 |
| 16 | Tu | Alpheratz mer. 10:29 p.m. ♀ ri. 4:24 a.m. | ♎ | 6:17 | 5:14 | sets | 6:07 | 5:24 | sets | 11:46 |
| 17 | We | Canis Minor ri. 11:31 p.m. ♆ sta. | ♎ | 6:19 | 5:12 | 6:03 | 6:08 | 5:23 | 6:18 | 12:38p |
| 18 | Th | Pollux ri. 10:04 p.m. | ♏ | 6:20 | 5:11 | 6:34 | 6:09 | 5:22 | 6:55 | 1:31 |
| 19 | Fr | Caph mer. 10:14 p.m. | ♏ | 6:21 | 5:09 | 7:09 | 6:10 | 5:21 | 7:36 | 2:24 |
| 20 | Sa | Capella mer. 3:20 a.m. | ♐ | 6:23 | 5:07 | 7:49 | 6:11 | 5:19 | 8:21 | 3:18 |
| **42. Twentieth Sunday after Pentecost - October 21, 2001** | | | | **L/Day 10h 42m - Twi. 1h 38m** | | | **L/Day 11h 07m - Twi. 1h 25m** | | | |
| 21 | Su | Perseus Double Cluster mer. 12:20 a.m. ☋ | ♐ | 6:24 | 5:06 | 8:36 | 6:11 | 5:18 | 9:10 | 4:12 |
| 22 | Mo | Beehive ri. 11:18 p.m.; ☿ ri. 5:04 a.m. ◡ | ♐ | 6:25 | 5:04 | 9:28 | 6:12 | 5:17 | 10:03 | 5:04 |
| 23 | Tu | Altair sets 12:14 a.m. | ♑ | 6:27 | 5:02 | 10:26 | 6:13 | 5:16 | 10:58 | 5:55 |
| 24 | We | Corvus ri. 5:01 a.m. | ♑ | 6:28 | 5:01 | 11:26 | 6:14 | 5:15 | 11:54 | 6:44 |
| 25 | Th | Pegasus sets 4:37 a.m. | ♒ | 6:29 | 4:59 | morn | 6:15 | 5:14 | morn | 7:30 |
| 26 | Fr | Rigel mer. 2:54 a.m.; ☽ apo. 3:00 p.m. | ♒ | 6:31 | 4:58 | 12:28 | 6:16 | 5:13 | 12:51 | 8:14 |
| 27 | Sa | Sirius ri. 11:13 p.m. | ♒ | 6:32 | 4:56 | 1:30 | 6:17 | 5:11 | 1:47 | 8:57 |
| **43. Twenty-first Sunday after Pentecost - October 28, 2001** | | | | **L/Day 10h 22m - Twi. 1h 38m** | | | **L/Day 10h 52m - Twi. 1h 25m** | | | |
| 28 | Su | Daylight Saving Time ends | ♓ | 6:33 | 4:55 | 2:32 | 6:18 | 5:10 | 2:43 | 9:38 |
| 29 | Mo | Spica ri. 5:28 a.m. ☿ gr. W. el. | ♓ | 6:35 | 4:53 | 3:35 | 6:19 | 5:09 | 3:39 | 10:20 |
| 30 | Tu | Arcturus ri. 4:34 a.m.; ♄ ri. 7:01 p.m. ⛢ sta. | ♈ | 6:36 | 4:52 | rises | 6:20 | 5:08 | rises | 11:02 |
| 31 | We | Halloween; Canes Venatici ri. 1:32 a.m. | ♈ | 6:38 | 4:50 | 4:58 | 6:20 | 5:07 | 5:09 | 11:46 |

BIRTHSTONE: Opal or Tourmaline, symbols of hope FLOWER: Calendula or Cosmos

**WEATHER FOLKLORE & LEGEND**

***A severe autumn denotes a windy summer; a windy winter a rainy spring.***

# WEATHER FORECAST
## ∞ OCTOBER 2001 ∞

ZONE

### ❶ Northeastern States

**1st-3rd.** Mostly fair, unseasonably chilly with widespread frosts. **4th-7th.** Squalls New York to Massachusetts, then clearing. Wet for the Mid-Atlantic States. **8th-11th.** Clearing skies over Maine, turning quite chilly everywhere else. **12th-15th.** Rain quickly spreads in from the West, followed just as quickly by clearing and colder weather. **16th-19th.** Fair, pleasant weather. **20th-23rd.** Squalls for New England, wet snow over higher terrain areas, then clearing. **24th-27th.** Initially, fair skies, then showers spread into New England by the 27th. **28th-31st.** Don't forget to set your clocks back one hour as we return to standard time on the 28th. Mostly fair skies.

### ❷ Great Lakes and Midwest

**1st-3rd.** Fair skies and unseasonably chilly, with widespread frosts. **4th-7th.** Wet weather for the Great Lakes. **8th-11th.** Turning quite chilly. **12th-15th.** Rain in Illinois, Michigan area spreading east, followed by clearing and colder weather. **16th-19th.** Fair initially, followed by stormy weather. **20th-23rd.** Clearing and turning much colder. **24th-27th.** Fair initially, then showers spread in from the West. **28th-31st.** Don't forget to set your clocks back one hour on the 28th as we return to standard time. Sunny to partly cloudy skies.

### ❸ Southeastern States

**1st-3rd.** Fair and unseasonably chilly with frosts into Tennessee. **4th-7th.** Wet for the Tennessee River Valley. Heavy rain for the Gulf Coast. **8th-11th.** Fair skies. **12th-15th.** Light showers, then fair. **16th-19th.** Dry and pleasant initially, then stormy weather shifts into Tennessee, Mississippi and Alabama by the 19th. **20th-23rd.** Rain clears, followed by fair and unseasonably cold conditions; frosts reach to the Gulf Coast. **24th-27th.** Showers sweep east to Georgia and Florida. **28th-31st.** Don't forget to set your clocks back one hour on the 28th as we return to standard time. Lots of sunshine.

### ❹ North Central States

**1st-3rd.** Mild, then showery. **4th-7th.** Some wet flurries; chilly for the Plains States. **8th-11th.** Fair and becoming milder. **12th-15th.** Showery, windy for Plains States, then fair and cold. **16th-19th.** Becoming stormy. **20th-23rd.** Dry and colder with widespread heavy frosts. **24th-27th.** Windy, then turning wet. **28th-31st.** Don't forget to set your clocks back one hour on the 28th as we return to standard time. Fair skies give way to very unsettled weather; light snow as far south and east as Kansas.

### ❺ South Central States

**1st-3rd.** Mild and dry, then showers develop. **4th-7th.** Some showers and/or wet flurries; chilly over the Plains. **8th-11th.** Fair skies and turning milder. **12th-15th.** Showery/windy for Plains States, then fair skies and cold. **16th-19th.** Stormy conditions spread east. **20th-23rd.** Dry and colder, with widespread heavy frosts, even along the Texas and Louisiana coasts. **24th-27th.** Windy, then turning wet; showers for the Southern Plains. **28th-31st.** Don't forget to set your clocks back one hour on the 28th as we return to standard time. Fair skies give way to very unsettled weather: light snow as far east as Oklahoma, rain showers farther south.

### ❻ Northwestern States

**1st-3rd.** Mild and showery. **4th-7th.** Chilly and showery. **8th-11th.** More showers for Washington and Oregon. **12th-15th.** Breezy, showers finally diminish, then fair and cold conditions. **16th-19th.** Becoming stormy. **20th-23rd.** Drier and colder. **24th-27th.** Turning windy, then wet. **28th-31st.** Don't forget to set your clocks back one hour on the 28th as we return to standard time. Any brief interval of fair weather again gives way to stormy conditions.

### ❼ Southwestern States

**1st-3rd.** Mild, dry weather, then showers. **4th-7th.** Chilly, but drier. **8th-11th.** Milder temperatures. **12th-15th.** A few showers, then turning fair and cold. **16th-19th.** Stormy conditions. **20th-23rd.** Drier and colder. **24th-27th.** Showers for California and points east. Windy. **28th-31st.** Don't forget to set your clocks back one hour as we return to standard time on the 28th. Turning unsettled again.

---

**MEMORABLE WEATHER EVENTS**

☛ **October 24th, 1973-Fatal Jersey Fog**—Sixty-five vehicles crashed on the New Jersey Turnpike.

11th Month **NOVEMBER 2001** 30 Days

♏ SCORPIO
October 23 to November 22

♐ SAGITTARIUS
November 22 to December 21

**TIME ON HIS WING FAST HASTES AWAY, AND CHILLS EACH WARM SUCCEED;
TO CAPRICORN SOL HASTES EACH DAY, SO NIGHTS THE DAYS EXCEED.**

**MOON'S PHASES**
EASTERN STANDARD TIME

| Phase | Date | Time |
|---|---|---|
| Full Moon | 1st | 12:41 a.m. |
| Last Quarter | 8th | 7:21 a.m. |
| New Moon | 15th | 1:40 a.m. |
| First Quarter | 22nd | 6:20 p.m. |
| Full Moon | 30th | 3:49 p.m. |

**SUN ON MERIDIAN CIVIL TIME**

| D. | H. | M. | S. |
|---|---|---|---|
| 1st | 11 | 43 | 37 |
| 8th | 11 | 43 | 46 |
| 15th | 11 | 44 | 38 |
| 22nd | 11 | 46 | 11 |
| 29th | 11 | 48 | 21 |

Calendar for NORTHERN STATES — *45°N. Lat. 75°W. Long.*

Calendar for SOUTHERN STATES — *35°N. Lat. 75°W. Long.*

| DATE | DAY | ASTRONOMY, CHURCH DAYS, ETC. | MOON'S PLACE | Northern Sun RISES | Northern Sun SETS | Northern Moon RISES | Southern Sun RISES | Southern Sun SETS | Southern Moon RISES | MOON'S SOUTHING OR MERIDIAN PASSAGE MORN |
|---|---|---|---|---|---|---|---|---|---|---|
| 1 | Th | All Saints' Day; Hunter's Moon | ♉ | 6:39 | 4:49 | 5:23 | 6:21 | 5:06 | 5:41 | morn |
| 2 | Fr | All Souls' Day; Canopus mer. 3:36 a.m. ♃ sta. | ♉ | 6:40 | 4:47 | 5:53 | 6:22 | 5:05 | 6:17 | 12:33 |
| 3 | Sa | Vega sets 12:39 a.m. ☽♄ cl. 6:45 p.m. | ♊ | 6:42 | 4:46 | 6:29 | 6:23 | 5:04 | 6:58 | 1:23 |
| **44. Twenty-second Sunday after Pentecost - November 4, 2001** | | | | L/Day 10h 02m - Twi. 1h 41m | | | L/Day 10h 39m - Twi. 1h 26m | | | |
| 4 | Su | Cepheus mer. 6:21 p.m. ☊ | ♊ | 6:43 | 4:45 | 7:12 | 6:24 | 5:03 | 7:46 | 2:16 |
| 5 | Mo | Fomalhaut mer. 8:03 p.m. | ♋ | 6:44 | 4:43 | 8:06 | 6:25 | 5:03 | 8:40 | 3:12 |
| 6 | Tu | **Election Day** ☽♃ cl. 1:02 a.m. ⌒ | ♋ | 6:46 | 4:42 | 9:09 | 6:26 | 5:02 | 9:42 | 4:10 |
| 7 | We | Regulus ri. 12:17 a.m.; ♂ sets 10:22 p.m. | ♌ | 6:47 | 4:41 | 10:19 | 6:27 | 5:01 | 10:48 | 5:08 |
| 8 | Th | Lyra sets 12:21 a.m. | ♌ | 6:49 | 4:39 | 11:34 | 6:28 | 5:00 | 11:56 | 6:05 |
| 9 | Fr | Aries mer. 11:12 p.m. | ♌ | 6:50 | 4:38 | morn | 6:29 | 4:59 | morn | 7:00 |
| 10 | Sa | Albireo sets 12:01 a.m./11:59 p.m. | ♍ | 6:51 | 4:37 | 12:50 | 6:30 | 4:58 | 1:06 | 7:53 |
| **45. Twenty-third Sunday after Pentecost - November 11, 2001** | | | | L/Day 9h 43m - Twi. 1h 42m | | | L/Day 10h 27m - Twi. 1h 28m | | | |
| 11 | Su | **Veterans' Day;** ☽ per. 12:00 p.m. | ♍ | 6:53 | 4:36 | 2:07 | 6:31 | 4:58 | 2:14 | 8:44 |
| 12 | Mo | Job's Coffin sets 12:00 a.m. | ♎ | 6:54 | 4:35 | 3:23 | 6:32 | 4:57 | 3:23 | 9:35 |
| 13 | Tu | Corvus ri. 3:43 a.m.; ♀ combust | ♎ | 6:55 | 4:34 | 4:39 | 6:33 | 4:56 | 4:31 | 10:25 |
| 14 | We | Spica ri. 4:25 a.m.; ☽☿ cl. 5:46 a.m. | ♏ | 6:57 | 4:33 | 5:55 | 6:34 | 4:55 | 5:40 | 11:17 |
| 15 | Th | Mirach mer. 9:32 p.m.; Procyon ri. 9:37 p.m. | ♏ | 6:58 | 4:32 | sets | 6:35 | 4:55 | sets | 12:09p |
| 16 | Fr | Betelgeuse mer. 2:12 a.m. | ♏ | 6:59 | 4:31 | 5:40 | 6:36 | 4:54 | 6:10 | 1:04 |
| 17 | Sa | Capella mer. 1:30 a.m. ☋ | ♐ | 7:01 | 4:30 | 6:24 | 6:37 | 4:54 | 6:58 | 1:58 |
| **46. Twenty-fourth Sunday after Pentecost - November 18, 2001** | | | | L/Day 9h 27m - Twi. 1h 43m | | | L/Day 10h 15m - Twi. 1h 29m | | | |
| 18 | Su | Great Andromeda Galaxy mer. 8:50 p.m. ◡ | ♐ | 7:02 | 4:29 | 7:15 | 6:38 | 4:53 | 7:50 | 2:53 |
| 19 | Mo | El Nath mer. 1:32 a.m. | ♑ | 7:03 | 4:28 | 8:12 | 6:39 | 4:53 | 8:45 | 3:46 |
| 20 | Tu | Bellatrix mer. 1:30 a.m. | ♑ | 7:05 | 4:27 | 9:12 | 6:40 | 4:52 | 9:42 | 4:36 |
| 21 | We | Alpheratz sets 4:01 a.m.; ♃ ri. 7:40 p.m. | ♑ | 7:06 | 4:26 | 10:14 | 6:41 | 4:52 | 10:39 | 5:24 |
| 22 | Th | **Thanksgiving Day;** Cancer ri. 9:16 p.m. | ♒ | 7:07 | 4:25 | 11:17 | 6:42 | 4:51 | 11:36 | 6:09 |
| 23 | Fr | Denebola ri. 12:45 a.m.; ☽ apo. 11:00 a.m. | ♒ | 7:09 | 4:25 | morn | 6:43 | 4:51 | morn | 6:52 |
| 24 | Sa | Caph mer. 7:52 p.m. | ♓ | 7:10 | 4:24 | 12:19 | 6:44 | 4:50 | 12:32 | 7:34 |
| **47. Christ the King Sunday - November 25, 2001** | | | | L/Day 9h 12m - Twi. 1h 45m | | | L/Day 10h 06m - Twi. 1h 29m | | | |
| 25 | Su | Castor ri. 7:03 p.m. | ♓ | 7:11 | 4:23 | 1:21 | 6:44 | 4:50 | 1:28 | 8:15 |
| 26 | Mo | Hyades mer. 12:00 a.m. | ♓ | 7:12 | 4:23 | 2:23 | 6:45 | 4:50 | 2:24 | 8:57 |
| 27 | Tu | Asteroid Vesta ☍ 12:00 p.m. | ♈ | 7:14 | 4:22 | 3:27 | 6:46 | 4:49 | 3:21 | 9:41 |
| 28 | We | Sirius mer. 2:17 a.m. | ♈ | 7:15 | 4:22 | 4:32 | 6:47 | 4:49 | 4:20 | 10:26 |
| 29 | Th | Beehive mer. 4:06 a.m.; ♄ ri. 4:55 p.m. | ♉ | 7:16 | 4:21 | rises | 6:48 | 4:49 | rises | 11:15 |
| 30 | Fr | ☽ Aldebaran cl. 5 p.m.; ♄ occ. 7:41 to 8:41 p.m. | ♉ | 7:17 | 4:21 | 4:26 | 6:49 | 4:49 | 4:53 | morn |

BIRTHSTONE: Topaz, symbol of fidelity FLOWER: Chrysanthemum

**WEATHER FOLKLORE & LEGEND**

***If the November goose bone be thick, so will the winter weather be;
If the November goose bone be thin, so will the winter weather be.***

# WEATHER FORECAST
## ∽ NOVEMBER 2001 ∽

### ZONE

### ❶ Northeastern States

**1st-3rd.** Stormy conditions, rain or wet snow. **4th-7th.** Much colder weather, clearing skies. **8th-11th.** Some showers spread across New England from the West, then fair and cold. **12th-15th.** Fair skies. **16th-19th.** Stormy for the New York, Massachusetts area and points northward, then fair and cold. **20th-23rd.** Wet Thanksgiving for New England. **24th-27th.** Fair skies and windy. **28th-30th.** Heavy snow (6" to 12") across much of the region; light amounts over the Mid-Atlantic States.

### ❷ Great Lakes and Midwest

**1st-3rd.** Stormy weather for the Great Lakes and points east. **4th-7th.** Skies clear, but it turns much colder. **8th-11th.** Some showery weather over the Great Lakes, giving way to clear and cold conditions. **12th-15th.** Snow, possibly heavy. **16th-19th.** Fair and cold. **20th-23rd.** Light snows for Thanksgiving. **24th-27th.** Fair weather, but also windy. **28th-30th.** Heavy snow (6" to 12"); lighter amounts over Kentucky.

### ❸ Southeastern States

**1st-3rd.** Heavy rain across Tennessee, Mississippi, Alabama, Florida Panhandle, Georgia, Carolinas. **4th-7th.** Drier, but much colder, with widespread frosts. **8th-11th.** Rain again across much of the Southeast, then fair and cold. **12th-15th.** Pleasant, tranquil. **16th-19th.** Changeable skies: mixed sunshine, clouds, with a risk of a shower. **20th-23rd.** Rain along Gulf Coast and much of the region for Thanksgiving. **24th-27th.** Fair skies. Gusty winds. **28th-30th.** Cold rain most of the region, but a storm out of the Texas, Oklahoma area also dumps significant snows across parts of Tennessee. Wintry mix for parts of the Carolinas.

### ❹ North Central States

**1st-3rd.** Clearing skies and colder. **4th-7th.** Cold weather gives way to more pleasant temperatures; however, unsettled conditions arrive by the 7th. **8th-11th.** Scattered showers for Dakotas, Nebraska area, then turning clear. **12th-15th.** Heavy snow for the Rockies and points east. **16th-19th.** Fair and cold. **20th-23rd.** Light snow for the Rockies and points east for Thanksgiving. **24th-27th.** Fair skies, then stormy weather moves in from the West, with a dose of heavy snow for the Plains States. **28th-30th.** Storms shift east, then clearing skies; blustery.

### ❺ South Central States

**1st-3rd.** Heavy rain Arkansas, Louisiana area. Elsewhere clearing and colder. **4th-7th.** Cold weather gives way to more pleasant temperatures; however, unsettled conditions arrive by the 7th. Light snow Southern Rockies. **8th-11th.** Scattered showers, then clearing. Rain Texas and points east, then turning fair, cold. **12th-15th.** Stormy weather New Mexico, points east to Louisiana. **16th-19th.** Fair skies, cold. **20th-23rd.** Some snow New Mexico and Texas. Rain farther east and along the Gulf Coast for Thanksgiving. **24th-27th.** Fair skies, then stormy from the West across New Mexico. **28th-30th.** Big storm moves across Texas, Oklahoma with a dose of heavy precipitation, then clearing, blustery conditions.

### ❻ Northwestern States

**1st-3rd.** Skies clear, turning chilly. **4th-7th.** Pleasant conditions, then turning unsettled. **8th-11th.** A few showers, then clearing. **12th-15th.** Becoming stormy Washington and Oregon. **16th-19th.** Fair and chilly. **20th-23rd.** Unsettled for Thanksgiving time. **24th-27th.** Fair skies initially, then stormy weather spreads in from the Pacific Coast. **28th-30th.** Clearing skies, windy.

### ❼ Southwestern States

**1st-3rd.** Clearing, colder, drier. **4th-7th.** Dry and pleasant, then showers. **8th-11th.** Scattered showers, then improving weather. **12th-15th.** Stormy in California and across the rest of the region. **16th-19th.** Fair and cold. **20th-23rd.** Some snow for Nevada, Utah, northern Arizona. Scattered showers elsewhere for Thanksgiving time. **24th-27th.** Fair weather gives way to very unsettled conditions moving in from the Pacific. **28th-30th.** Skies clear with gusty winds.

---

### MEMORABLE WEATHER EVENTS

☞ **NOVEMBER 13th, 1933-First "Dust Bowl" Storm**—Spread dust pall from the Great Plains to New York State.

---

♐ **SAGITTARIUS**
November 22 to December 21

♑ **CAPRICORN**
December 21 to January 20

**COLD BLOWS THE WIND, THE FROZEN RAIN AND FLEECY SNOW DESCEND;**
**FOR, FREEZING WINTER'S COME AGAIN, AND SO THE YEAR DOES END.**

### MOON'S PHASES
EASTERN STANDARD TIME

| | | |
|---|---|---|
| ☽ Last Quarter | 7th | 2:51 p.m. |
| ● New Moon | 14th | 3:47 p.m. |
| ☽ First Quarter | 22nd | 3:56 p.m. |
| ○ Full Moon | 30th | 5:40 a.m. |

Subtract hour(s) for other time zones
–1h for C.S.T. –2h for M.S.T. –3h for P.S.T.

### SUN ON MERIDIAN CIVIL TIME

| D. | H. | M. | S. |
|---|---|---|---|
| 1st | 11 | 49 | 05 |
| 8th | 11 | 51 | 57 |
| 15th | 11 | 55 | 12 |
| 22nd | 11 | 58 | 39 |
| 29th | 12 | 02 | 06 |

| | | Calendar for NORTHERN STATES 45°N. Lat. 75°W. Long. | | | Calendar for SOUTHERN STATES 35°N. Lat. 75°W. Long. | | | MOON'S SOUTHING OR MERIDIAN PASSAGE |
|---|---|---|---|---|---|---|---|---|
| DATE | DAY | ASTRONOMY, CHURCH DAYS, ETC. | MOON'S PLACE | Sun RISES | Sun SETS | Moon RISES | Sun RISES | Sun SETS | Moon RISES | **MORN** |

| DATE | DAY | ASTRONOMY, CHURCH DAYS, ETC. | MOON'S PLACE | Sun RISES | Sun SETS | Moon RISES | Sun RISES | Sun SETS | Moon RISES | MORN |
|---|---|---|---|---|---|---|---|---|---|---|
| 1 | Sa | Messier 42 mer. 12:56 a.m. | ♊ | 7:18 | 4:20 | 5:07 | 6:50 | 4:49 | 5:39 | 12:07 |

**48. First Sunday of Advent - December 2, 2001**   L/Day 9h 01m - Twi. 1h 46m   L/Day 9h 57m - Twi. 1h 30m

| DATE | DAY | ASTRONOMY, CHURCH DAYS, ETC. | MOON'S PLACE | Sun RISES | Sun SETS | Moon RISES | Sun RISES | Sun SETS | Moon RISES | MORN |
|---|---|---|---|---|---|---|---|---|---|---|
| 2 | Su | Seven Sisters mer. 11:00 p.m. ☊ | ♊ | 7:19 | 4:20 | 5:58 | 6:51 | 4:48 | 6:33 | 1:04 |
| 3 | Mo | ☽ Pollux cl. 10:06 p.m. ♄☐♂ | ♋ | 7:21 | 4:20 | 7:00 | 6:52 | 4:48 | 7:34 | 2:03 |
| 4 | Tu | Hamal mer. 9:10 p.m. ☿ sup. ♂ | ♋ | 7:22 | 4:19 | 8:09 | 6:53 | 4:48 | 8:40 | 3:02 |
| 5 | We | Canis Minor mer. 2:42 a.m. | ♌ | 7:23 | 4:19 | 9:23 | 6:53 | 4:48 | 9:48 | 4:01 |
| 6 | Th | Virgo ri. 2:32 a.m.; ☽ per. 6:00 p.m. | ♌ | 7:24 | 4:19 | 10:39 | 6:54 | 4:48 | 10:57 | 4:57 |
| 7 | Fr | Arcturus ri. 1:59 a.m. ♇☐⊙ | ♍ | 7:25 | 4:19 | 11:55 | 6:55 | 4:48 | morn | 5:50 |
| 8 | Sa | Conception B.V.M.; Menkar mer. 9:53 p.m. | ♍ | 7:26 | 4:19 | morn | 6:56 | 4:48 | 12:05 | 6:41 |

**49. Second Sunday of Advent - December 9, 2001**   L/Day 8h 52m - Twi. 1h 46m   L/Day 9h 52m - Twi. 1h 31m

| DATE | DAY | ASTRONOMY, CHURCH DAYS, ETC. | MOON'S PLACE | Sun RISES | Sun SETS | Moon RISES | Sun RISES | Sun SETS | Moon RISES | MORN |
|---|---|---|---|---|---|---|---|---|---|---|
| 9 | Su | Capella mer. 12:00 a.m.; ♂ sets 10:15 p.m. | ♎ | 7:27 | 4:19 | 1:09 | 6:57 | 4:49 | 1:12 | 7:30 |
| 10 | Mo | Chanukah; Deneb sets 1:24 a.m. | ♎ | 7:28 | 4:19 | 2:23 | 6:57 | 4:49 | 2:19 | 8:19 |
| 11 | Tu | Corvus ri. 1:53 a.m. | ♏ | 7:28 | 4:19 | 3:37 | 6:58 | 4:49 | 3:25 | 9:08 |
| 12 | We | Libra ri. 4:34 a.m. | ♏ | 7:29 | 4:19 | 4:51 | 6:59 | 4:49 | 4:31 | 9:59 |
| 13 | Th | Taurus mer. 10:53 p.m. | ♏ | 7:30 | 4:19 | 6:03 | 7:00 | 4:49 | 5:37 | 10:52 |
| 14 | Fr | Eclipse - Pacific/Central America 3:52 p.m. ☋ | ♐ | 7:31 | 4:19 | sets | 7:00 | 4:49 | sets | 11:45 |
| 15 | Sa | Dog Star ri. 8:00 p.m. | ♐ | 7:32 | 4:19 | 5:03 | 7:01 | 4:50 | 5:38 | 12:40p |

**50. Third Sunday of Advent - December 16, 2001**   L/Day 8h 47m - Twi. 1h 47m   L/Day 9h 48m - Twi. 1h 31m

| DATE | DAY | ASTRONOMY, CHURCH DAYS, ETC. | MOON'S PLACE | Sun RISES | Sun SETS | Moon RISES | Sun RISES | Sun SETS | Moon RISES | MORN |
|---|---|---|---|---|---|---|---|---|---|---|
| 16 | Su | Rasalgethi ri. 4:40 a.m. ☋ | ♑ | 7:32 | 4:19 | 5:57 | 7:02 | 4:50 | 6:32 | 1:34 |
| 17 | Mo | Sickle ri. 9:46 p.m. | ♑ | 7:33 | 4:20 | 6:57 | 7:03 | 4:50 | 7:29 | 2:26 |
| 18 | Tu | Orion's Belt mer. 11:46 p.m. | ♒ | 7:34 | 4:20 | 7:59 | 7:03 | 4:51 | 8:27 | 3:16 |
| 19 | We | Ember Day; Vega sets 9:36 p.m. | ♒ | 7:34 | 4:20 | 9:02 | 7:03 | 4:51 | 9:24 | 4:03 |
| 20 | Th | Crab Nebula mer. 11:35 p.m. ☽☐⊙ cl. 9:41 p.m. | ♒ | 7:35 | 4:21 | 10:05 | 7:04 | 4:51 | 10:21 | 4:47 |
| 21 | Fr | Ember Day; ☽ apo. 8:00 a.m. | ♓ | 7:35 | 4:21 | 11:07 | 7:04 | 4:52 | 11:17 | 5:29 |
| 22 | Sa | Ember Day; ♃ ri. 5:23 p.m. | ♓ | 7:36 | 4:22 | morn | 7:05 | 4:52 | morn | 6:10 |

**51. Fourth Sunday of Advent - December 23, 2001**   L/Day 8h 46m - Twi. 1h 47m   L/Day 9h 48m - Twi. 1h 31m

| DATE | DAY | ASTRONOMY, CHURCH DAYS, ETC. | MOON'S PLACE | Sun RISES | Sun SETS | Moon RISES | Sun RISES | Sun SETS | Moon RISES | MORN |
|---|---|---|---|---|---|---|---|---|---|---|
| 23 | Su | Dubhe mer. 4:55 a.m. | ♓ | 7:36 | 4:22 | 12:08 | 7:05 | 4:53 | 12:12 | 6:50 |
| 24 | Mo | Rigel mer. 10:59 p.m. | ♈ | 7:37 | 4:23 | 1:11 | 7:06 | 4:53 | 1:08 | 7:32 |
| 25 | Tu | **Christmas Day** | ♈ | 7:37 | 4:23 | 2:14 | 7:06 | 4:54 | 2:05 | 8:16 |
| 26 | We | Procyon mer. 1:19 a.m. | ♉ | 7:37 | 4:24 | 3:20 | 7:07 | 4:54 | 3:04 | 9:03 |
| 27 | Th | ♄ sets 5:19 a.m.; Leo ri. 9:27 p.m. | ♉ | 7:38 | 4:25 | 4:29 | 7:07 | 4:55 | 4:06 | 9:54 |
| 28 | Fr | ☽Aldebaran cl. 5:00 a.m.; ♄occ.4:01 to 4:38 a.m. | ♊ | 7:38 | 4:26 | 5:39 | 7:07 | 4:56 | 5:11 | 10:49 |
| 29 | Sa | Arcturus ri. 12:34 a.m. ♌ | ♊ | 7:38 | 4:26 | rises | 7:08 | 4:57 | rises | 11:48 |

**52. First Sunday after Christmas - December 30, 2001**   L/Day 8h 49m - Twi. 1h 46m   L/Day 9h 50m - Twi. 1h 30m

| DATE | DAY | ASTRONOMY, CHURCH DAYS, ETC. | MOON'S PLACE | Sun RISES | Sun SETS | Moon RISES | Sun RISES | Sun SETS | Moon RISES | MORN |
|---|---|---|---|---|---|---|---|---|---|---|
| 30 | Su | Capella mer. 10:37 p.m. ⌒ | ♋ | 7:38 | 4:27 | 4:44 | 7:08 | 4:58 | 5:19 | morn |
| 31 | Mo | New Year's Eve; Procyon mer. 1:04 a.m. | ♋ | 7:38 | 4:28 | 5:53 | 7:08 | 4:58 | 6:25 | 12:49 |

BIRTHSTONE: Turquoise, Lapis Lazuli or Zircon, symbols of success and prosperity   FLOWER: Narcissus or Holly

### WEATHER FOLKLORE & LEGEND
*If Christmas day on Tuesday be, a dry summer that year shall be.*

# WEATHER FORECAST
## ∽ DECEMBER 2001 ∽

ZONE

### ❶ *Northeastern States*

**1st-3rd.** Clearing skies, cold. **4th-7th.** Fair, snow flurries, then clearing skies. **8th-11th.** Mostly fair and cold. **12th-15th.** Heavy snow for much of the region; lighter snowfall Mid-Atlantic States, then fair and cold everywhere. **16th-19th.** Mostly fair, cold. **20th-23rd.** Light snow spreads across New York area and points northward, then fair. **24th-27th.** This could turn out to be a white Christmas for some: heavy snow (8" to 12") spreads across New England; cold rain for Virginia, Maryland and a wintry mix for those places in between. **28th-31st.** Fair and cold.

### ❷ *Great Lakes and Midwest*

**1st-3rd.** Fair skies. **4th-7th.** Quick changes: fair, then flurries, then back to fair again. **8th-11th.** Sun gives way to clouds. **12th-15th.** Stormy for Illinois, Michigan area, then clearing and colder. **16th-19th.** Flurries spread east to Great Lakes. **20th-23rd.** Light snow Ohio, moves east, then fair skies. **24th-27th.** A white Christmas? Heavy snow (8" to 12") through Great Lakes. **28th-31st.** Fair and cold.

### ❸ *Southeastern States*

**1st-3rd.** Skies clear, but cold temperatures. **4th-7th.** Squally weather spreads in from the West. **8th-11th.** Mostly fair and cold. **12th-15th.** Some snow Tennessee and parts of the Carolinas. Elsewhere look for cold rains and winds, then clearing, colder weather down into the Gulf Coast. **16th-19th.** Sunny to partly cloudy skies and cold. **20th-23rd.** Showers from Gulf Coast through the rest of the Southeast. **24th-27th.** Rain for Gulf Coast, all points east and north to the Carolinas. **28th-31st.** Fair, cold. Frosts down to the Gulf Coast.

### ❹ *North Central States*

**1st-3rd.** Clear and pleasant. **4th-7th.** Unsettled for Rocky Mountain States, then clearing. Fair, snow flurries for the Plains, then clearing by the 7th. **8th-11th.** Fair, then stormy weather. **12th-15th.** Fair and colder. **16th-19th.** Wet over the Rockies. Flurries over the Plains. **20th-23rd.** Fair weather initially, then squally weather spreads from West into the Rockies. **24th-27th.** Heavy snow (8" to 12") for the Plains, spreading eastward. **28th-31st.** Light snow Rockies.

### ❺ *South Central States*

**1st-3rd.** Pleasant, fair weather. **4th-7th.** Squalls spread east to Arkansas, Louisiana, then turning mostly fair. **8th-11th.** Fair, then stormy weather as far east as Texas. **12th-15th.** Stormy conditions shift east, otherwise fair and colder conditions, even down to the Texas, Louisiana Gulf Coasts. **16th-19th.** Wet weather spreads as far east as Louisiana, Arkansas area. **20th-23rd.** Showers linger for a while along the Texas, Louisiana Gulf Coasts, then turning fair. Elsewhere fair weather initially, then squally weather spreads from West into the Southern Rockies. **24th-27th.** Stormy weather spreads east to Texas, then turning fair and cold. Rain lingers along Louisiana coast. **28th-31st.** Frosts down to the Texas, Louisiana Gulf Coasts. Light snow, flurries for Southern Rockies.

### ❻ *Northwestern States*

**1st-3rd.** Fair, pleasant. **4th-7th.** Unsettled Washington and Oregon, then clearing. **8th-11th.** Fair, then stormy conditions. **12th-15th.** Fair, much chillier. **16th-19th.** Fair, then unsettled with showers, especially near and along the coast. **20th-23rd.** Fair, then squally weather moves in from the Pacific. **24th-27th.** Slowly clearing skies. **28th-31st.** Showers for Washington and Oregon.

### ❼ *Southwestern States*

**1st-3rd.** Fair, tranquil. **4th-7th.** Squalls over the South Plateau, spreading east. **8th-11th.** Initially fair and pleasant, then stormy weather spreads east. **12th-15th.** Fair and colder. **16th-19th.** Showery/wet for the South Plateau and all points east. **20th-23rd.** Fair, then turning very unsettled. **24th-27th.** Stormy for Arizona and points east. Slow improvement elsewhere. **28th-31st.** Blustery most of Southwest, especially Nevada.

---

**MEMORABLE WEATHER EVENTS**

☛ **December 25th, 1980 - Cold Christmas in Northeast**—Sharp cold front moved southeast during the predawn hours; Old Forge, N.Y., -38°F; Boston, MA, dropped from midnight 32°F to 7°F; New York City, NY, from 37°F to -1°F.

**AU GRATIN:** Topped with crumbs and/or cheese and browned in the oven or under the broiler.

**AU JUS:** Served in its own juices.

**BASTE:** To moisten foods during cooking with pan drippings or a special sauce. It adds flavor and prevents drying.

**BLANCH:** To immerse in rapidly boiling water and allow to cook slightly.

**CREAM:** To soften a fat, by beating it at room temperature.

**CRIMP:** To seal the edges of a two-crust pie either by pinching them together at intervals with the fingers or by pressing with the tines of a fork.

**DREDGE:** To coat lightly with flour, cornmeal, etc.

**FOLD:** To combine a delicate substance, such as whipped cream or beaten egg whites, with another substance, without releasing air bubbles. A rubber spatula is used to gently bring part of the mixture from the bottom of the bowl to the top. The process is repeated, while slowly rotating the bowl, until the ingredients are thoroughly blended.

**JULIENNE:** To cut vegetables, fruits, or cheeses into matchstick-shaped slivers.

**MARINATE:** To allow food to stand in a liquid to tenderize or to add flavor.

# TERMS USED IN
# Cooking

**MINCE:** To chop or cut food into very small pieces.

**PARBOIL:** To boil until partially cooked; to blanch. Usually this procedure is followed by a final cooking in a seasoned sauce.

**PARE:** To remove the outermost skin of a fruit or vegetable; to peel.

**POACH:** To cook very gently in a hot liquid kept just at the boiling point.

**PUREE:** To mash foods until perfectly smooth; by hand, by rubbing through a sieve or food mill, or by whirling in a blender or food processor.

**REFRESH:** To run cold water over food that has been blanched, to quickly stop the cooking process.

**SAUTÉ:** To cook and/or brown food in a small quantity of fat (oil, butter, shortening, etc.).

**SCALD:** To heat to just below the boiling point, so that tiny bubbles appear at the edge of the saucepan.

**SIMMER:** To cook in liquid just at the boiling point. The surface of the liquid should be barely moving, broken from time to time by slowly rising bubbles.

**STEEP:** To let food stand in a (usually hot) liquid to extract or to enhance flavor, like tea in hot water, or poached fruits in sugar syrup.

**TOSS:** To combine ingredients with a lifting motion.

**WHIP:** To beat rapidly to combine with air and produce expansion; used for heavy cream or egg whites.

# VEGETABLE COOKING TIMES

| VEGETABLE | COOKING METHOD | TIME |
|---|---|---|
| Asparagus tips | Boiled | 10-15 minutes |
| Artichokes | Boiled | 40 minutes |
| Artichokes | Steamed | 45-60 minutes |
| Beans, lima | Boiled | 20-40 minutes |
| Beans, lima | Steamed | 60 minutes |
| Beans, string | Boiled | 15-35 minutes |
| Beans, string | Steamed | 60 minutes |
| Beets, *young with skin* | Boiled | 30 minutes |
| Beets, *young with skin* | Steamed | 60 minutes |
| Beets, *young with skin* | Baked | 70-90 minutes |
| Broccoli, *flowerets* | Boiled | 5-10 minutes |
| Brussels sprouts | Boiled | 20-30 minutes |
| Cabbage, *chopped* | Boiled | 10-20 minutes |
| Cabbage, *chopped* | Steamed | 25 minutes |
| Cauliflower, *stem down* | Boiled | 20-30 minutes |
| Cauliflower, *flowerets* | Boiled | 8-10 minutes |
| Carrots, *cut across* | Boiled | 8-10 minutes |
| Carrots, *cut across* | Steamed | 40 minutes |
| Corn on the cob | Boiled | 8-10 minutes |
| Corn on the cob | Steamed | 15 minutes |
| Eggplant, *whole* | Boiled | 30 minutes |
| Eggplant, *whole* | Steamed | 40 minutes |
| Eggplant, *whole* | Baked | 45 minutes |
| Peas, green | Boiled or Steamed | 5-15 minutes |
| Potatoes | Boiled | 20-40 minutes |
| Potatoes | Steamed | 60 minutes |
| Potatoes | Baked | 45-60 minutes |
| Pumpkin or Squash | Boiled | 20-40 minutes |
| Pumpkin or Squash | Steamed | 45 minutes |
| Pumpkin or Squash | Baked | 60 minutes |
| Turnips | Boiled | 25-40 minutes |

## COOKING TIME FOR DRIED FRUITS

| Fruit | Cooking Time | Amount of Sugar or Honey |
|---|---|---|
| Apricots | About 40 minutes | 1/4 cup for each cup of fruit |
| Figs | About 30 minutes | 1 tablespoon for each cup of fruit |
| Peaches | About 45 minutes | 1/4 cup for each cup of fruit |
| Prunes | About 45 minutes | 2 tablespoons for each cup of fruit |

*From the*

# FARMERS' ALMANAC

# Kitchen

**Do you have a favorite recipe you'd like to share? E-mail us at: recipes@farmersalmanac.com. We will notify you if we decide to publish it.**

## Bodacious Breakfast

### Cream Cheese Muffins

*Creamy Sweet Treat!*

1/2 cup sugar
1 tsp. cinnamon
1/8 tsp. almond extract
1/4 cup margarine (or butter), melted
1/2 tsp. vanilla
1 (7.5 oz.) can buttermilk or country refrigerator biscuits
1 (3 oz.) package of cream cheese, cut into 10 cubes

In a small bowl, combine the sugar, cinnamon, and almond extract. In another bowl, combine margarine and vanilla. Separate the refrigerator rolls into 10 individual biscuits. Press each biscuit into a 3-inch circle. Roll each cheese cube in the margarine and then the sugar mixture. Place one cube in the center of each pressed biscuit. Fold dough over cheese, cover completely and seal well. Shape each filled biscuit into a ball and then roll in the margarine, then the sugar. Place seam-side down in an ungreased muffin pan cup. Bake at 375°F for 12-18 minutes.

*Marion Sampaio*
*Bethlehem Twp., New Jersey*

128

## Luscious Lunches

### Spinach Pie

*Cheese And Quiche Lovers Will LOVE This One!*

2 boxes frozen spinach (1 1/2 lb. fresh)
1 large onion, chopped
2 tbsp. oil
4 eggs, beaten
3/4 lb. Muenster cheese, chopped or shredded
Salt and pepper to taste
9-inch prebaked pie crust (optional)

Thaw (or clean) and drain spinach. Sauté spinach and chopped onion in oil until cooked. Remove from heat. Add eggs, cheese, salt and pepper to the spinach and onions. Pour into a prebaked pie shell or a greased pie plate. Bake at 350°F for 35 minutes. Let set 5-10 minutes. Slice and serve.

*Donna Lewis*
*Belleville, New Jersey*

*Something Different!*

### Fresh Tomato Casserole

2 strips of bacon
3 slices soft bread, cubed
1 large onion, chopped
6 fresh tomatoes, peeled and chopped
1 tbsp. sugar
2 tbsp. flour
Salt and pepper to taste
1 cup American cheese, cubed

Fry bacon, remove from pan and drain. Toss bread cubes in skillet with bacon fat. Add onion and sauté. Put the tomatoes in a greased casserole. Add the bread mixture. Combine the sugar, flour, salt and pepper and add to casserole. Mix lightly. Stir in cheese. Crumble bacon and sprinkle on top. Bake at 350°F for 20 minutes.

*Amanda Green*
*South Bend, Indiana*

## Party Pleasers

### Dill Boat

2 loaves of round rye or pumpernickel
  bread, unsliced
1 pint sour cream
1/2 cup mayonnaise
2 tsp. dill weed
1 small onion, chopped
1 package chopped beef,
  chopped more finely

*Dip With Style*

Carve out the middle of each loaf of bread, leaving a hollow circle. (Save the cut portion to use for dipping.) Mix the rest of the ingredients together and place in the carved-out breads. For best results, make the dip ahead of time and refrigerate (before you place it in the bread) for at least one hour.

*Dianne DeAngelis*
*Lebanon, New Jersey*

### Crab Stuffed Celery

1 small package cream cheese, softened
1 can crabmeat
Onion juice (to taste)
Celery sticks

Blend cream cheese, crabmeat and onion juice. Stuff celery. *Easy And Tasty!*

*David Ryan*
*Portland, Oregon*

*continued*

| ⊰— Measurement Equivalents —⊱ | |
|---|---|
| Pinch | 1/8 teaspoon |
| 3 teaspoons | 1 tablespoon |
| 4 tablespoons | 1/4 cup |
| 8 tablespoons | 1/2 cup |
| 12 tablespoons | 3/4 cup |
| 16 tablespoons | 1 cup |
| 2 cups | 1 pint |
| 4 cups | 1 quart |
| 4 quarts | 1 gallon |
| 8 quarts | 1 peck |
| 4 pecks | 1 bushel |
| 16 ounces | 1 pound |
| 1 ounce liquid | 2 tablespoons |
| 8 ounces liquid | 1 cup |
| 32 ounces liquid | 1 quart |

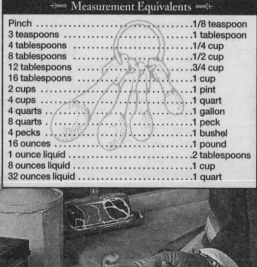

## Delectable Dinners

### Crock-Pot Kielbasa

2 or 3 kielbasa links (cut into one-inch pieces)
1/2 cup brown sugar
1/3 cup white sugar
2 tbsp. prepared mustard
2 tbsp. corn starch
1/2 cup white vinegar
8 oz. jellied cranberry sauce
1/4 cup light corn syrup

*Super For Potluck Dinners.*

Mix all ingredients together, and simmer for about 2 hours (if using a Crock-Pot, simmer all day).

*Chrissy Olson*
*Lewiston, Maine*

### Fried Rice with Shrimp

*A Flavorful Combination*

1 cup rice, cooked
4 eggs
2 tsp. water
2 tsp. butter
2 tsp. oil
1/2 cup celery, finely chopped
1/2 cup scallions, cut into thin strips
2 tsp. parsley, chopped
1/2 cup smoked ham, cubed
Salt and pepper to taste
3 tsp. soy sauce, or to taste
2 cups shrimp, cooked and shelled

Cook rice, then cool. Beat the eggs and water together. Melt butter in skillet. Pour eggs into skillet and cook without stirring or turning over. Then remove eggs from heat. Heat oil in separate large skillet and add vegetables. Cook quickly, stirring for about 3 to 4 minutes. Add rice and ham. Mix well. Add more oil if necessary. Season to taste with salt and pepper and soy sauce. Add shrimp, stir, and cook until thoroughly heated. Cut eggs into thin strips and place over fried rice.

*Jill Snivly*
*Elverson, Pennsylvania*

### New England Brown Bread

1 cup sour milk
1/2 cup molasses
1 cup graham flour (whole wheat)
1/2 cup white flour
1 tsp. baking soda
1/2 tsp. salt
1/2 cup dates or currants, chopped (optional)
1/2 cup nuts, chopped (optional)

*Great With Beans*

Mix milk and molasses. Add dry ingredients and mix well. Stir in dates and nuts. Pour into two greased 4" x 8" loaf pans. Bake at 350°F for 45 minutes.

*Georgette Dutil*
*Winslow, Maine*

## Delicious Desserts

### Chocolate Lazy Cake

**Easy and great for people allergic to dairy products!**

1 1/2 cups flour
1 cup sugar
3 tbsp. cocoa
1 tsp. baking soda
1/2 tsp. salt
1 tbsp. vanilla
1 tbsp. vinegar
6 tbsp. salad oil
1 cup water

*You Won't Believe How Easy!*

Mix all dry ingredients together. Make a well in the dry ingredients and add the vanilla, vinegar, and oil. Stir, add the water and mix again. Pour into a greased 9" x 9" square baking pan. Bake at 350°F for 30-35 minutes. (You can frost this cake, but it is so rich it really doesn't need a frosting.)

*Virginia Walker*
*Brunswick, Maine*

## Grandmother's Oatmeal Cookies

3 eggs
1 tsp. vanilla
1 cup raisins
1 cup shortening or butter
1 cup light brown sugar
1 cup sugar
2 1/2 cups sifted flour
1 tsp. salt
2 tsp. baking soda
1 tsp. cinnamon
2 cups oatmeal
1/2 cup nuts, chopped (pecans work well)
1 (12 oz.) package of chocolate chips

*Traditional With A Modern Touch!*

In a small bowl, beat the eggs and vanilla together. Add the raisins and let the mixture stand for 1 hour. (Don't skip this step!) Blend together the shortening and the brown and white sugars until fluffy. Sift the flour, salt, soda, and cinnamon into the sugar mixture and mix well. Blend in the egg and raisin mixture, combine well.

Next, add the oatmeal. The batter will be very thick and dry at this point; you may need to use your hands to mix it. Finally, add the nuts and chocolate chips. Place heaping teaspoons of dough on an ungreased cookie sheet—or roll with your hands into small balls. Bake for 10-15 minutes at 350°F. Cookies should be lightly browned. Do not overcook.

*Julia Forbes*
*Baltimore, Maryland*

### ⇒ Emergency Substitutions ⇒

1 tablespoon cornstarch = 2 tablespoons flour

1 square of chocolate (1 oz.) = 3 tablespoons cocoa plus 1 tablespoon butter

1 whole egg = 2 egg yolks plus 1 tablespoon of water

1 cup sour milk = 1 tablespoon lemon juice or vinegar plus sweet milk to make 1 cup. Let stand for 5 minutes.

1 cup milk = 1/2 cup evaporated milk plus 1/2 cup water

## Apple Cake

1 cup sugar
1/4 cup butter
1 large egg
4 cups Granny Smith apples, cut up
1 cup flour
1/2 tsp. baking powder
1/2 tsp. baking soda
1/2 tsp. salt
1/2 tsp. cinnamon
1 cup walnuts, chopped

*Move Over Coffee Cake!*

Cream sugar with butter. Beat in egg. Stir in apples. In another bowl, sift flour with baking powder, baking soda, salt, and cinnamon. Mix dry ingredients with wet ingredients. Pour into Bundt pan. Add chopped walnuts on top. Bake at 350°F for about 1 hour.

*Cindy Katz*
*Carmel, New York*

## Kansas Pear Pie

*A Fruity Delight!*

6 cups pears, peeled and coarsely chopped
3/4 cup sugar
2 tbsp. minute tapioca mix
1/2 tsp. cinnamon
1/4 tsp. nutmeg
2 nine-inch pie crusts
1 tbsp. butter

Mix pears, sugar, tapioca, cinnamon and nutmeg in a large bowl. Let stand for 15 minutes. Fill pastry-lined pie plate with fruit mixture. Dot with 1 tablespoon butter. Cover pie with top crust and seal. Flute edge and cut several slits to allow steam to escape. Bake at 400° F for 1 hour.

*Meghan Goudie*
*Hamilton, New Jersey*

# Wheat *to* Bread

## It's more than what you think...

What invention of this new millennium do you think might become "the greatest thing since sliced bread"? It will have to be good, whatever it is. This homespun adage speaks to availability, reliability, convenience, and necessity.

As we rush to embrace the microwonders of the twenty-first century, we take sliced bread for granted. But it is the ultimate canvas for peanut-butter-and-jelly art, the indispensable wrapping for a freshly sliced tomato, and the perfect post-Thanksgiving companion for turkey leftovers. It satisfies wee toddlers and feeds mighty construction workers. Sliced bread is ubiquitous; it is consistent; it is always there, just like the sky.

## by Glenn Morris
### Freelance author located in Lansdale, Pennsylvania.

## BAKING BASICS

Most of us don't give this readily available, mass-produced bread a second thought (except immediately following a winter storm warning, when all bread vanishes in a frenzy). The fact is, sliced bread is not so simple after all; it neither grows in plastic bags ready to eat, nor does it, in the words of one baking executive, "auto-magically" appear on the shelves.

Baking bread involves combining flour, water, sugar, and salt to make dough. The leavening agent, the yeast, ferments with the starches and sugars in the flour to release carbon dioxide. This gas is trapped in the elastic dough, causing it to rise. The risen dough goes into an oven, bakes, and comes out as bread. Add some proportions to these ingredients; allow some time for the different steps, and you have a recipe.

Occasionally baking bread for one's self is a homey pleasure that requires mostly time. Baking nearly identical loaves of bread to keep store shelves filled year-round is altogether different. There are two reasons for the difference: the volume of production, and consumer expectations.

According to Mark Dirkes of the Interstate Baking Corporation in Kansas City, Missouri, people expect consistency in a brand-name bread. Interstate bakes Wonderbread, the largest selling brand in the country. Dirkes, Vice President of Marketing, speaks of the importance of providing a predictable product, "Trust is everything with bread."

## HARD WHEAT IS GOOD TO FIND

The foundation of that trust is found in the midwestern wheat fields. Finding sufficient flour for one's occasional personal

baking is, pun intended, a piece of cake. Supplying railroad-car-sized quantities of suitable flour to commercial bakeries across the country is not.

"We look for functionality in flour," states Dirkes, meaning, "can you bake bread with it?" While baking corporations keep one eye on the production lines, they keep the other on the wheat harvests. Good wheat means good baking, because not just any wheat will do.

Hundreds of varieties of wheat are grown in the United States, classified by two distinct seasons, winter and spring. Winter wheats are sown in the fall and mature in spring or summer; spring wheats are planted in the spring and harvested in late summer or fall. Further classification is based on the color of the kernels, red or white, and their hardness. For sliced bread purposes, the wheats of choice are hard red winter wheat and hard red spring wheat; wheats that have a high percentage of the elastic protein "gluten." When you sing about amber waves of grain, you salute the Great Plains states of Kansas, North Dakota and Montana, which are our leading bread wheat producers.

If it's dry enough to plant; if there's enough moisture to grow the crop; if no hail or high winds break the straw; if rain doesn't mire the fields at harvest—then the combines reap. The wheat goes into storage in grain elevators until flour mills need it. (Grain elevators lift and load grains into the top, and empty stored grains from the bottom.) By harvest, the bakeries and mills they partner with know right down to individual fields where the wheat grew.

## THE SAME OLD GRIND

Mills, of course, take wheats and grind them into flour. That may seem simple
*continued*

enough, but bakeries have very specific expectations for flours that are derived from the mills' production processes. Some mills custom blend wheats before milling; others may blend the flours of different wheats after milling. Mills also test-bake with their flours during processing as a matter of quality control.

## THE GENERAL CONVEYOR-BELT WALTZ OF WHEAT-TO-FLOUR GOES LIKE THIS:

The wheats are inspected, classified by type, and then chemically analyzed for, among other things, their protein quality and quantity. Sometimes wheats are blended after this step. Then magnetic separators remove any iron or steel particles before another separator, using fine reciprocating screens, eliminates debris such as stones and sticks.

An aspirator uses air currents to remove lighter impurities. A disc separator eliminates barley, oats and other foreign materials before a scourer, rotating beaters in a screen cylinder, scours off impurities and roughage.

The now-purer wheats are tempered with moisture, which toughens the bran coating for later removal from the kernel, or wheat berry. (Some mills blend wheats at this step.)

Another scourer removes unsound kernels, the cleaned wheats then go into a grinding bin, where corrugated rollers break the berries into coarse particles. The broken kernels are sifted through successively finer screens. After the sifter, a succession of purifiers and reducing rolls removes the bran and the germ, and reduces the middlings, the remaining portion of the kernels, to flour. The new flour is sifted and purified further. Then it is bleached, so the color is neutralized (unbleached flour does not go through this step). Following

bleaching, flour is stored in bulk prior to any enriching and shipping to the bakeries, or it is enriched and packaged to be distributed for home use.

At Interstate Bakeries, Theresa Cogswell, Vice President of Research and Development, oversees the final batch-specific testing of flours before they arrive at any of Interstate's 67 bakeries. "It's our job to give the bakeries a heads up when a flour is different," she states. "They use this to fine-tune the baking, so that the product is consistent." Only when the testing is over is it time to bake bread.

## FLOUR IS AS FLOUR DOES

Regardless of bakery size and location, the mixing room is where the art and science of baking come together. "Garbage out of the mixing room," says Cogswell, "garbage out of the bakery." Bigger, faster, more efficient machines haven't eliminated the personal face of baking. "You will never get away from the guy standing there squeezing the dough," echoes Dale Mediate, of Flowers Industries, Inc. in Thomasville, Georgia, bakers of Southern favorites, Bunny Bread and the Cobblestone Mills brands. "The mixers are the guys who have to know what they are doing. They know–from experience–how to tweak it, what to do when it's hot and the humidity is high."

Wess Rhodes of Flowers, with nineteen years of baking experience, sketched the baking process. The first step is the ferment, where flour, water, and yeast are combined in large vats to start the yeast working. Some mixers make a "sponge," which uses 80 percent of the total flour needed for the bread. Other mixers prefer a "brew," a ferment which uses about 50 percent of the total bread flour.

There are advantages to each style: a brew can be piped to the next stage while sponges need to be transported in large carts.

The same brand of bread can be made from either, according to Rhodes, but the sponge technique yields a silkier texture that some consumers prefer. The ferment takes about two to three hours, and the mixture can expand to six times its original volume.

The sponge or brew is sent to a mixer machine, where the remaining ingredients are added and the dough is kneaded. Kneading is the important step that develops the elasticity of the flour protein. The elasticity is needed to trap the gases released by the yeast's action. This entrapment makes bread rise. Some mixers can mix 3,000 pounds at one time, the weight of a Volkswagen Beetle.

The Old Mill at Guilford in Oak Ridge, NC

A divider then parcels the dough into the correct amounts for loaves, a process called scaling: too little dough and a loaf looks short; too much, and it puffs too large for the wrapper. The divided dough is shaped and placed in individual pans to enter a proof box, for the final rising.

The proof box maintains a heat/humidity range of 110 to 112 degrees Fahrenheit and 88 to 98 percent humidity to control the rise. After rising approximately one hour, the dough is ready to be baked for 14 to 16 minutes at 400 to 425 degrees Fahrenheit. Rhodes notes that the interior temperature of the baking dough must reach between 198 to 202 degrees Fahrenheit to "set the starch" and to help the loaf retain its shape.

Out of the oven, suction lifters "depan" the bread, and it goes for a 40-minute cooling ride on a conveyor belt, bringing the internal temperature down to 104 degrees. The next stop is the bread slicer. Blades initiate slicing on a bottom corner and zip through each loaf to make–what else– sliced bread. Then, each loaf is stuffed into a wrapper and loaded onto a truck. Start to finish, the process takes about 4 1/2 to 5 hours.

## A MILLER TELLS HIS TALE

"Like a big baker, I am tied to my flour source for baking success, and I have a secret ingredient," reveals Charles Parnell, the chipper, perpetually flour-dusted proprietor of the Old Mill at Guilford in Oak Ridge, North Carolina. Parnell makes flour the "slow-fashioned" way—a waterpowered wheel turns a generator that whirls massive millstones which powder Montana wheat into Hi-Gluten Flour. In addition to his expertise, the only thing added to the flour is the paper sack which holds it.

Scottish by birth and resolute by temperament, Parnell is definite about what bread needs to be kneaded. "You need high-protein wheat, it's that simple. That's what makes bread elastic and able to rise," he says with a hint of a burr, adding, "The best wheat comes from high latitudes and to bake good bread you need between 14.8 and 16.8 percent protein in the wheat."

I don't know from percentages nor can I confirm Parnell's science, but I do know that his Hi-Gluten Flour pushes back when you knead it. It would push back too much for a commercial production line, but bakes the kind of bread I like to bake.

With all of this spelled out for you, here is a challenge: try going two weeks without "store-bought" bread. Take out the mixing bowl and do some productive "loafing" in the home kitchen and eat what you bake. It might make you appreciate all of the steps that go into a product that we often take for granted—sliced bread.

The editorial staff at the *Farmers' Almanac* is once again challenging students in grades K-8 to become published authors. If you are a student (or know of a student) and think you've got what it takes to be published in next year's *Farmers' Almanac*, you must complete this thought, *"Once upon a time, there was this invention"* TO ENTER: All stories must be original and written by a student in grades K-8. Stories must be less than 225 words and received by March 1, 2001. Teachers are encouraged to send in class entries. Each entry must include: author's name, age, grade, home address, school and teacher's name, and school's address. All entries become the property of Almanac Publishing Company and will not be returned. Winning entries will be published in the 2002 *Farmers' Almanac*, and each winning author will receive an advance, complimentary copy of the 2002 edition, and a special, personalized writing journal. SEND YOUR ENTRY TO: *Farmers' Almanac* Challenge, Mt. Hope Ave., P.O. Box 1609 Lewiston, ME 04241 or enter through our Web site at www.farmersalmanac.com GOOD WRITING!

# 2000 CHALLENGE WINNERS

Last year we asked students to complete this thought: "What life was like 100 years ago." Out of the 2,000 entries we received, here are the winners of last year's *Farmers' Almanac* Challenge:

### *What life was like 100 years ago*

William McKinley was president until 1901,
When Leon Czolgosz assassinated him with a gun.
Teddy Roosevelt was next in line,
He served as president until 1909.
The Open Door Policy was started by John Hay,
Before it began, the Boxer Rebellion took it away.
Motion pictures had just begun,
All thanks to Thomas Edison.
In 1900, the first glider was built by the brothers
Wright, by 1903 they would take their first flight.
By the 1900s times were lush,
Thanks to the Klondike gold rush.
The average life expectancy was 50,
To live beyond that would be nifty.
A corset a woman had to wear,
Leave home without it, she wouldn't dare.
Basketball was played in college,
Now the students can have fun while
gaining some knowledge.
In 1900, AT&T bought Bell Telephone,
Everyone could communicate without feeling alone.
As Henry Ford popularized the car,
Cecil B. De Mille was looking for the right star.
Health insurance became available to all,
Back then a doctor would even make a house call.
Not many teenagers were enrolled in school,
By the current standards, that wasn't cool.
If you put the absence of TVs and VCRs into the mix,
I'm sure glad that I was born in 1986!

KATHLEEN MOORE
Grade 8, Age 13, Crest Memorial School
Wildwood Crest, New Jersey

## If I lived 100 years ago

If I lived a 100 years ago, my life would be different because . . . There weren't any buses or cars to ride in. So, I would ride a horse or a pony. If there wasn't pop, I would drink anything I like. If there weren't any computers, I would just make my own games, like hide-and-seek or duck-duck-goose. If there weren't any radios, I would make up my own songs. I would like that if I lived 100 years ago.

CLAIRE CARROLL
Grade 2, Age 7
Indian Hills Elementary School,
Washington Twp., Michigan

## Through the eyes of a horse

The early nineteen hundreds were very strenuous years for us horses. Many changes were beginning to happen that improved our lives. One of the difficulties was caused by the lack of vehicles. Field horses had to plow. Everywhere you looked horses were hauling around carriages. Horses became quite exhausted tugging gallons of water in fire wagons to infernos.

Things changed as people discovered new inventions. Automobiles improved horses' lives immensely. Telephones prevented people from having to travel across the country to talk to relatives. Electricity in houses and stables provided light. Conclusively, life in the early nineteen hundreds was difficult. Life and work were almost unbearable. Fortunately, new inventions gave us hope for an easier life in the future.

SALLY SIGMON
Grade 6, Age 11, New Covenant School,
Anderson, South Carolina

## Life without technology

Life was very different 100 years ago. Most people didn't have cars—they rode horses. They didn't have televisions, refrigerators and dishwashers. They washed dishes by hand. They didn't have washers and dryers—they did their laundry by hand. There were no fans or air-conditioning. Many people lived on farms—they raised animals and grew gardens for food.

ERIN LINDSAY McCULLEY
Grade 2, Age 7
Powderhorn Elementary
Littleton, Colorado

## 100 years ago

Let's take a trip, yes, here we go,
Back to 100 years ago!
There were no cars to go
from place to place,
They used a horse and carriage,
yes, that was the case.
There was no computer and no TV,
No VCR or DVD.
They used iceboxes, not refrigerators,
They didn't even use calculators!
The first plane was flown
by Orville Wright,
12 seconds lasted the entire flight.
Oklahoma became the 47th state,
It caused another flag to be out of date.
The light bulb, Thomas Edison
did invent,
Theodore Roosevelt became president.
100 years ago was much
different than today,
No matter how you look at it,
any which way!

MATT MICHALSKI
Grade 5, Age 11
University Heights School,
Trenton, New Jersey

*continued*

## Long ago

Long dirt roads. Grassy fields and a house every couple of miles or so. There are no cars, no giant buildings, just cool, clean air and the open fields. No clutter, no trash. A small girl in a checkered dress and pigtails emerges from one of the little farms to start her morning chores. Her mama is inside cooking breakfast. Her papa is upstairs getting dressed to go into town to vote. Only a man can vote for president. Her older brother is outside in overalls hitching up the wagon for papa.

Papa walks out and climbs into the wagon. He drives down the bumpy dirt road into a bustling town. There are no TV stores, no shopping malls, no grocery stores. Instead there are butchers on every curb selling fresh meat, women displaying quilts, and, in a small store, fruits and vegetables can be bought. Papa rides to the largest wooden building and walks inside. He strides into a small booth and votes for William McKinley. This is life. This is 1900.

ERIN GOSSELIN
Grade 6, Age 11,
Montello Elementary School,
Lewiston, Maine

## Life one hundred years ago

A hundred years ago, America
was the place to be,
A country where others were
accepted and free.
It was a place of opportunities
and hope,
A place where even the
poorest could cope.
But everything wasn't perfect in
this great land,
It's like people's heads
were in the sand.
African-Americans wanted to be
equal and were willing to fight,
To stand up and be heard
for what was right.
African-Americans were treated
unfairly because of their race,
In America, everyone deserves
their own place.
Where people are respected
no matter what color they are,
Maybe after one hundred years
we've sadly not come that far.

LAUREN FRASCELLA
Grade 5, Age 11
University Heights School
Trenton, New Jersey

## 100 years of growth

A hundred years ago today, I know just what I'd see,
This pine tree deep inside the woods, a hundred years would be,
Atop a hill, by a tiny stream, it still lives, so peacefully,
and I'd sit for all those years there, the tree looking down on me,
This tree is so old, among growth anew, all its seeds springing up annually,
It seems so much, I wonder still, how old it will grow to be.

LAURA de BOER
Grade 7, Age 13,
Hants West Middle School,
Brooklyn, Hants Co., Nova Scotia, Canada

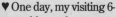

♥ One day, my visiting 6-year-old granddaughter Elizabeth was trying to make a grape drink from a packaged drink mix. When I asked her how she was doing, she said with a loud sigh, "Not so good, Grandma. I'm having a problem getting the water into the envelope!"
—Suzan L. Wiener

♥ When my 6-year-old grandson Billy was once being mischievous, his mother told him, "When you do bad things, you have to live with the consequences." Without a pause, he asked eagerly, "Do they have a pool?"
— Suzan L. Wiener

♥ One day, my 12-year-old grandson Danny told his 10-year-old brother Bobby that he had heard on television that a naked lady was going to ride a white horse in a parade. "Oh, boy," said his brother excitedly. "I never saw a white horse!"
— Mrs. Sherri Brown

*O*ften, children come out with the funniest, yet most innocent of comments. The following are some "juvenile jewels" that were sent in by readers.

♥ While visiting family in another town, we went to their church. Our 4–year-old Jack went to their Sunday School with his customary quarter in his pocket (in our church, the teacher passes a little church bank around for the children's offerings).

After the service, Jack came running out of the Sunday School room, very excited. Holding up his quarter, he shouted, "Look, Mom, they liked me so much they let me in for free!"
— Mrs. Jack L. Shreves

♥ My mother's friend was visiting her grown daughter on her grandson's first day of school. When he got home, his grandmother asked what he thought of school. He replied seriously, "It's OK, but it's sure gonna take up a lot of my time!"
— Beverly Snyder

♥ I was headed for the car wash in my customarily hand-washed car, and invited my little girl to come along. She always enjoyed going with her dad in his truck, even though the last time there had been a little mishap when her window was accidentally left open a bit.

Although she was just 4, I knew she'd be a big help, and asked her if she could guide me through the wash. She replied, "Oh sure, Mom. The easy part is putting the quarters in. The hard part is getting soap in your eyes."
— Joyce McClain

Hear any good ones lately? Send your favorite "juvenile jewel" to *Farmers' Almanac*, Box 1609, Mt. Hope Ave., Lewiston, ME 04241. Winning submissions will be published in next year's Almanac. Winners will be paid $15 for each statement published. All submissions must be received by March 1, 2001.

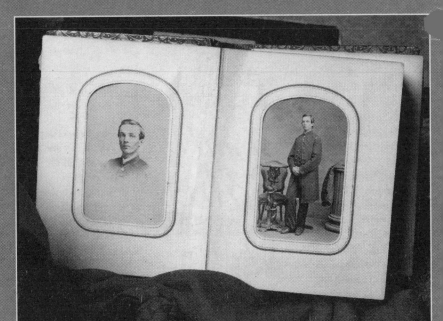

# Keeping The Past Alive.

## by Gloria Troyer
Freelance author located in Guelph, Ontario

*Tips on caring for personal papers and keepsakes*

**M**any folks in North America have caught a disease that has no cure—the Genealogy Bug. To trace their roots, they spend endless hours searching through dusty files, rummaging through church records, writing letters, and traveling for miles. If you were to ask these diligent researchers to show you their own personal family papers, you might be presented with one of the following storage methods: a cardboard box, a plastic shopping bag, or a wooden crate. Inside, you would find loose photographs, bunches of letters (either tied with string or held together with elastic bands), diaries, and scrapbooks, with a few books thrown on top to act as paperweights.

The family papers we save in our lifetime can become the treasures of future generations. Letters, diaries, day journals, legal documents (including birth, death, marriage certificates, divorce decrees, wills, commissions, and mortgages), photographs, and publications are paper, a self-destructive substance. All paper will deteriorate if mistreated or stored improperly. If we value these objects, we should take steps to preserve them. There are easy methods you can follow to protect these important connections to the past and to ensure their future.

To provide long-term protection, storage containers and enclosures should be made of materials that are strong, durable, and chemically inert. Archival supplies are recommended and can be purchased through library and archival supply companies, craft stores, art supply shops, and stationery stores. Here are some tips and suggestions on ways you can preserve and protect your family's important memorabilia.

What supplies do you need? File folders, acid-free • Clear plastic enclosures Sleeves for negatives and photos • Envelopes, acid-free • Tissue, acid-free Storage boxes, acid-free • Soft brush for cleaning • Labels • Glue stick, nonacidic, nontoxic • Photo corners • Unbleached cloth tying strips • Nylon or cotton gloves • Kneadable groomstick • Pencil, soft-lead • Desiccant (a drying agent)

## Caring for *Papers*

Handle all paper carefully, wear gloves. • Remove loose surface dirt from your papers using a soft brush. Be careful not to abrade the paper, do not rub in any way. • Remove all paper clips, rubber bands, ties, staples, and pins, wrapping paper, and old folders. Replace staples or metal clips with plastic paper clips, only if necessary. • Wherever possible, unfold and flatten papers without breaking or tearing the creases, folds, and bent corners. • Remove letters from envelopes. Keep the envelopes or folders, only if they offer important information or if they are valuable. • Lay papers carefully in an acid-free file folder. Make sure that the papers are not slipping out of the file at the edge or at the corners. • Place badly damaged items in individual folders and set them aside for professional conservation treatment. Unless you have received training, do not undertake repairs. • If it is necessary to place identifying information on an item, use a pencil and write in the lower right margin. Place identification on folders, using acid-free labels. Never use ballpoint or felt-tip pens. • Store all paper materials in

*continued*

## Caring for
# Photographs

Photographs are found throughout our homes. They are taken for granted, but are actually fragile and easily damaged. Unfortunately, the deterioration of photographs is often out of our control because of the instability of certain photographic processes and materials. They are also vulnerable to many environmental hazards, such as fluctuating temperature or humidity levels, poor air quality, excessive light, molds, fungi, insects, and rodents. The greatest danger to the longevity of family photographs is improper handling. So here are some steps you should take to help protect your pictures.

acid-free folders and boxes. • Keep light levels in the storage area low. Avoid leaving paper exposed to light for long periods of time. • All boxes should be placed in environments with a stable temperature and relative humidity. They should be strong enough to support the weight of the contents, have reinforced corners, and covers tight enough to prevent soil and pollutants from entering. • Watch for insects, like silverfish and earwigs; or rodents like mice, rats, chipmunks, and squirrels that shred paper for nesting materials.

When handling pictures, wear nylon or white cotton gloves at all times, since dirt, dust, and oils from your fingers can cause permanent damage. Handle prints and negatives along the edges. Never touch the face of a photograph or the emulsion side of a negative. • If it is possible to do without causing damage, remove photographs and negatives from poor quality enclosures. Do not remove the frames from photographs without checking the type and condition of the image first. • Remove all extraneous materials such as paper clips, rubber bands, and string. Any notes or clippings should be stored separately. • Do not try to unroll large or long photographs, or film strips that resist. Seek the advice of an expert. Write gently on the backs of photographs, using only a soft-lead pencil. Felt-tipped pens and ballpoint pens should never be used because the inks are destructive. Use acid-free enclosures made especially for negatives and photos. Use buffered paper for newer black-and-white prints only. Old black-and-white pictures, and color prints and films should be placed in acid-free pH-neutral materials. • It is best to place each print in an individual enclosure, or use archival interleaves between them. Photographs that are viewed often may be placed in enclosures that allow the image to be readily seen. • Place plastic sleeves or envelopes in folders or boxes that are acid-free. • Storage boxes should be strong, have reinforced corners, and match the size of the prints. • If you have a traditional older photo album that you want to preserve intact (because the prints cannot be removed without damage), you can place it inside an acid-free box and store it flat. If the photographs face each other, interleaving sheets can be placed between the pages to act as a barrier. • Photographs are best preserved by storing them in the dark and under cover. Minimize ultraviolet and high-energy light in the storage area. Humidity and moisture can damage paper through warping, mold, or foxing (which leaves permanent brown spots). Photographs can be ruined by moisture. When possible keep photographic materials out of damp basements or rooms with no temperature control or air circulation.

## Caring for
# Mementos

A memento is an object that is kept as a very personal individual keepsake, a reminder, or a souvenir of a person or an event.

## Caring for
# Books

These easy and inexpensive methods can be used to protect the books in your personal collection.

Segregate objects that are made from several kinds of material. Each part may have a particular preservation problem that needs to be addressed separately. • Clean objects with a small, soft, brush to remove dust and debris. • Do not store mementos in the same containers with papers and photographs, since a small box mixed in with larger file folders could cause damage to the objects in the folders. Likewise, heavy objects may crush fragile papers. A separate, acid-free box with dividers is best for items that are not flat. • Use acid-free envelopes for locks of hair. • A small, deep, box with acid-free tissue can be used for textile pieces, or jewelery. Roll textiles loosely rather than folding them. • Postcards can be stored in acid-free envelopes or attached to acid-free scrapbook pages with archival photo corners. • Attach newspaper clippings to buffered, acid-free scrapbook pages with a water-soluble or washable nontoxic glue stick. • Flowers and other objects can be put in polyethylene bags. • Make sure that you identify the origin of your memento, providing a date, source of the item, and names and places on a label on top of your container. Keep your collections dry and out of direct sunlight.

※

Prepare books for storage by removing all types of plastic, envelopes, brown paper bags, loose cardboard backings, newspaper wrappings, staples, pins, paper clips, or any other metal attachments. • Enclosures for books can range from wrapping the books in archival papers, to custom-made boxes for either the most fragile or most valuable books. • Books in good condition may not require enclosures and can be placed on shelves as they are. If the text is important, and the binding is weak, the book may be adequately protected by rebinding. Books should be shelved snugly enough to support each other, but loosely enough so that drawing one from the shelf does not stress adjacent volumes. Store like sizes together. • Thick, heavy, oversized books should be stored flat when possible. If a book is oversized and cannot be placed on its tail (the bottom of the page), lay it on its side so the weight of the text will not work against the spine. Oversized books should be placed on shelves large enough to support the books completely. • If you are not trained in book repair, it is better to tie or box a damaged book than to experiment and risk damage. This is especially true if the book is valuable or has historic significance for your family (i.e. a family Bible). Use unbleached cotton cloth strips to tie up unbound issues of journals or damaged books. • Book boxes are the most sophisticated protection for fragile or valuable books. They are available in various styles or designs. Some have hinged lids and sides. Book boxes are expensive. Where book and box sizes can be matched, a less expensive option may be to use flat boxes intended for other documents, textiles, or photographs.

*continued*

## Keep an *Inventory*

Few individuals today have the time to describe each item in their collection; item-level description is simply too time-consuming a task for its worth. However, an accurate and detailed inventory (list) of your collection can be useful as a quick finding aid, instead of going through your boxes and files one by one. Make sure that you keep at least two copies of your inventory, one with the collection and one as a security copy, preferably in a different building. If you are creating your list on a computer, remember to make extra copies of the electronic files and backup disks. Store backup disks in a safe place, and be sure to update them as you add new information to your inventory.

This method of record keeping also can be used with your present-day papers and certificates. There's no need to wait for later to organize important documents that are going to be passed on to your children when they reach adulthood. In a separate box, start files for records such as birth certificates, baptismal papers, school report cards, immunization cards, mementos, etc.

## Basic inventory *Elements*

List the physical forms of the collection: correspondence, journals, diaries, photographs, books, or mementos. • Dates, inclusive dates of the material from the oldest document to the most recent. If there are gaps, be as specific as possible about the dates. For example, if you only have one letter from 1850 and all of the rest of your papers are from the twentieth century, use the dates "1850, 1900-1999," instead of "1850-99." If there is no date at all, use "n.d." Physical descriptions, including whether something is damaged or fragile, and quantity (i.e. 3 boxes, 4 books, 13 photographs, 20 letters, 2 diaries). • Biographical or historical information, including significant information about the owners or previous owners or creators of the items you are preserving. Include things such as date and place of birth or death, residence, occupation, original or maiden names, significant accomplishments. Combine the various elements described above to create the inventory of your family papers.

There can be a great deal of pleasure and satisfaction in organizing your family papers. Not only will the above guidelines ensure a future for your past, but you will also be creating a treasure of family details that generations to come will cherish as part of their legacy.

## What is Archival?

Most paper products, pen inks, string, and adhesives are or become acidic (pH lower than 7), and self-destruct when exposed to light, air pollution, and wide variations of temperature and humidity. Paper clips, staples, pins, and other material fasteners corrode and stain, or damage objects by abrading, puncturing, and tearing. Wood and plastics, like those made from polyvinyl chlorides (PVCs), give off gases which cause and increase the rate of deterioration. In high humidity, rubber bands soften and become sticky; in low humidity, they dry out and leave a dark brown residue on surfaces. They also can bend, crease, or tear papers. Light (particularly ultraviolet) accelerates destructive chemical reactions and makes colors fade.

Archival materials should be chemically inert and pH neutral, or balanced to counter a destructive chemical condition. For example, acid-free papers contain no residual chemicals (bleaches) or wood materials (lignin) that cause acids to form. They have a pH that is neutral (7) or higher (7.1+). Buffered papers are not only acid-free, but are made alkaline (pH 7.1+) to inhibit the formation and migration of acid compounds.

Plastics should be chemically inert and should not emit plasticizers (which "smell" like plastic). Only polyethylene, polypropylene, and polyester (Mylar) are chemically stable and considered archival.

Temperature directly affects deterioration; the higher the temperature the faster the destruction. Maximum temperatures should not exceed 77° F. Color film (slides and negatives) and prints are very unstable and should be kept colder than 50° F. Currently, cold storage below freezing 32° F is recommended for all color photographic materials.

High humidity fosters the growth of fungi (mold and mildews), increases acidification and corrosion, weakens fibers, and can cause photographic emulsions to lift off their supports. Low humidity makes materials more brittle, curls photos and films, and allows paper to oxidize, which is a very slow form of burning that turns paper brown.

When materials are mixed, a relative humidity of 30% is most appropriate. If levels are too high, dehumidifiers and desiccants can absorb much of the excess. When levels are too low, a humidifier can be used.

If it is possible, use an air cleaner to keep dirt, fungi spores, and pollutant levels low, and the air circulating where collections are stored. Low-wattage (60-watts or less) incandescent lights emit the least ultraviolet. If a stronger light is needed, a spotlight with a narrow beam is the best choice. An alternative is to filter out ultraviolet rays by putting UV shields on fluorescent tubes, and using UV-protection glass or acrylic in display cases, picture frames, or windows.

# Sauerkraut
## It's not just for hot dogs

*From meatballs to cake, sauerkraut is a surprisingly tasty ingredient that your kitchen shouldn't be without.*

## Kraut Is Healthy!

The healthful qualities of sauerkraut were recognized as early as 200 B.C. According to historical records, sauerkraut was doled out to the laborers working on the Great Wall of China.

Sauerkraut was also well thought of during the Civil War. Its popularity can be attributed not only to its taste, but more importantly, to the fact that it prevented attacks of scurvy during the North's long winters. In June 1863, when Southern troops captured the town of Chambersburg, PA, one of the things demanded was 25 barrels of sauerkraut. It seems that many of the men were suffering from scurvy, and the South's commander had heard that kraut was an effective cure and a preventative for that "troublesome disease."

## Good Old-fashioned Sauerkraut

To make sauerkraut, place a 2-3 inch layer of thinly shredded cabbage in a large stone or earthenware crock. Sprinkle lightly with noniodized salt (use 3 1/2 tbsp. of salt per 5 pounds of cabbage). Pound vigorously with a potato masher or wooden "stomper." Repeat this process until the crock is almost full. Cover with a clean cloth and place a round board on top. Place something on top of the board to weigh it down. Set in a warm place to ferment. After about 6 days, remove the scum that has formed on top. Wash the cloth in cold water, replace it and move the crock to a cool place. In about two weeks, the sauerkraut will be ready.

**COOKING SUGGESTION:** To retain its full flavor, sauerkraut should be served raw or barely heated through. Cooking makes the flavor milder.

# Corned Beef Sauerkraut Puffs

12 oz. corned beef, chopped very fine
1 cup sauerkraut, drained and chopped
2 tbsp. mayonnaise
3-4 tbsp. (or to taste) horseradish

Mix all ingredients together. May be made ahead and refrigerated.

*Cream Puffs (Shells)*
1 cup water
1/2 cup butter
1/4 tsp. salt
1 cup flour
4 eggs

In a saucepan, heat on high: water, butter, and salt. Stir until it boils. Then mix in the flour until it forms a ball and pulls away from the sides of the pan. Remove from heat. Beat in eggs until blended well. Drop small mounds of dough onto a greased cookie sheet, about 3 inches apart. Bake for 60 minutes at 375° F, or until golden brown. Cool. Cut part way across. Stuff with mixture. Serve cold.

*Margaret Connor, Savannah, Georgia*

# Easy Kraut

5 slices bacon, browned & diced
4 cups sauerkraut
4 cups cabbage, chopped
1 cup onion, diced
1 tbsp. margarine
1 tsp. sugar
1/2 tsp. salt
1/8 tsp. pepper
Bacon drippings

In a slow cooker, combine bacon with all ingredients except for bacon drippings. Pour bacon drippings over all. Cover and cook on low for 3 to 5 hours. Serves 4 to 6.

*Winnie Dalgewicz, Stockton, New Jersey*

# Crazy Cocktail Meatballs

2 lbs. ground beef
2 slices dry bread, crumbled
1 package of dry onion soup mix
Water

Mix all ingredients with enough water to hold together. Shape into meatballs and bake for 20-30 minutes at 350° F.

*Meatball Glaze*
1 cup sauerkraut
1 cup whole cranberries or cranberry sauce
8 oz. bottle chili sauce
1 cup brown sugar

Mix together and pour over meatballs. Bake for an additional 30-40 minutes at 350° F, or place in a Crock-Pot and simmer for at least 2 hours.

*Bettie Herzstein, Ewing, New Jersey*

# Sauerkraut Casserole

2 lbs. mild Italian sausage links, cut into 1" slices
1 large onion, chopped
2 apples, peeled and quartered
4 cups sauerkraut, undrained
1 cup water
1/2 cup packed brown sugar
1 tsp. caraway seed (optional)

In a skillet, cook sausage and onion until sausage is brown and onion is tender; drain. Stir in apples, sauerkraut, water, brown sugar, and caraway seed. Transfer to 2 1/2 quart baking dish. Cover and bake at 350° F for one hour.

*Susan Ely, Newtown, Pennsylvania*

*continued*

# Sauerkraut Mushroom Soup

**4 oz. dried mushrooms**
**1 cup sauerkraut, drained**
**4 qts. water**
**2 lbs. fresh Polish sausage**
**1 onion, sliced**
**Dash of salt and pepper**
**1/2 cup millet seed**
**(or cooked rice or barley)**

Boil mushrooms for 2 to 3 minutes in a large soup pot. Drain off water. To the mushrooms, add the rest of the ingredients except millet seed. Simmer for 2 to 2 1/2 hours. Add the millet seed and cook for 5 more minutes.

*Chet Dalgewicz, Stockton, New Jersey*

# Sauerkraut Surprise Cake

**1/2 cup butter or margarine**
**1 1/2 cups white sugar**
**3 eggs**
**1 tsp. vanilla extract**
**2 cups all-purpose flour**
**1 tsp. baking powder**
**1 tsp. baking soda**
**1/2 tsp. salt**
**1/2 cup unsweetened cocoa powder**
**1 cup water**
**1 cup sauerkraut, very finely chopped**

Grease and flour one 13" x 9" cake pan. In a large mixing bowl, cream the butter or margarine and sugar until light. Beat in eggs, one at a time, then add vanilla.

Sift together flour, baking powder, baking soda, salt, and cocoa powder. Add to creamed mixture, alternating with water, and beating after each addition. Stir in sauerkraut. Pour batter into prepared pan. Bake at 350° F for 35 to 40 minutes. Let cake cool in pan. Frost with Sour Cream Chocolate Frosting. Cut into squares to serve.

*Sour Cream Chocolate Frosting*
**16 oz. semisweet chocolate chips**
**4 tbsp. butter or margarine**
**1/2 cup sour cream**
**1 tsp. vanilla**
**1/4 tsp. salt**
**2 3/4 cups confectioners' sugar**

Melt the semisweet chocolate pieces and butter or margarine over low heat. Remove from heat. Blend in the sour cream, vanilla, and salt. Gradually add enough sifted confectioners' sugar to make frosting spreadable. Beat well. Spread over cooled cake.

*Wynona D. Lurie, Nashville, Tennessee*

# Sweetened Sauerkraut Salad

**2 1/2 cups sauerkraut, rinsed & drained**
**1 large sweet red onion, sliced**
**1 large pepper, cut in strips**
**1 small jar chopped red pimentos**
**2 cups celery, chopped**

Mix all ingredients well.

*Dressing:*
**1 cup sugar**
**1 tsp. salt**
**1/2 cup white vinegar**
**1/2 tsp. celery seed**

Heat the dressing ingredients in a medium pot over medium heat. Once warm, pour over sauerkraut mixture and let stand overnight. Serve cold.

*Eleanor Raddar, Elma, New York*

# Medicinal and other uses for Herbs

| | MAIN USE | MEDICINAL USE |
|---|---|---|
| **Basil** | Salads, soups, and casseroles with tomatoes, fish, chicken, or lamb. | A tonic against rheumatism, eases stomach pains. |
| **Bay Leaf** | Used to flavor soups, meats, tomato sauces, and casseroles. | Used externally for sprains and bruises. |
| **Caraway** | Breads, cakes, and salads. | Prevents colds, eases upset stomachs and throat infections. |
| **Chamomile** | Herbal teas, cosmetics, and hair preparations. | Helps combat headaches, toothaches, earaches and neuralgia. |
| **Chervil** | Egg and fish dishes, sauces, salads, and butters. | Lowers blood pressure, diuretic. |
| **Chives** | Egg, cheese, and vegetable dishes, soups, and salads. | Appetite enhancer. |
| **Cilantro** | Sauces, curries, and chutney. | Good for digestion. |
| **Dill** | Potatoes, salmon, pickles, sour cream sauces. | Aids digestion. |
| **Fennel** | Anise flavor used in pickles, biscuits, fish, or pork. | Appetite stimulant. |
| **Lavender** | Fruit salads, and grilled meats. Best known for its use in cosmetics and toiletries. | Antidepressant in aromatherapy, lowers blood pressure. |
| **Lemon Balm** | Stuffings, salad dressings, and potpourris. | Treats fever, aids poor digestion and nausea. |
| **Parsley** | Garnishes, flavoring for many foods. | General tonic, bad breath. |
| **Thyme** | Stuffings, roasts. Oil of thyme is used for perfumes. | An expectorant, antibacterial, and antiseptic. Gargle to ease sore throat. |

# A
## *Maple Sugaring*
# ACCOUNT

Engravings courtesy of
North Wind Picture Archives

*by* **JEAN GRIGSBY**
FREELANCE WRITER FROM WINTHROP, MAINE

**M**aple sugaring is a uniquely North American avocation. The process depends chiefly upon the sweet, watery sap of the sugar maple tree, *Acer saccharum*, also known as hard or rock maple, which is native to eastern North America. The sweet-water sap of the sugar maple is clear, thin, and only slightly sweet. The golden color and sweet, distinctive taste of maple sugar comes, almost magically, through the evaporation process.

While other varieties of maples are also used for syrup production, they produce saps with lower sugar contents. Many individuals have been bitterly disappointed when the red or silver maples they tapped failed to produce the liquid gold they craved. In addition, not all sugar maples are equal. Some have sap that runs more sweetly than others. It takes fewer gallons of this sweeter sap to make a gallon of syrup. Efforts to genetically predict and reproduce these sweet trees have already met with some success.

## A Taste of History

Prior to the arrival of European settlers, the Native Americans of the Great Lakes and St. Lawrence River regions of eastern North America produced maple syrup.

The Algonquin called it sinzibuckwud, which means "drawn from wood." Legend has it that the Native Americans discovered the sweetness of the maple tree by eating "sapsicles," icicles of frozen sap that form at the end of a broken maple twig. As the icicle forms, some of its water evaporates, leaving an icy sweet hanging from the tree.

Maple syrup production for the Native Americans was not radically different from sapsicle formation. They made notches in the trunks of maples and inserted reeds or concave pieces of bark to run the sap into birch-bark buckets. The sap was concentrated by throwing hot stones into the buckets. The mixture was boiled down into maple sugar, because it was easier to store solid sugar than syrup.

## From Sugarbushes to Sugarhouses

Native Americans taught early European settlers how to make maple sugar. Like the Native Americans, these settlers set up camps in maple groves, known as sugarbushes, but they also introduced many innovations and new materials to the maple sugaring process. They bored holes in the trees and hung their buckets on homemade spouts. They gathered their sap in wooden buckets and boiled it in a

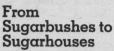

*continued*

series of large, iron kettles hanging over a fire. As the sap got thicker in one kettle, they ladled it into the next one and added fresh sap to the first kettle. In this way, they had the last kettle full of nearly completed sugar. They stirred the thickened, yet still liquid, sugar until it began to crystallize, then poured it into wooden molds.

Maple sugar became the most widely used sugar in early American households. Its production was especially important because the other types of sugar were more expensive and difficult to obtain. Thomas Jefferson and Benjamin Franklin were said to have advocated maple sugar production in order to make the Colonies less dependent on European sources of sugar.

By the late 1700s, an import tax on cane sugar was lifted, and, as a result, cane sugar quickly began to outsell maple sugar. This is when maple syrup became popular. Soon, maple syrup was being made and sold, though the production process was still affectionately referred to as maple sugaring, as it is to this day.

Although the fundamentals of maple sugar production have remained the same, the process has gone through some changes over time. One of the most notable changes was the introduction of the sugar evaporator, a flat pan with channels for the sap to flow through as it boils. The evaporator allows fresh sap to be added to one end and finished syrup to be drawn off the other. Also, a contained fire may be built under the evaporator, making the process more efficient by exposing a greater surface area to the heat of the fire. Other alterations have included the

building of shelters, known as sugarhouses or sugar shacks, where the sap is boiled. The sap must be boiled the same day it is gathered or it will sour. A sugarhouse allows a hot and steady fire to stay burning.

In recent years maple sugaring, especially as a commercial endeavor, has been modernized: sanitary methods for filtering and handling sap have been adopted; elaborate pipe or tubing systems are used to transport sap to storage tanks; and central evaporator plants have been established to serve whole communities of maple producers.

Today, there are more than 15,000 maple producers in the United States and Canada. Commercial quantities of maple syrup are produced (in order of amount) in Quebec, Vermont, New York, Ontario, Wisconsin, Ohio, Michigan, New Hampshire, Pennsylvania, Massachusetts, and Maine. Although those who manufacture them would argue this point vehemently, maple products are similar in quality over the different areas.

## Delicious and Nutritious

The best-known and most widely enjoyed maple product is, of course, table syrup for pancakes, French toast, and waffles. Maple syrup is boiled even further to produce maple cream, sugar, and candy; it takes one gallon of syrup to produce eight pounds of candy or sugar. And there are a staggering number of other maple products available today, including butters, dips, dressings, jams, jellies, mustards, sauces, and teas. Maple products are also used to add flavor to apples, bacon, baked beans, carrots, donuts, ham, squash, sweet potatoes, and more.

Consumers should be mindful that pure maple products will be labeled as such. Many maple products have corn or cane sugars added to the maple. Pure maple syrup has about the same number of calories per tablespoon as cane sugar (50), but also contains significant amounts of potassium (35 mg/tbsp), calcium (21 mg/tbsp), small amounts of iron and phosphorus, and trace amounts of B vitamins.

## "Mapling" the Grade

In the United States, pure maple syrup is graded on color and flavor in accordance with federal regulations. Some states use slightly different terminologies to describe the grades. Canadian grades, also regulated by the government, are similar to those used in the United States, but are based on the color of and the percentage of light that passes through the syrup, rather than the flavor. For example: Grade A Light Amber syrup is sometimes called Fancy Grade, and in Canada, it is called No. 1 Extra Light. Pure maple syrup is not graded based upon quality; therefore, one grade of maple syrup is not better than another.

Because sap production is a natural process, producers cannot control the syrup grade they make. As the season progresses, changes in the

**GRADE A LIGHT AMBER** is very light, has a mild, more delicate maple flavor, and is used for making maple candy and maple cream.
**GRADE A MEDIUM AMBER** is a bit darker, has a bit more maple flavor and is the most popular grade of table syrup.
**GRADE A DARK AMBER**, is darker yet, with a stronger maple flavor.
**GRADE B**, sometimes called cooking syrup, is very dark, with a very strong maple flavor, as well as some caramel flavor. Because of its strong flavor, it is most often used for baking, cooking, and as flavoring in specialty foods, although some prefer it for table use as well.

weather and in the maple trees themselves cause differences in maple syrups. As a rule of thumb, lighter syrup is made earlier in the season, and darker syrup is made later. Lighter syrup has a more delicate flavor; darker is more "mapley." During some years, most of the annual crop generated is light amber syrup, while other years yield almost no light syrup at all. Medium and dark amber are the most widely available grades.

## It's Sugar Time!

Exclusively a North American phenomenon, the maple sugaring season occurs in early spring when days are sunny and warm, 35 to 45 degrees (Fahrenheit), while nights are still below freezing. When several of these days occur in succession, the sap begins to flow. The season can begin as early as mid-January and end as late as mid-April, but it generally lasts four to six weeks. The sap flows throughout the season, but is heavy for only 10 to 20 days. Sap flowing in high volumes is called a "run." Warmer weather in the late spring, when nights remain above freezing and days warm into the 50s, causes leaf buds to swell. Budding alters the flavor of the syrup, and signals the end of the sugaring season.

*continued*

It takes only a few sugar maples to make a backyard sugarbush, because sugarbushes are measured not by the number of maple trees, but by the number of taps. Opinions vary about the size a tree needs to be for tapping and the number of taps per tree. Under the best conditions, sugar maples are tappable at 40 to 45 years of age and at least 12" in diameter at chest height. For each additional 8" to 10" diameter, another tap may be added. Some old maples may have as many as four taps. Each tap yields about ten gallons of sap over the whole season, which makes about one quart of syrup. On average, 30 to 50 gallons of sap are needed to make one gallon of syrup. If care is taken, tapping causes no permanent damage to the tree. Since only about 10% of the tree's sap is collected each year, a carefully tapped tree may yield sap for a century or more.

## See it for Yourself

During the season, many sugarhouses allow the public to observe the maple sugar production process and to indulge in a delicacy known as "sugar on snow," a rich taffy made by pouring hot, thick syrup over clean, fresh snow. Some sugarhouses serve pancakes or waffles covered with their freshly made pure maple syrup, as well as many other fresh maple treats.

Those who have visited a sugarhouse and witnessed the fascinating process of maple sugaring may undoubtedly want to try their hands at it. Maple sugaring can be done at home. There is an abundance of information available in books, through extension services, on the Internet, and from maple producers. Maple sugaring is a particularly good pastime to pursue with children; it has plenty of science and sweet results for them to savor.

# The many helpful uses of Baking Soda

### ☞ DOING DISHES?

Don't forget the baking soda. Add 2 heaping tablespoons of baking soda to your dishwater. It will help cut grease and loosen food on dishes, pots, and pans. For cooked-on, baked-on foods, soak in a baking soda and detergent mixture, then use dry baking soda on a damp sponge or cloth as a scratchless scouring powder.

### ☞ CLEANER FRUITS AND VEGETABLES

The experts agree—you should wash produce before consuming it. To clean more of the dirt, chemical residues, and waxes from all varieties of fruits and vegetables, use baking soda. Shake some onto wet produce, scrub, then rinse. Works better than water alone.

### ☞ REMOVE HAIR BUILDUP

For extraclean hair, try adding a small amount of baking soda (about the size of a quarter) to your shampoo. Wash, rinse, and condition as you normally would. The baking soda helps remove built-up residues from styling products and mineral-abundant waters.

### ☞ GREAT FOR DENTAL GEAR

Baking soda works well as a cleaner for dentures, retainers, or mouthguards. Add 2 teaspoons of baking soda to a bowl of water. Then soak dental gear for 5-10 minutes. Rinse with cold water after soaking.

---

### WHAT IS BAKING SODA?

Baking soda is sodium bicarbonate, a naturally occurring substance present in all living things. It helps living things maintain the pH balance necessary for life. Baking soda is made from soda ash, which is sodium carbonate. For more useful hints, check out www.armhammer.com

---

### ☞ CAMPING NECESSITY

Baking soda is a must for any camper. It can serve as a dish washer, pot scrubber, hand cleanser, deodorant, toothpaste, fire extinguisher, and first aid treatment for insect bites, sunburn and poison ivy, as well as much more. Plus, it saves space (one box compared to many products!).

### ☞ LAWN FURNITURE CLEANER

To clean and deodorize lawn and pool furniture, mix a solution of 1/4 cup baking soda to 1 quart of warm water. Wipe the furniture with this solution, then rinse clean. For tougher stains, sprinkle baking soda directly onto a damp sponge, scrub with it and rinse.

### ☞ FIRST AID

Relieve the itching and pain of an insect bite with a baking soda paste. After you have removed any stinger, make a paste by combining 3 parts baking soda to 1 part water. Apply it to the affected area and let it dry. Wash it off and repeat, if needed.

### ☞ NO MORE SMELLY DOGS

Instead of heading for the bathtub every time Fido smells, try giving him periodic dry baths. Rub dry baking soda into his fur, then comb or brush it through and out. Baking soda is nontoxic and safe for use on and around your pets.

The walls of a crumbling building lie along a tumbleweed-strewn trail. Winds howl through the bare timbers, while dark clouds loom over deserted horizons. What's left of a door creaks and groans in the winds, weathered from years of neglect and nature's fury. Nearby, the ground is barely marked with foundations of what were once homes, stores, hotels, and saloons. Remnants of rusted mining tools and cans are scattered among fragments of broken bottles and crockery that litter the landscape.

The faint whistle of an approaching narrow-gauge steam engine can almost be heard through the din of gunfighters cursing. Music from a piano pierces the crisp air, only to fade into oblivion. But the only voices left at this location are in the now-deserted cemetery, where fragile headstones lay unreadable, and heroes and villains lie forgotten. So many people lived and died here. Now, the only residents are hungry coyotes and rodents.

# GHOST TOWNS

## by TODD UNDERWOOD

Professional ghost towner and freelance writer located in Glendale, Arizona

## HOLLYWOOD SCENE OR ACTUAL TOWN?

While this description may seem more like a scene in an old Western movie, it actually depicts several thousand deserted places called ghost towns, located in the United States and Canada. Most of these ghost towns, once booming with activity, have vanished, returning to the elements from which they came. A few, however, still have a small number of residents hanging on to what once was.

## WHAT IS A GHOST TOWN?

Loosely defined, a ghost town is a location where people once lived, or are still living, that is a shadow of its past glory. Some, such as Bodie, California, appear just like a movie set. Others, such as Virginia City, Nevada, still have many residents and tourists. Still others, such as Meesville, Arizona, are hidden, or have vanished in a remote wilderness, taking all of their copious secrets with them.

No one knows the exact origin of the term "ghost town"; however, the phrase "ghost city" was popularized in the mid-1950s by the residents of Jerome, Arizona. They advertised their town as "the largest ghost city in America."

Most places now referred to as ghost towns lived and died in the mid to late 1800s. Their raison d'être is not as much of a puzzle as one might think. Most owe their existence to the mining booms of the 19th century. A small percentage originated because of agriculture or lumbering, and about the same percentage lived and died as stage stops along the Old West's frontier trails.

## THE LURE OF GHOST TOWNS

These broken-down, abandoned places are often as mysterious as their names. After all, who were the people who lived there; what were their names; where did they go; why did they leave; what brought them there in the first place are questions left unanswered.

The desire to answer these questions is often the motivation for people to search for and visit ghost towns, or even become "ghost towners." To many, there is simply nothing like the thrill of seeing and discovering the reasons behind a place and its people, especially those that are shrouded in mystery.

Visiting a ghost town allows one to reminisce about what it must have been like to have lived in the days of the "Old West"—when hopeful prospectors scoured the countryside in search of gold and other precious metals or gemstones.

Once a strike was located, a town could spring up almost overnight. Winding, dusty trails were made by wagons full of ebullient people and a plethora of equipment. As the mines were worked, streets were cleared, tents set up, and buildings and outhouses hastily constructed. In no more than a few weeks, there would be saloons, hotels, general stores, brothels, Chinese laundries, stables, and more. Some towns were lucky enough to become stops on the ever-increasing railroad routes. Such good fortune almost always meant growth and stability.

Unfortunately for the hard-working prospectors of yesterday, the precious ores they sought were not usually

*continued*

found in the most livable or accessible areas. The locations of most ghost towns make it apparent that the lust for gold and silver transcended all obstacles. Some ghost towns are perched on the sides of 14,000-foot mountain peaks that are buried under snow almost the entire year. Others are found in the harshest desert climates, miles from the nearest water.

**WHAT YOU MIGHT SEE** Ghost towns today vary widely in how much remains. The towns differed significantly in the construction techniques and materials which were used. In the mountainous areas, most towns were built of logs and had slanted roofs. There, neither wood nor water was scarce. Much thought was put into keeping warm and safe, especially if residents were to remain through the cold season. One of the most interesting characteristics of the mountain ghost town is the two-story outhouse, such as one in Lundbreck, Alberta (since moved). The not-uncommon ten-foot-plus snow drifts of the winter necessitated a second story for winter accessibility. Ironically, it is the winter snows that have preserved some of the mountains' ghost towns.

The desert region's towns were generally characterized by adobe walls and flat roofs. Wood and water were scarce there. It was rare to see wood buildings in the desert. On the rare occasion wood was used, the resourceful residents would disassemble their abodes and cart them off with them to the next town. Some desert towns have been completely obliterated due to flash floods and other harsh desert weather conditions.

**EASY COME... EASY GO** Most things in life don't last forever, especially the veins of ore that kept these towns alive. As the mines played out, people left in search of the next bonanza. Anxious residents often vacated these locations faster than they built them. Some towns were abandoned so quickly that food was left on kitchen tables and books were left on nightstands. Others were boarded up, as if there were thoughts of returning someday.

Ghost towns reveal the past. As we visit these historic reminders of our heritage and hear the echoes from days gone by, we need to remember the ghost towner's motto: "Take nothing but photographs, leave nothing but footprints."

## WHERE CAN YOU FIND MORE INFORMATION?

There are many resources available for people (or ghost towners) seeking to unravel the mysteries of specific ghost towns. The most comprehensive of these resources, for both American and Canadian ghost towns, is a Web site entitled Ghost towns (www.ghosttowns.com). This site not only lists ghost towns in the United States and Canada, but also contains pictures, histories, and locations. It is also a great place for ghost towners to communicate their findings, and share questions and experiences. Another great resource is the Web site called Frontier Trails (www.frontiertrails.com). Frontier Trails covers many of the events and circumstances which preceded the founding of the old towns, such as what stage routes and pioneer trails were used before the railroads began to cross the West.

**FAVORITE Quotations**

From the 1901 FARMERS' ALMANAC

"It is a secret known to but few, yet of no small use in the conduct of life, that when you fall into a man's conversation, the first thing you should consider is whether he has a greater inclination to hear you, or that you should hear him."

"The more we have read, the more we have learned, the more we have meditated, the better conditioned we are to affirm that we know nothing."

"Money never made a man happy yet, nor will it. There is nothing in its nature to produce happiness. The more a man has, the more he wants. Instead of its filling a vacuum, it makes one. If it satisfies one want, it doubles and trebles that want another way. That is a true proverb of the wise man, rely upon it: 'Better is little with the fear of the Lord, than great treasure and trouble therewith.' "

"Happiness must be cultivated. It is not a thing to be safely left alone for a moment, as it will run to weeds."

"It is not work that kills men, it is worry. Work is healthy; you can hardly put more upon a man than he can bear. Worry is rust upon the blade. It is not the revolution that destroys the machinery, but the friction. Fear secretes acids, but love and trust are sweet juices."

"Many people take no care of their money till they have come nearly to the end of it, and others do just the same with their time."

"Judgment is not a swift growing plant; it requires time and culture to mature it, while fancy often springs up and blossoms in a single hour. The fragrance of the first, however, is lasting, while that of the latter is as transient as its stem is fragile."

"Joy wholly from without is false, precarious and short. From without it may be gathered; but, like gathered flowers, though fair and sweet for a season, it must soon wither, and become offensive. Joy from within is like smelling the rose on the tree; it is more sweet and fair, it is lasting; and, I must add, immortal."

# Love Lobsters?

By Gordon Browne
Canadian travel writer.

## *Head for* **Prince Edward Island**

You only have to know three words to be well fed on Prince Edward Island: *Love That Lobster.* This province prides itself on its many community and church-sponsored lobster suppers that not only attract the locals but also the tourists. The star of these events is the Atlantic lobster, the tastiest of all the fruits of the sea. For most seafood lovers, lobster is number one.

Serious "scoffing," as the islanders call it, officially starts on the long holiday weekend in May and carries on well into October. "We never really get enough," said one happy diner, who had a wonderful mess of cracked, succulent lobster on her plate.

Community lobster suppers occur from one end of the island to the other. The "lobster trail" crisscrosses the island from Tignish in the north to Elmira or Souris (pronounced soo-ree) in the east. During the season, local newspapers carry announcements of the next church or community lobster supper.

"Mother's Day is one of our biggest days," says the New Glasgow's Sterling MacRae, describing the scene when hundreds come to PEI's oldest lobster supper restaurant. Mother's Day is the unofficial start of the spring lobster supper ritual, because it coincides with the start of the lobstering season.

## Lobsters go way back

Lobstering in PEI dates back over 200 years. Originally, lobsters were so plentiful fishermen just scooped them up from the shore in nets. Often they were spread across farmlands as fertilizer. Once canning was invented, thousands of tons were shipped across the ocean to meet European demand. As the lobster population declined in later years, traps were introduced, and lobstermen had to venture farther out to sea for the best catches.

Today, the season is closely regulated. There are about 1300 lobstering licenses issued in PEI. Mostly, it is a family business, with parents and older children working the gear, which includes the familiar wood-slatted traps. There are two seasons to fish for lobster; the first starts in May and goes until the end of June, and the second goes from mid-August until October.

## From rags to riches

Although lobster has long been a staple, stories abound on PEI about how lobster was the poor people's food, and how kids were embarrassed when they took lobster sandwiches to school. Yet somewhere along the way, the lobster gained full recognition for its distinctive taste—it is now prized as a delicacy by people around the globe.

## PEI's traditional suppers

Lobster suppers originally started as community events in small towns and villages as a way to help raise money for community activities and needs. They were officially introduced in PEI during the late 1950s. The New Glasgow Lobster Suppers are recognized as the first on the island. Although now operated as a family-owned, open-air restaurant, the first New Glasgow Lobster Supper in 1958 was a fundraising event held by the Junior Farmers of PEI. According to one of the founders, a current co-owner, the early lobster feasts served about 100 people at a time, a couple of times a year. The New Glasgow now serves over 50,000 pounds of lobster annually.

*continued*

While the New Glasgow was one of the first lobster supper events in PEI, the Fisherman's Wharf Lobster Suppers, located in the fishing community of North Rustico a few miles from New Glasgow,

**Ellie and Rosemary Macdonald, organizing the Little Pond Lobster Suppers since 1966.**

is a main competitor. It is known not only for its high-quality lobsters, but also for a 60-foot salad bar and the unlimited chowder served as part of the meal. The Fisherman's Wharf served its first lobster event on Mother's Day 1980.

Traditional lobster suppers continue to be a mainstay as fundraising events, supporting community centres or churches, in places like Tignish, Alberton, St. Margarets, Little Pond and others. However, to meet the growing demand (mostly from tourists), commercially run lobster suppers such as the New Glasgow and the Fisherman's Wharf have become very popular.

## Lobster done your way

Of course, there are many ways to enjoy PEI lobster. Julie Watson, island resident and author of the book, *Largely Lobster*, recalls that the very best lobster she ever had was at the home of a friend's parents, where they cooked up a huge pot full of lobster over a fire in the backyard. "They used sea water, brought in on the boat, and lobster caught that morn-

ing. The table was covered with layers of newspaper. We had big, wooden chopping blocks and a bunch of cleavers to whack the lobster and break the shells with. All they served with it was vinegar, mayonnaise, rolls and butter. No plates, just rolls of paper towels . . . was I stuffed. Think I ate 10 or 12 lobsters that night."

## Where can you find these feasts?

Watch for the local community ads in newspapers and on bulletin boards. They list smaller, community suppers. The large commercial restaurants are open every day from early June until Columbus Day.

Well-known lobster suppers (all within a half-hour drive from Charlottetown, PEI's capital city) include: • New Glasgow Lobster Suppers • World-Famous Fisherman's Wharf Lobster Suppers, North Rustico • St. Anne Lobster Suppers • St. Margaret's Lobster Suppers.

## Getting there

The major airlines have flights to Halifax, Nova Scotia, with connections, or direct flights, into Charlottetown, PEI's capital. If you're traveling by car from the mainland, cross from New Brunswick on the Confederation Bridge, which takes about 15 minutes.

# The Island

Prince Edward Island, on Canada's east coast, is its smallest province, only 174 miles long and about 37 miles wide. It is an ideal province for touring by car or bike. Aside from lobster, PEI is known for potatoes, Malpeque oysters, and wonderful cultured mussels. With dozens of bed-and-breakfasts, and a growing reputation for outstanding cuisine, dining is something around which visitors can easily plan a vacation.

---

**TABLE TIPS:** At the table, eating lobster is a delightfully messy affair. A bib, lemon and clarified butter for dipping, a shell cracker, and a lobster fork are essential. It's mostly a hands-on affair, but using the fork you can pick out the small morsels from the legs, claws and knuckles. The bib gives protection from the wonderful juices that burst from the recesses and hollows when a lobster is pulled apart. The tail is split with a knife and pried open, and the meat is eaten with a fork, if there's one handy.

**The best lobsters are freshly cooked, usually about ten minutes in a pot of boiling, salted water.** One-pound lobsters are widely served, although a one and one-half or two-pounder is a special treat. Some lobster lovers prefer their lobster cold or grilled, rather than boiled. A true lobster supper includes mashed potatoes, potato salad or cole slaw, vegetables, and a delicious dessert.

Twist off the claws.

Insert a fork where the flippers broke off and push.

Crack each claw with a nutcracker.

Unhinge the back from body. This contains the "tomalley" or liver.

Separate the tailpiece from the body by arching the back until it cracks.

Open the remaining part of the body by cracking sideways. Good meat here.

Bend back and break the flippers off the tail.

The small claws are excellent eating. The meat can be sucked out.

*It's not what you think it is.*

# The Grange

**by RICHARD WEISS**

**From potluck suppers to town hall meetings to poetry, writing, photography, and art competitions, the Grange offers family-oriented alternatives to malls, movies, coffee bars, and other forms of entertainment...**

Throughout the American countryside, there are certain structures that are almost automatically identified with rural communities, and which conjure up images of our agricultural heritage: the courthouse standing tall in the town square, the co-op with its brimming silos, perhaps a library, and, in thousands of rural communities, the Grange hall. While most people easily associate these symbolic buildings with certain functions; governance, trade, or education; for many, the Grange hall remains a mystery.

A friend once asked, "I see these Grange halls all over the place. What are they? Who are these people? What do they do?" That friend is not alone in asking those questions. Some people often say, "The Grange is the best kept secret in town."

## What is the Grange?

Many familiar only with the name think of it as a farmers' organization. When founded in 1867 by Oliver Kelley, an employee of the then newly created Department of Agriculture, it was to be a fraternal organization composed of farmers from all over the country.

Its mission was to help heal the scars caused by the Civil War and to improve the farmers' economic and social positions.

While still a champion of farmers' rights, today's Grange is a surprising combination of social, civic, bipartisan political and educational activities.

The Grange is an advocacy organization for all rural Americans, not just farmers. In addition to addressing farm-specific issues, the Grange's "Blueprint for Rural America" includes platforms for using federal resources to improve rural education, delegating utility deregulation to the states, and improving rural healthcare through rates and services competitive with urban areas. Through a very sophisticated resolution system, starting at the Subordinate (local) Grange level, Granges determine what issues the organization will be involved in at the local, county, state, and national level. The Grange is truly a grassroots organization.

The Grange's current 300,000 members are proof of its evolution to a broad organization. Today's Granges are made up of insurance agents, hospital administrators, homemakers, lawyers, teachers, and many others involved in the rural community. Men and women have always had equal voices and votes in the Grange, and today women hold national, state, and local offices, including President or "Master," as the office is termed in the Grange.

> **The Grange's current 300,000 members are proof of its evolution to a broad organization.**

## Community service, the Grange's heart and soul

The Grange is much more than an advocacy organization. Granges serve as vehicles for those who want to give something back to their communities. Community service is the heart and soul of every local Grange. Programs vary from town to town, but there is an emphasis on helping the disadvantaged, improving community infrastructures, and recognizing community servants. Granges adopt roads, clean parks, build bus shelters, visit the elderly, make stuffed toys for disadvantaged children and children dealing with trauma, and help feed the poor in 3,600 Grange localities in 37 states. Local, county, and state Granges also help implement the national health project, Deaf Activities, that serves thousands of hearing-impaired people.

## A nurturing place for the young

Young people are important to the Grange. The Junior Grange is a distinct unit open to children ages 5 to 14. Junior Grangers have their own rituals and degree work, conduct education hours at their meetings, provide wholesome social activities, and undertake community service projects of their own, all guided by a Subordinate Grange adult. Upon reaching 14 years of age, most Junior Grangers graduate into the parent Grange. At that stage, they participate in the full range of Grange programs, as well as enjoy special youth and young adult

*continued*

programs, such as camps, conferences, essay writing and speaking contests, and many other activities that prepare them for adulthood. Young Grangers also have an opportunity to participate in the National Youth Team, which travels the country helping other Granges with their youth programs.

## Creative competition

The Grange is also a place where one can demonstrate a creative talent and perhaps gain national recognition. Each year, the Grange sponsors competitions in art, photography, prose or poetry writing, sewing, knitting, and stuffed toy making. Entries from the Subordinate Granges are judged at state levels, and state winners are sent to the National Convention, where their entries are judged and national awards are presented. While the sewing, knitting, and stuffed toy competitions are sponsored by the Women's Activities Department, they are open to everyone, men included. The Women's Activities competitions are also open to non-members, and serve as a means of introducing the Grange to the general public.

## An annual celebration

The annual convention is a celebration held each fall, always in a different Grange state. It draws close to 5,000 members. While delegates continue the resolution process to identify the coming year's issues, members and the public roam the exhibit hall viewing the winning entries in community service projects, and the arts and crafts. The weeklong convention is a festive affair. It includes a talent show, a public speaking contest, banquets, and a "Sign-a-Song" contest for singing a song in sign language.

## Origins of the Grange

Southern agriculture lay in ruins after the Civil War. Many farms, with no men to work them, had become overgrown with weed and thatch. Retreating or invading troops had devastated other farms, and confiscated and eaten most of the livestock in the South. Large plantation owners, formerly dependent on slave labor, faced dim prospects for finding workers from a male population decimated by the war. One of Oliver Kelley's first Department of Agriculture assignments was a commission from President Johnson.

**Oliver Kelley**
GRANGE FOUNDER

His job was to survey Southern farm conditions following the Civil War, with a view to mending the rifts between North and South, and to creating a united farm community. Though a farmer himself, Kelley was regarded suspiciously because he was a Northerner, and so he could not create farmer-to-farmer dialogues. Eventually, he realized that many Southern farmers were Masons like him. By invoking this brotherhood, Kelley was able to communicate as Mason to Mason.

That experience gave Kelley the idea of using a brotherhood or fraternity to bring farmers back together. As he put it, "Politicians would never restore peace in the country; if it came at all, it must be through fraternity. The people North and South must know each other as members of the same great family, and all sectionalism be abolished." Besides mending North-South relations, Kelley reasoned that such an organization would give all farmers more leverage in the marketplace, where they were at the mercy of equipment suppliers, the railroads, and assorted middlemen.

## A farmers' fraternity with a woman's touch

One of the first people to hear Kelley's idea was his niece Caroline A. Hall. She is credited with convincing Kelley to make the Grange the first national fraternal organization to admit women, and to give them equal standing with men. On December 4, 1867, the Patrons of Husbandry was founded by seven men and Hall, in Washington, D.C.

The group decided that the term "Grange," which means farm or farmhouse, was to apply to local units. Kelley immediately resigned his government position and devoted his time to establishing Subordinate Granges throughout the country. The dues from those Subordinates paid his $2,000 per year salary. Initially, he had little success. Not until he arrived in Minnesota and started promoting the Grange as a means for farmers to purchase supplies and equipment on a group basis (thus avoiding middlemen, and forcing suppliers to give quantity discounts), did the Grange concept catch on. Soon it was being hailed as the farmers' protector. By the end of 1873, there were over 1,000 Granges in 31 states.

## Degrees and ritual

The Grange founders were very concerned that American farmers in the mid-19th century were not keeping up with progressive farming methods and were ignorant of the basics of agricultural science. In an 1867 letter to fellow founder William Saunders, Kelley wrote, "Of the science of agriculture, the natural laws that govern growth of plants and kindred subjects of pleasing and vital interest to farmers, when once they turn their attention to them, there was ninety percent who were totally ignorant." The founders made farmer education an important Grange mission.

Achieving that mission was not so easy in the 1860s and 1870s. Literacy among farmers was low, and even though there were many farm publications, "book farming" was limited

*continued*

to a few. How, then, to transmit this wealth of knowledge to simple farmers? Kelley and the founders determined that to become full-fledged Grange members, candidates had to earn "degrees" by participating in a series of rituals that were like short plays, each demonstrating some aspect of agriculture. The rituals also expressed the underlying Grange philosophy of self-improvement through cooperative effort and each carried a moral message. The degree rituals and the meeting-opening ceremony are still the same in all 3,600 Granges across the country. Just as in the beginning, the rituals and ceremonies give the Order of Patrons of Husbandry a unique identification in this day and age.

One must achieve the first four degrees, conveyed at the Subordinate level, to be considered a full-fledged Grange member. The four rituals are based on the four seasons, and, though held indoors, all four are held in a farm-like setting, using fruits, flowers and grains as parts of the ceremonies.

While many of today's Granges have "undegreed" members, they are encouraged to participate in the rituals and receive the four degrees. The rituals contain prose, poetry and music. They are very positive, and convey some very basic moral messages that apply today just as they did 133 years ago.

## A new century—A new Grange

As the new century unfolds, the 133-year-old Grange looks forward to new growth and prosperity. As it has in the past, the Grange will adjust to the needs and wants of an evolving society. New programs and services, such as low-cost, long-distance calling and Internet access, insurance and other benefits, will appeal to newcomers. But it is likely to be the old core values of family, friendship, community service, and charity that will sustain the Grange through the 21st century. More and more Americans want to strengthen their family ties, while helping others and improving their communities. What better vehicle is there to achieving these goals than the "new" Grange?

Richard Weiss is a communications consultant to the National Grange, and the proprietor of The Weiss Consultancy, a communications firm based in Washington, D.C. To get more information about the Grange, check out www.nationalgrange.org or call 1-888-447-2643.

## Norm Dvoskin's
# WEATHER WIT

- **ICY COMMUTE**
  Crawl Waiting

- **TORNADO FORECASTERS**
  Windfall Prophets

- **VERNAL EQUINOX**
  Season's Greenings

- **EARTH CELEBRATION**
  Groundhug Day

- **CHRISTMAS FORECAST**
  Toynadoes

- **EXORBITANT**
  An expensive satellite that has fallen

- **NORWEGIAN METEOROLOGIST**
  A Fjordcaster

- **SPRING**
  When golfers get that fairway look in their eyes

- **JUNE THUNDERSTORMS**
  Summer come loudly

- **WINTER DRIVING CLOTHES**
  Long Honda Wear

- **APRIL SHOWERS**
  Petal Pushers

- **COLORFUL SUNRISE**
  Hues on First

# *Don't* Throw It Away!

## Here are some easy and useful ways to reuse and recycle!

### Coffee Cans

Empty coffee cans (1 lb.) make great:

✔ Storage places for nails, screws, and small tools (write contents on plastic lid).

✔ Outdoor citronella candles. Place candle in can and light. When not in use, let candle cool then top with plastic lid.

✔ Baking pans. Bake breads (pumpkin, banana, etc.) in can. Good size and if you decorate the can, it can serve as a great gift.

✔ Fund-raisers. Decorate empty coffee cans and fill with cookies/brownies. Sell at bake sales and other fund-raising events.

### Spice Jars

✔ Empty spice jars that have perforated inner lids can be reused for your own cinnamon and sugar mixture; cornstarch or flour for making gravy; or dispensing sprinkles.

### Empty Jelly Or Honey Jars

✔ Great jars for homemade salad dressings, homemade mustards, and homemade candy. The fancier they are, the better.

### Large Clear Jars

✔ Good food keepers, especially in the refrigerator. Make it easy to see what's in there!

### Wrapping Paper Cardboard Tubes

✔ Wrap your holiday lights around empty tubes. Prevents tangling —easy storage.

### Empty Paper Towel Tubes

✔ Use to store tongs in drawers. Keeps tongs closed, so they take up less room.

### Plastic Milk Containers

✔ Store sugar. Easy to pour and sugar won't lump.

✔ Fill with rice, small pasta, dried beans, used lemons (yes, used lemons).

✔ Save partly used lemons, put them in your dishwater. They make the water, dishes and your hands smell good. Also cut grease.

"Never shampoo a carpet when it's new. It will get dirty faster."

Carpets don't get dirty faster after first shampoo if you do it correctly. Follow directions.

"Toothpaste and peanut butter remove black marks" (walls).

They remove black marks but are abrasive and leave dull patches, especially on enamel paint.

## Is there any truth to these *Old Wives' Tales?*

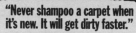

# FARMERS' ALMANAC™
# STORE

The *Farmers' Almanac* Store combines good old-fashioned value with priceless gems of nostalgia. We offer a friendly, hometown way for you to purchase your favorite *Farmers' Almanac* products, without having to leave the comfort of your own home. If you prefer to shop online, check out www.farmersalmanac.com

### 2001 *Farmers' Almanac*

Best known for its weather forecasts, the *Farmers' Almanac* also contains useful information, bits of nostalgia, gardening tips, seasonal recipes, humor, best fishing days, entertaining short stories and much more.

**$4.99 FA-01 FARET**

### *Farmers' Almanac* Weather Stick

Straight from the Maine woods, this balsam fir weather forecaster really works! Hang it from an outside wall or door casing and watch it bend down to predict foul weather, up to predict good weather!

**$4.95 FA03**

### *Farmers' Almanac* Cap

Whether you're sipping coffee on the deck, or taking on bolder outdoor pursuits, our attractive *Farmers' Almanac* cap will stylishly shade your head and eyes from the sun.

**$6.95 FA05**

## Farmers' Almanac Norman Rockwell 2001 Calendar

Talk about two all-time American favorites! This calendar combines the charm and appeal of Norman Rockwell's famous illustrations with wise-old weather predictions, wit, and wisdom from the *Farmers' Almanac*.

**$5.99 FA-01 FAROCK**

## Farmers' Almanac Sampler 2001 Calendar

Monthly morsels to enjoy and employ are what you'll find in this old-time calendar that reflects on simpler times. Each month features a 19th-century steel engraving of a nostalgic scene, along with recipes, zodiac readings, weather predictions and more.

**$6.99 FA-01 FASAMP**

---

### TO ORDER: Please complete the order form and mail to:

**Farmers' Almanac Order Desk, Mt. Hope Ave., Lewiston, Maine 04240.**

**(PLEASE DO NOT USE A P.O. BOX. PLEASE PRINT CLEARLY.)**

## CREDIT CARD ORDERS CALL: 1-888-222-4276

Please check your payment method: ☐ Check (No cash or C.O.D.)  ☐ MasterCard  ☐ VISA  ☐ AMERICAN EXPRESS

Card Number: _____  Exp. Date: _____  Signature: _____

SHIP TO: Name _____

| Address | City | State | Zip | | |
|---|---|---|---|---|---|

| Item No. | Description | Price Each | Quantity | Total |
|---|---|---|---|---|
| | | | | |
| | | | | |
| | | | | |
| | | | | |
| | | | | |

| | SHIPPING CHARGES | | |
|---|---|---|---|
| All orders shipped UPS Ground or U.S. Mail. Please call for expedited shipping charges or information. | Up to $4.99–$1.95<br>$5.00 to $13.99–$2.95<br>$14.00 to $24.99–$3.95<br>$25.00 to $49.99–$4.95 | Merchandise Total | |
| | | Applicable Sales Tax | |
| | | Shipping (see left) | |
| | | **TOTAL** | |

## RICHARD LEDERER

# Our Seaworthy Language

Richard Lederer is a contributing editor for the *Farmers' Almanac* and a well-known verbalist.

Relatively few of us go down to the seas anymore, and even fewer of us get to steer a tall ship. Having lost our intimacy with the sea and with sailing, we no longer taste the salty flavor of the metaphors that ebb and flow through our language.

Consider our use of the word *ship*. We continue to ship goods, even when that shipping is done by truck, train, or plane. We compliment someone on "running a tight ship," even when that "ship" is an office or a classroom. And many things besides ships can be shipshape or sinking ships.

The lapping of the sea at our language is not a difficult concept to fathom. When we try to *fathom* an idea, we are making poetic use of an old word that originally meant "the span between two outstretched arms." Then the word came to mean "a unit of six feet used for measuring the depth of water." By poetic extension the verb *to fathom* now means "to get to the bottom of" something, and that something doesn't have to be the ocean.

To help you learn the ropes and get

*In "Sea Fever" (1902), the poet JOHN MASEFIELD sang:*

*I must down to the seas again, to the lonely sea and the sky, And all I ask is a tall ship and a star to steer her by*

your bearings with seafaring metaphors, take a turn at the helm. The coast is clear for you to sound out the lay of the land by taking a different tack and playing a landmark game. Don't go overboard by barging ahead. If you feel all washed up, on the rocks, in over your head, and sinking fast in a wave of confusion, try to stay on an even keel. As your friendly anchorman, I won't rock the boat by lowering the boom on you.

Now that you get my drift, consider how the following idioms of sailing and the sea sprinkle salt on our tongues: *shape up or ship out, to take the wind out of his sails, the tide turns, a sea of faces, down the hatch, hit the deck, to steer clear of, don't rock the boat, to harbor a grudge,* and *to give a wide berth to.* For ancient mariners, *by and large* was a command that meant "to sail slightly off the wind," in contrast to "full and by." When we say *by and large* today, we mean "in general; for the most part" because we do not wish to sail directly into the topic. The expression *taken aback* probably conjures up in your mind an image of a person caught off guard and staggering backwards. But the origin of the phrase is nautical, too: *sailing by and large* left an inexperienced helmsman in less danger of being *taken aback,* which meant "to catch the wind on the wrong side of the sails."

I trust you won't be taken aback by the armada of additional salty words and seafaring metaphors:

From the Greek word for "ship," we inherit a word that means "illness" but that originally signified "seasickness." That word is *nauseated.* Feeling nauseated on shipboard can force one to go below deck to recover. That's where we get the expression *under the weather.*

The long, narrow central hall of a cruciform church gets its name from *navis,* the Latin word for "ship," because the church is thought of as an ark for its congregants. Many of these long corridors do indeed resemble upside-down ships, and ships are often built bottoms up. These corridors are called *naves.*

The lee is the side of the ship sheltered from the wind. Hence, when we make things easy for others, we give them *leeway.*

On sailing ships of yesteryear, the "butt" was a popular term for the large, lidded casks that held drinking water. These butts were equipped with "scuttles," openings through which sailors ladled out the water. Just as today's office workers gather about a water cooler to exchange chitchat and rumor, crewmen stood about the scuttled butts to trade *scuttlebutt.*

Old salts used to describe a ship in shallow water touching bottom from time to time with the phrase which has been extended to designate any precarious situation

as *touch and go.* A much worse situation is one in which a ship strikes bottom and is held tight, unable to proceed. Today, we use the expression *hard and fast* to identify any rigid rule or opinion.

The doldrums are those parts of the ocean near the Equator that are noted for calm and neutral weather. They pose no difficulty for fuel-driven vessels, but for sailing ships they mean a dead standstill. When we are stuck in boredom or depression, we are *in the doldrums.*

Like a vessel driven ashore beyond the normal high-water mark, one who is abandoned or rejected is left *high and dry.*

Ships' colors used to be raised and lowered a peg at a time. The higher the colors, the greater the honor. Nowadays, we diminish others' self-esteem by *taking them down a peg.*

In sailing parlance, "devil" is not he of the forked tail, but a nautical term for the seam between two planks in the hull of a ship, on or below the water line. Anyone who had to caulk such a "devil" was figuratively caught between a rock and a hard place, or *between the devil and the deep blue sea.*

For sailors, "sheets" refer to the lines attached to the lower corner of a sail. When all three sheets of an old sailing vessel were allowed to run free, they were said to be "in the wind," and the ship would lurch and stagger. That's why we call an unsteady state of drunkenness *three sheets to the wind.*

Seafaring folk called the posts they secured cables to "bitts," and the turn of the cable around the bitts the "bitter." When a ship rides out a gale, the anchor cable is let out to just the place that this article has reached—*the bitter end.*

# 2001 ATLANTIC COAST TIDE TABLES

## COMPARED TO THE BATTERY

### BY THE NATIONAL OCEANIC & ATMOSPHERIC ADMINISTRATION

These are average values. To find the approximate time of high tide at any given point on the Atlantic Coast, find the time of high tide at the Battery, N.Y., on the date desired and then add or subtract the difference in time as indicated in the tables below. Note: Conventional Daylight Saving Time is used.

**REFERENCE STATIONS — CORR. H. M.**

| Station | Corr. | Station | Corr. | Station | Corr. |
|---|---|---|---|---|---|
| Bar Harbor, Me. | +2 20 | Newport, R.I. | -1 05 | Atlantic City, N.J. | -1 05 |
| Eastport, Me. | +2 25 | Point Judith, R.I. | -55 | Cape May, N.J. | -45 |
| Portland, Me. | +2 35 | Providence, R.I. | -55 | Newark, N.J. | +50 |
| Rockland, Me. | +2 20 | Block Isl. Hbr., R.I. | -1 05 | Toms River, N.J. | +4 05 |
| Portsmouth, N.H. | +2 55 | Bridgeport, Conn. | +2 55 | Ocean City, Md. | -1 05 |
| Isle of Shoals, N.H. | +2 40 | New London, Conn. | +1 05 | Norfolk, Va. | +1 00 |
| Barnstable, Mass. | +3 05 | New Haven, Conn. | +2 50 | Beaufort, N.C. | -05 |
| Boston, Mass. | +2 45 | Stamford, Conn. | +2 55 | Cape Hatteras, N.C. | -1 15 |
| Falmouth, Mass. | +2 05 | Bayshore, L.I., N.Y. | +2 00 | Southport, N.C. | -25 |
| Gloucester, Mass. | +2 40 | Orient, L.I., N.Y. | +1 45 | Beaufort, S.C. | +35 |
| Harwichport, Mass. | +3 20 | Oyster Bay, N.Y. | +3 00 | Charleston, S.C. | -30 |
| Edgartown, Mass. | +3 25 | Sag Harbor, N.Y. | +2 05 | Georgetown, S.C. | +1 25 |
| Nantucket, Mass. | +3 35 | Asbury Park, N.J. | -55 | Brunswick, Ga. | +25 |
| Plymouth, Mass. | +2 45 | | | Savannah, Ga. | +20 |
| New Bedford, Mass. | -55 | | | Jacks'ville (Bdg.), Fla. | +2 05 |
| Newburyport, Mass. | +3 25 | | | Miami Yht. Ban., Fla. | +1 25 |
| Vineyd. Hvn., Mass. | +2 55 | | | Palm Beach (OCEAN), Fla. | -35 |
| Salem, Mass. | +2 40 | | | Fort Pierce (CITY DOCK), Fla. | +1 45 |
| Wellfleet, Mass. | +3 05 | | | Daytona Beach (OCEAN), Fla. | -35 |

- SHADED AREA = DST
- **+** DATE OF HIGHEST HIGH TIDE
- **-** DATE OF LOWEST LOW TIDE
- **A** TIME CHANGES FROM P.M. TO A.M.
- **P** TIME CHANGES FROM A.M. TO P.M.

## 2001 DAYLIGHT HIGH TIDES (EST) FOR NEW YORK CITY AT THE BATTERY
### Converted to Daylight Saving Time - April 1 through October 27

| Day | JAN | FEB | MAR | APR | MAY | JUN | JUL | AUG | SEP | OCT | NOV | DEC |
|---|---|---|---|---|---|---|---|---|---|---|---|---|
| 1 | 12:27 P | 1:20 P | 12:04 P | 3:05 P | 4:13 P | 5:55 P | 6:25 P | 7:22 A | 8:28 A | 8:35 A | 8:07 A | 8:14 A |
| 2 | 1:10 | 2:20 | 12:57 | 4:21 | 5:18 | 6:48 | 7:15 | 8:09 | 9:06 | 9:09 | 8:38 | 8:54 |
| 3 | 2:01 | 3:38 | 2:02 | 5:33 | 6:17 | 7:11 A | 7:41 A | 8:52 | 9:42 | 9:41 | 9:11 | 9:41 |
| 4 | 3:02 | 4:59 | 3:24 | 6:36 | 7:09 | 8:00 | 8:28 | 9:33 | 10:17 | 10:10 | 9:50 | 10:36 |
| 5 | 4:14 | 6:05 | 4:45 | 6:59 | 7:32 A | 8:46 | 9:12 | 10:13 | 10:50 | 10:39 | 10:40 | 11:37 |
| 6 | 5:22 | 6:30 A | 5:51 | 7:52 A | 8:20+ | 9:31 | 9:56 | 10:53 | 11:20 | 11:12 | 11:40 | 12:37 P |
| 7 | 6:20 | 7:24 | 6:16 A | 8:40 | 9:06- | 10:17 | 10:41 | 11:32 | 11:51 | 11:55 | 12:43 P | 1:36 |
| 8 | 6:46 A | 8:15+ | 7:09 | 9:28+- | 9:52 | 11:05 | 11:26 | 12:08 P | 12:28 P | 12:48 P | 1:48 | 2:38 |
| 9 | 7:37 | 9:07- | 7:59+ | 10:15 | 10:39 | 11:54 | 12:10 P | 12:43 | 1:13 | 1:48 | 2:55 | 3:42 |
| 10 | 8:29+- | 10:01 | 8:49- | 11:04 | 11:29 | 12:42 P | 12:52 | 1:17 | 2:07 | 2:56 | 4:03 | 4:44 |
| 11 | 9:23 | 10:54 | 9:39 | 11:54 | 12:19 P | 1:28 | 1:31 | 1:55 | 3:10 | 4:10 | 5:05 | 5:42 |
| 12 | 10:19 | 11:47 | 10:29 | 12:44 P | 1:09 | 2:12 | 2:08 | 2:41 | 4:24 | 5:22 | 6:01 | 6:12 A |
| 13 | 11:16 | 12:39 P | 11:20 | 1:35 | 1:59 | 2:56 | 2:47 | 3:49 | 5:39 | 6:25 | 6:30 A | 7:44+- |
| 14 | 12:12 P | 1:31 | 12:11 P | 2:27 | 2:49 | 3:42 | 3:32 | 4:48 | 6:43 | 7:20 | 7:17 | 8:28 |
| 15 | 1:06 | 2:26 | 1:02 | 3:22 | 3:40 | 4:31 | 4:26 | 5:58 | 7:17 A | 7:50 A | 8:02+- | 9:13 |
| 16 | 2:00 | 3:25 | 1:55 | 4:20 | 4:34 | 5:22 | 5:26 | 6:59 | 8:09 | 8:37 | 8:48 | 9:58 |
| 17 | 2:57 | 4:29 | 2:53 | 5:20 | 5:26 | 6:12 | 6:25 | 7:33 A | 8:58+ | 9:24- | 9:34 | 10:43 |
| 18 | 3:57 | 5:28 | 3:57 | 6:13 | 6:14 | 6:59 | 6:54 A | 8:27 | 9:47- | 10:11+ | 10:23 | 11:29 |
| 19 | 4:58 | 6:18 | 4:58 | 6:59 | 6:57 | 7:23 A | 7:50 | 9:18+ | 10:37 | 11:00 | 11:13 | 12:13 P |
| 20 | 5:53 | 6:37 A | 5:50 | 7:14 A | 7:15 A | 8:11 | 8:43 | 10:11 | 11:30 | 11:52 | 12:03 P | 12:56 |
| 21 | 6:42 | 7:18 | 6:07 A | 7:54 | 7:57 | 9:00 | 9:36+ | 11:05- | 12:23 P | 12:44 P | 12:52 | 1:40 |
| 22 | 7:01 A | 7:57 | 6:50 | 8:32 | 8:38 | 9:52+ | 10:32- | 11:59 | 1:16 | 1:37 | 1:42 | 2:27 |
| 23 | 7:41 | 8:33 | 7:29 | 9:08 | 9:19 | 10:49- | 11:30 | 12:53 P | 2:09 | 2:29 | 2:33 | 3:22 |
| 24 | 8:20 | 9:08 | 8:05 | 9:44 | 10:06 | 11:49 | 12:26 P | 1:46 | 3:04 | 3:24 | 3:28 | 4:21 |
| 25 | 8:57 | 9:40 | 8:39 | 10:22 | 11:00 | 12:48 P | 1:21 | 2:40 | 4:01 | 4:21 | 4:23 | 5:18 |
| 26 | 9:33 | 10:11 | 9:12 | 11:03 | 12:01 P | 1:44 | 2:15 | 3:35 | 5:02 | 5:18 | 5:14 | 6:08 |
| 27 | 10:08 | 10:42 | 9:44 | 12:02 P | 1:01 | 2:39 | 3:09 | 4:34 | 5:59 | 6:11 | 6:00 | 6:08 |
| 28 | 10:40 | 11:19 | 10:20 | 1:03 | 2:00 | 3:35 | 4:05 | 5:35 | 6:49 | 5:57 | 6:25 A | 6:31 A |
| 29 | 11:12 | | 11:04 | 2:04 | 2:58 | 4:32 | 5:04 | 6:30 | 7:19 A | 6:25 A | 7:02 | 7:13 |
| 30 | 11:48 | | 11:56 | 3:07 | 3:57 | 5:30 | 6:01 | 7:18 | 7:59 | 7:01 | 7:38 | 7:57 |
| 31 | 12:30 P | | 12:57 P | | 4:57 | | 6:54 | 7:47 | | 7:35 | | 8:43 |

# 2001 PACIFIC COAST TIDE TABLES

## COMPARED TO REFERENCE STATIONS

These are average values. To find the approximate time of high tide at any given point on the Pacific Coast, find the time of high tide at the reference station on the date desired and then add or subtract the difference in time as indicated in the tables below. Note: Conventional Daylight Saving Time is used.

| REFERENCE STATIONS | CORR. H. M. |
|---|---|
| **SAN FRANCISCO** | |
| Santa Cruz, Calif. | -1 10 |
| Oakland, Calif. | +35 |
| San Mateo, Calif. | +1 05 |
| Richmond, Calif. | +25 |
| Vallejo, Calif. | +1 55 |
| Port Chicago, Calif. | +3 05 |
| Eureka, Calif. | +55 |
| Wedderburn, Oregon | +30 |
| Coos Bay, Oregon | +1 55 |
| Newport, Oregon | +35 |
| Astoria, Oregon | +1 35 |
| Ilwaco, Wash. | +1 45 |
| South Bend, Wash. | +1 35 |
| Aberdeen, Wash. | +1 45 |
| Neah Bay, Wash. | +1 05 |

| | |
|---|---|
| **LOS ANGELES** | |
| San Diego, Calif. | +10 |
| Santa Monica, Calif. | +1 20 |
| Ventura, Calif. | +10 |
| Catalina Harbor, Calif. | +10 |
| Port San Luis, Calif. | +50 |
| **SEATTLE** | |
| Port Townsend, Wash. | -50 |
| Bremerton, Wash. | +10 |
| Tacoma, Wash. | +05 |
| Olympia, Wash. | +45 |
| Everett, Wash. | -05 |
| Anacortes, Wash. | -20 |
| Bellingham, Wash. | +10 |

- □ SHADED AREA = DST
- \+ DATE OF HIGHEST HIGH TIDE
- – DATE OF LOWEST LOW TIDE
- A TIME CHANGES FROM P.M. TO A.M.
- P TIME CHANGES FROM A.M. TO P.M.

The data provided in the following tables were derived from the computer program TIDES developed by Mr. Edward P. Wallner. For more information about this program, contact him at: 32 Barney Hill Road, Wayland, Mass. 01778. Tide predictions for many other reference stations are listed at the National Ocean Services (NOS) Web site, www.opsd.nos.noaa.gov/tp4days.html Estimations derived from the following tables are not to be used for navigation. *Farmers' Almanac* accepts no responsibility for errors or any consequences ensuing from use of these tables.

## 2001 DAYLIGHT HIGH TIDES (PST) SAN FRANCISCO AT GOLDEN GATE
### Converted to Daylight Saving Time - April 1 through October 27

| Day | JAN h m | FEB h m | MAR h m | APR h m | MAY h m | JUN h m | JUL h m | AUG h m | SEP h m | OCT h m | NOV h m | DEC h m |
|---|---|---|---|---|---|---|---|---|---|---|---|---|
| 1 | 3:23 P | 6:02 P | 4:22 P | 8:20 P | 8:36 P | 8:53 A | 10:13 A | 11:57 A | 12:31 P | 12:04 P | 11:03 A | 10:59 A |
| 2 | 4:40 | 5:41 A | 6:06 | 6:38 A | 7:40 A | 10:06 | 11:16 | 12:38 P | 12:57 | 12:27 | 11:32 | 11:37 |
| 3 | 6:14 | 6:34 | 7:41 | 7:52 | 8:55 | 11:11 | 12:11 P | 1:14 | 1:22 | 12:51 | 12:04 P | 12:20 P |
| 4 | 6:36 A | 7:29 | 6:01 A | 9:01 | 10:02 | 12:10 P | 12:59 | 1:46 | 1:46 | 1:16 | 12:40 | 1:08 |
| 5 | 7:18 | 8:24 | 7:07 | 10:04 | 11:04 | 1:04 | 1:43 | 2:15 | 2:11 | 1:45 | 1:24 | 2:04 |
| 6 | 8:01 | 9:18 | 8:11 | 11:02 | 12:02 P | 1:54 | 2:23 | 2:43 | 2:38 | 2:18 | 2:18 | 3:09 |
| 7 | 8:46 | 10:11+ | 9:09 | 11:58 | 12:58 | 2:43 | 3:00 | 3:10 | 3:09 | 2:57 | 3:24 | 4:26 |
| 8 | 9:32 | 11:02- | 10:05+- | 12:52 P | 1:53 | 3:30 | 3:35 | 3:38 | 3:46 | 3:46 | 4:41 | 5:52 |
| 9 | 10:20+ | 11:54 | 10:58 | 1:47 | 2:47 | 4:17 | 4:09 | 4:10 | 4:31 | 4:49 | 6:02 | 7:06 A |
| 10 | 11:09- | 12:47 P | 11:51 | 2:43+ | 3:43 | 5:02 | 4:42 | 4:45 | 5:26 | 6:02 | 7:48 A | 7:48 |
| 11 | 12:00 P | 1:43 | 12:45 P | 3:44 | 4:42 | 5:45 | 5:15 | 5:26 | 6:29 | 7:17 | 8:28 | 8:29 |
| 12 | 12:53 | 2:44 | 1:41 | 4:53 | 5:43 | 6:25 | 5:51 | 6:13 | 7:36 | 9:29 A | 9:05 | 9:09 |
| 13 | 1:49 | 3:57 | 2:42 | 6:10 | 6:42 | 7:01 | 6:28 | 7:06 | 10:05 A | 10:08 | 9:41 | 9:48+ |
| 14 | 2:52 | 5:27 | 3:54 | 7:26 | 7:31 | 7:35 | 7:08 | 9:37 A | 10:46 | 10:44 | 10:17 | 10:26- |
| 15 | 4:05 | 7:07 | 5:22 | 8:27 | 8:11 | 7:19 A | 8:24 A | 10:33 | 11:23+ | 11:19 | 10:54+- | 11:04 |
| 16 | 5:32 | 6:02 A | 6:54 | 6:28 A | 6:47 A | 8:41 | 9:47 | 11:19 | 12:00 P | 11:54 | 11:30 | 11:42 |
| 17 | 5:59 A | 6:58 | 5:12 A | 7:37 | 8:00 | 9:55 | 10:50 | 12:00 P+ | 12:36 | 12:30 P | 12:07 P | 12:19 P |
| 18 | 6:48 | 7:51 | 6:16 | 8:40 | 9:07 | 10:57 | 11:42 | 12:39 | 1:12 | 1:06+- | 12:46 | 12:58 |
| 19 | 7:35 | 8:39 | 7:18 | 9:36 | 10:08 | 11:53 | 12:28 P | 1:17- | 1:49 | 1:43 | 1:28 | 1:40 |
| 20 | 8:20 | 9:23 | 8:13 | 10:26 | 11:04 | 12:44 P | 1:12+ | 1:56 | 2:28 | 2:24 | 2:15 | 2:28 |
| 21 | 9:02 | 10:03 | 9:01 | 11:13 | 11:56 | 1:33 | 1:54- | 2:35 | 3:10 | 3:08 | 3:11 | 3:25 |
| 22 | 9:41 | 10:40 | 9:45 | 11:59 | 12:48 P | 2:21+ | 2:37 | 3:16 | 3:56 | 4:00 | 4:17 | 4:37 |
| 23 | 10:18 | 11:16 | 10:26 | 12:46 P | 1:39+ | 3:09- | 3:20 | 3:59 | 4:49 | 5:02 | 5:32 | 6:03 |
| 24 | 10:53 | 11:53 | 11:06 | 1:35 | 2:32 | 3:57 | 4:03 | 4:46 | 5:50 | 6:12 | 7:27 A | 6:51 A |
| 25 | 11:28 | 12:31 P | 11:47 | 2:27 | 3:26- | 4:46 | 4:48 | 5:38 | 6:57 | 7:23 | 7:57 | 7:26 |
| 26 | 12:03 P | 1:12 | 12:30 P | 3:25 | 4:23 | 5:34 | 5:35 | 6:34 | 8:02 | 9:26 A | 8:25 | 8:02 |
| 27 | 12:29 | 2:01 | 1:17 | 4:29- | 5:20 | 6:23 | 6:25 | 7:33 | 10:12 A | 9:56 | 8:53 | 8:39 |
| 28 | 1:18 | 3:01 | 2:11 | 5:39 | 6:15 | 7:10 | 7:15 | 10:00 A | 10:46 | 9:22 | 9:22 | 9:17 |
| 29 | 2:04 | | 3:17 | 6:48 | 7:07 | 7:29 A | 9:01 A | 10:48 | 11:15 | 9:46 | 9:52 | 9:57 |
| 30 | 3:01 | | 4:37 | 7:47 | 7:54 | 8:57 | 10:13 | 11:28 | 11:40 | 10:11 | 10:25 | 10:39 |
| 31 | 4:18 | | 6:06 | | 7:32 A | | 11:10 | 12:01 P | | 10:37 | | 11:23 |

# 2001 DAYLIGHT HIGH TIDES (PST) LOS ANGELES, CA., AT OUTER HARBOR
### Converted to Daylight Saving Time - April 1 through October 27

| Day | JAN h m | FEB h m | MAR h m | APR h m | MAY h m | JUN h m | JUL h m | AUG h m | SEP h m | OCT h m | NOV h m | DEC h m |
|---|---|---|---|---|---|---|---|---|---|---|---|---|
| 1 | 12:43 P | 3:38 P | 1:27 P | 6:43 P | 6:41 P | 7:11 P | 7:19 P | 9:35 A | 9:57 A | 9:32 A | 8:33 A | 8:35 A |
| 2 | 2:15 | 5:38 | 3:58 | 7:20 | 7:15 | 7:46 A | 8:51 A | 10:07 | 10:18 | 9:52 | 8:59 | 9:10- |
| 3 | 4:03 | 6:47 | 5:56 | 6:00 A | 7:46 | 8:41 | 9:39 | 10:35 | 10:40 | 10:14 | 9:28 | 9:50 |
| 4 | 5:33 | 5:32 A | 6:44 | 7:03 | 7:49 A | 9:32 | 10:21 | 11:02 | 11:03 | 10:36 | 10:01 | 10:37 |
| 5 | 6:41 | 6:24 | 5:14 A | 7:56- | 8:40 | 10:19 | 11:00 | 11:30 | 11:27 | 11:01 | 10:42 | 11:33 |
| 6 | 5:58 A | 7:13 | 6:13 | 8:46 | 9:28 | 11:06 | 11:37 | 11:57 | 11:52 | 11:30 | 11:37 | 12:46 P |
| 7 | 6:39 | 8:01- | 7:05 | 9:32 | 10:16 | 11:53 | 12:14 P | 12:27 P | 12:21 P | 12:07 P | 12:56 P | 2:16 |
| 8 | 7:23 | 8:48+ | 7:54+ | 10:19+ | 11:04 | 12:43 P | 12:53 | 12:58 | 12:57 | 12:57 | 2:37 | 3:51 |
| 9 | 8:07 | 9:35 | 8:40 | 11:05 | 11:54 | 1:39 | 1:33 | 1:32 | 1:47 | 2:17 | 4:08 | 5:12 |
| 10 | 8:53+ | 10:22 | 9:26 | 11:55 | 12:52 P | 2:41 | 2:16 | 2:13 | 3:01 | 4:00 | 5:20 | 6:21 |
| 11 | 9:41 | 11:13 | 10:13 | 12:52 P | 2:04 | 3:44 | 3:00 | 3:03 | 4:28 | 5:26 | 6:21 | 6:21 A |
| 12 | 10:31 | 12:09 P | 11:02 | 2:08 | 3:41 | 4:36 | 3:45 | 4:03 | 5:44 | 6:32 | 6:30 A | 6:57 |
| 13 | 11:24 | 1:31 | 11:57 | 4:11 | 5:13 | 5:15 | 4:28 | 5:06 | 6:45 | 7:28 | 7:22 | 7:32 |
| 14 | 12:26 P | 3:07 | 1:10 P | 6:18 | 6:01 | 5:47 | 5:10 | 6:04 | 7:38 | 8:23 A- | 7:55 | 8:06 |
| 15 | 1:41 | 5:18 | 3:08 | 7:02 | 6:30 | 6:15 | 5:52 | 6:58 | 8:57 A+ | 8:54 | 8:28+ | 8:41 |
| 16 | 3:19 | 6:44 | 5:35 | 7:28 | 6:53 | 6:43 | 6:34 | 7:48 | 9:30- | 9:26 | 9:01 | 9:16 |
| 17 | 5:05 | 5:17 A | 6:38 | 7:49 | 7:14 | 7:13 | 7:17 | 9:28 A | 10:03 | 9:59+ | 9:36 | 9:51 |
| 18 | 6:30 | 6:07 | 4:44 A | 6:55 A | 7:04 A | 8:24 A | 9:07 A | 10:05+- | 10:38 | 10:33 | 10:12 | 10:27 |
| 19 | 5:43 A | 6:48 | 5:43 | 7:38 | 7:51 | 9:13 | 9:51 | 10:42 | 11:09 | 11:09 | 10:51 | 11:07 |
| 20 | 6:24 | 7:23 | 6:28 | 8:15 | 8:34 | 10:01 | 10:34+ | 11:20 | 11:52 | 11:46 | 11:38 | 11:54 |
| 21 | 7:01 | 7:55 | 7:05 | 8:52 | 9:18 | 10:49+ | 11:16- | 12:00 P | 12:34 P | 12:30 P | 12:44 P | 12:57 P |
| 22 | 7:34 | 8:26 | 7:38 | 9:28 | 10:03 | 11:39- | 12:01 P | 12:43 | 1:24 | 1:27 | 2:18 | 2:27 |
| 23 | 8:06 | 8:56 | 8:10 | 10:06 | 10:50+ | 12:32 P | 12:47 | 1:30 | 2:30 | 2:54 | 3:50 | 4:06 |
| 24 | 8:37 | 9:27 | 8:42 | 10:48 | 11:43- | 1:28 | 1:36 | 2:25 | 3:57 | 4:34 | 5:01 | 5:27 |
| 25 | 9:08 | 9:58 | 9:15 | 11:34 | 12:43 P | 2:26 | 2:28 | 3:30 | 5:21 | 5:48 | 5:56 | 6:30 |
| 26 | 9:39 | 10:33 | 9:50 | 12:31 P | 1:53 | 3:25 | 3:24 | 4:42 | 6:25 | 6:42 | 6:44 | 6:03 A |
| 27 | 10:10 | 11:12 | 10:29 | 1:46 | 3:09 | 4:20 | 4:23 | 5:50 | 7:12 | 7:26 | 6:44 A | 6:34 |
| 28 | 10:44 | 12:04 P | 11:16 | 3:28 | 4:18 | 5:11 | 5:20 | 6:46 | 8:51 | 7:09 A | 7:08 | 7:07 |
| 29 | 11:22 | | 12:18 P | 5:06 | 5:13 | 5:57 | 6:13 | 7:31 | 8:54 A | 7:28 | 7:34 | 7:43 |
| 30 | 12:11 P | | 2:00 | 6:02 | 5:57 | 6:40 | 7:01 | 9:11 A | 9:13 | 7:48 | 8:03 | 8:22+ |
| 31 | 1:30 | | 4:31 | | 6:36 | | 8:57 A | 9:35 | | 8:10 | | 9:03 |

# 2001 DAYLIGHT HIGH TIDES (PST) SEATTLE, WASHINGTON
### Converted to Daylight Saving Time - April 1 through October 27

| Day | JAN | FEB | MAR | APR | MAY | JUN | JUL | AUG | SEP | OCT | NOV | DEC |
|---|---|---|---|---|---|---|---|---|---|---|---|---|
| 1 | 9:47 A | 9:52 A | 8:19 A | 10:05 A | 11:20 A | 2:42 P | 4:07 P | 5:40 P | 6:08 P | 5:32 P | 4:13 P | 3:55 P |
| 2 | 10:21 | 10:31 | 8:55 | 11:19 | 12:56 P | 3:59 | 5:06 | 6:18 | 6:31 | 5:50 | 4:38 | 4:31 |
| 3 | 10:56 | 11:17 | 9:41 | 12:45 P | 2:25 | 5:02 | 5:56 | 6:50 | 6:51 | 6:10 | 5:07 | 5:12 |
| 4 | 11:31 | 12:10 P | 10:39 | 2:09 | 3:42 | 5:55 | 6:38 | 7:19 | 7:11 | 6:33 | 5:40 | 8:09 A |
| 5 | 12:09 P | 1:07 | 11:48 | 3:24 | 4:47 | 6:43 | 7:16 | 7:44 | 6:55 A | 6:58 | 8:19 A | 8:58 |
| 6 | 12:49 | 2:07 | 1:01 P | 4:30 | 5:44 | 7:27 | 7:51 | 6:12 A | 7:41 | 7:27 | 9:17 | 9:48 |
| 7 | 1:33 | 3:07- | 2:10- | 5:30+ | 6:37 | 8:08 | 8:24 | 6:56 | 8:32 | 9:23 A | 10:18 | 10:37 |
| 8 | 2:20 | 4:06 | 3:15 | 6:26 | 7:26 | 5:55 A | 6:16 A | 7:45 | 9:30 | 10:27 | 11:18 | 11:24 |
| 9 | 3:09 | 5:05 | 4:16 | 7:20 | 5:59 A | 6:55 | 7:01 | 8:39 | 10:38 | 11:39 | 12:12 P | 12:09 P |
| 10 | 4:02- | 6:05+ | 5:15+ | 6:48 A | 6:32 | 7:15 | 7:52 | 9:42 | 11:57 | 12:53 P | 12:58 | 12:51 |
| 11 | 4:58 | 7:27 A | 6:13 | 7:20 | 7:07 | 8:05 | 8:51 | 10:55 | 1:23 P | 1:56 | 1:39 | 1:31 |
| 12 | 5:57 | 8:04 | 6:39 A | 7:54 | 7:46 | 9:08 | 10:00 | 12:19 P | 2:36 | 2:47 | 2:16+ | 2:10 |
| 13 | 8:10 A+ | 8:42 | 7:12 | 8:32 | 8:33 | 10:25 | 11:20 | 1:51 | 3:32 | 3:28 | 2:51 | 2:47 |
| 14 | 8:51 | 9:22 | 7:48 | 9:17 | 9:35 | 11:53 | 12:49 P | 3:10 | 4:15 | 4:05 | 3:25 | 3:25 |
| 15 | 9:33 | 10:06 | 8:26 | 10:16 | 10:57 | 1:23 P | 2:19 | 4:09 | 4:53- | 4:39+ | 3:59 | 4:02 |
| 16 | 10:16 | 10:55 | 9:10 | 11:34 | 12:28 P | 2:45 | 3:36 | 4:55 | 5:27 | 5:11 | 4:33- | 4:40 |
| 17 | 11:00 | 11:50 | 10:04 | 1:00 P | 1:54 | 3:53 | 4:34 | 5:35 | 6:00+ | 5:44 | 5:09 | 5:19 |
| 18 | 11:46 | 12:48 P | 11:11 | 2:17 | 3:06 | 4:48 | 5:22 | 6:11- | 6:33 | 6:17 | 7:45 A | 8:10 A |
| 19 | 12:31 P | 1:43 | 12:25 P | 3:20 | 4:04 | 5:36 | 6:05 | 6:47 | 7:07 | 6:51- | 8:35 | 8:50 |
| 20 | 1:16 | 2:32 | 1:32 | 4:12 | 4:55 | 6:21 | 6:45 | 7:22+ | 7:50 A | 6:28 | 9:28 | 9:29 |
| 21 | 2:40 | 3:16 | 2:28 | 4:58 | 5:40 | 7:04 | 7:24- | 6:41 A | 8:54 | 9:52 A | 10:20 | 10:08 |
| 22 | 3:19 | 3:57 | 3:15 | 5:41 | 6:25 | 7:48- | 8:03 | 7:44 | 10:03 | 10:57 | 11:11 | 10:45 |
| 23 | 3:58 | 4:38 | 3:59 | 6:24 | 7:09 | 8:32 | 6:32 A+ | 8:52 | 11:20 | 12:05 P | 11:57 | 11:21 |
| 24 | 4:37 | 5:20 | 4:40 | 7:08 | 7:56 A | 6:28 A | 7:36 | 10:08 | 12:42 P | 1:09 | 12:36 P | 11:54 |
| 25 | 5:19 | 6:04 | 5:22 | 6:03 A | 5:55 A | 7:29+ | 8:47 | 11:34 | 1:56 | 2:03 | 1:09 | 12:27 P |
| 26 | 7:23 A | 6:54 A | 6:06 | 6:33 | 6:39 | 8:39 | 10:08 | 1:07 P | 2:57 | 2:46 | 1:37 | 12:59 |
| 27 | 7:48 | 7:19 | 5:57 A | 7:08- | 7:30+ | 10:02 | 11:40 | 2:31 | 3:44 | 3:20 | 2:03 | 1:32 |
| 28 | 8:16 | 7:47 | 6:24 | 7:49 | 8:33 | 11:38 | 1:20 P | 3:36 | 4:21 | 2:47 | 2:28 | 2:08 |
| 29 | 8:45 | | 6:53 | 8:41 | 9:54 | 1:20 P | 2:50 | 4:27 | 4:50 | 3:09 | 2:54 | 2:46 |
| 30 | 9:17 | | 7:28 | 9:51 | 11:29 | 2:53 | 4:00 | 5:08 | 5:13 | 3:29 | 3:23 | 3:28 |
| 31 | 9:34 | | 8:10 | | 1:10 P | | 4:55 | 5:41 | | 3:50 | | 4:14+ |

# WEATHER FOLKLORE
## FROM 1899

A rosy sky at **SUNSET**, fine weather; an Indian-red tint, rain.

•

A red sky in the **MORNING**, bad weather; much wind, perhaps rain; a gray sky, fine weather.

•

Soft-looking **CLOUDS**, fine weather; hard-edged, oily-looking clouds, wind; small, inky-looking clouds, rain.

•

A dark, gloomy blue **SKY**, windy; a light, bright blue sky, fine weather; a bright yellow sky at sunset presages wind; a pale yellow sky, wet weather; a greenish sky, wind and rain.

# Weather SIGNS

The formula of popular weather signs which is most kindly treated by the official observers is that adopted by the Farmers' Club of the American Institute a number of years ago.

**1.** When the temperature falls suddenly, there is a storm forming south of you.

**2.** When the temperature rises suddenly, there is a storm forming north of you.

**3.** The wind always blows from a region of fair weather towards a region where a storm is forming.

**4.** Cirrus clouds always move from a region where a storm is in progress towards a region of fair weather.

**5.** Cumulus clouds always move from a region where a storm is forming.

**6.** When cirrus clouds are moving rapidly from the north or northeast, there will be rain within twenty-four hours, no matter how cold it is.

**7.** When cirrus clouds are moving rapidly from the south or southeast, there will be a cold hailstorm on the morrow if it be in the summer, and if it be in the winter, there will be a snowstorm.

**8.** The wind always blows in a circle around a storm, and when it blows from the north, the heaviest rain is east of you; if it blows from the south, the heaviest rain is west of you; if it blows from the east, the heaviest rain is south.

**9.** The wind never blows unless rain or snow is falling within 1,000 miles of you.

**10.** Whenever heavy, white frost occurs, a storm is forming within 1,000 miles north or northwest of you.

# WIND SPEED CLASSIFICATIONS

| WIND SPEED MPH | KNOTS | BEAUFORT NUMBER | NATIONAL WEATHER SERVICE DESCRIPTION | EFFECT OF THE WIND ON LAND | EFFECT OF THE WIND ON THE SEA | WAVE HEIGHT |
|---|---|---|---|---|---|---|
| 0-1 | 0-1 | 0 | CALM | Smoke rises vertically | Sea appears mirrorlike | Calm |
| 1-3 | 1-3 | 1 | LIGHT AIR | Direction shown by smoke drift; vane still | Ripples with an appearance of scales; no foam | 0.25 ft |
| 4-7 | 4-6 | 2 | LIGHT BREEZE | Leaves rustle; weathervane moves | Small wavelets; crests of glassy appearance, not breaking | 0.5-1 ft |
| 8-12 | 7-10 | 3 | GENTLE BREEZE | Leaves in constant motion; wind will extend a light flag | Large wavelets; crests begin to break; scattered whitecaps | 2-3 ft |
| 13-18 | 11-16 | 4 | MODERATE BREEZE | Raises dust; small branches move | Small waves, becoming longer; numerous whitecaps | 3-5 ft |
| 19-24 | 17-21 | 5 | FRESH BREEZE | Small trees with leaves begin to sway | Moderate waves, taking longer forms; many whitecaps, some spray | 6-8 ft |
| 25-31 | 22-27 | 6 | STRONG BREEZE | Large branches in motion; difficult to control an umbrella | Larger waves forming; whitecaps everywhere; more spray | 9-13 ft |
| 32-38 | 28-33 | 7 | MODERATE GALE | Whole trees in motion; noticeable difficulty in walking | Sea heaps up; white foam from breaking waves begins to be blown in streaks | 13-19 ft |
| 39-46 | 34-40 | 8 | FRESH GALE | Small branches may be broken; walking against the wind becomes very difficult | Moderately high waves of greater length; edges of crests begin to break into spindrift; foam is blown in well-marked streaks | 18-25 ft |
| 47-54 | 41-47 | 9 | STRONG GALE | Slight damage to structures; shingles blown off roofs | High waves; sea begins to roll; dense streaks of foam; spray may begin to reduce visibility | 23-32 ft |
| 55-63 | 48-55 | 10 | GALE | Considerable damage to structures; trees uprooted | Very high waves with overhanging crests; sea takes white appearance as foam is blown in very dense streaks; rolling is heavy and visibility is reduced | 29-41 ft |
| 64-74 | 56-64 | 11 | STORM | Widespread damage to structures; rarely occurs inland | Exceptionally high waves; sea covered with white foam patches; visibility further reduced | 37-52 ft |
| 75+ | 65+ | 12 | HURRICANE | Extreme destruction | Air filled with foam; sea completely white with driving spray; visibility greatly reduced | 45 ft+ |

*A scale devised by British Rear Admiral, Sir Frances Beaufort in 1805 based on observations of the effects of the wind.

# TEMPERATURE CONVERSIONS

To convert degrees Fahrenheit into degrees Celsius, subtract 32,
multiply by 5, and divide by 9. To convert degrees Celsius into degrees Fahrenheit,
multiply by 9, divide by 5, and add 32.

Source: U.S. Department of Commerce, National Bureau of Standards.

| °F | °C | °F | °C | °F | °C | °F | °C |
|---|---|---|---|---|---|---|---|
| -40 | -40 | 45 | 7.2 | 69.8 | 21 | 93.2 | 34 |
| -35 | -37.2 | 46 | 7.8 | 70 | 21.1 | 94 | 34.4 |
| -31 | -35 | 46.4 | 8 | 71 | 21.7 | 95 | 35 |
| -30 | -34.4 | 47 | 8.3 | 71.6 | 22 | 96 | 35.6 |
| -25 | -31.7 | 48 | 8.9 | 72 | 22.2 | 96.8 | 36 |
| -22 | -30 | 48.2 | 9 | 73 | 22.8 | 97 | 36.1 |
| -20 | -28.9 | 49 | 9.4 | 73.4 | 23 | 98 | 36.7 |
| -15 | -26.1 | 50 | 10 | 74 | 23.3 | 98.6 | 37 |
| -13 | -25 | 51 | 10.6 | 75 | 23.9 | 99 | 37.2 |
| -10 | -23.3 | 51.8 | 11 | 75.2 | 24 | 100 | 37.8 |
| -5 | -20.6 | 52 | 11.1 | 76 | 24.4 | 100.4 | 38 |
| -4 | -20 | 53 | 11.7 | 77 | 25 | 101 | 38.3 |
| 0 | -17.8 | 53.6 | 12 | 78 | 25.6 | 102 | 38.9 |
| 5 | -15 | 54 | 12.2 | 78.8 | 26 | 102.2 | 39 |
| 10 | -12.2 | 55 | 12.8 | 79 | 26.1 | 103 | 39.4 |
| 14 | -10 | 55.4 | 13 | 80 | 26.7 | 104 | 40 |
| 15 | -9.4 | 56 | 13.3 | 80.6 | 27 | 105 | 40.6 |
| 20 | -6.7 | 57 | 13.9 | 81 | 27.2 | 105.8 | 41 |
| 23 | -5 | 57.2 | 14 | 82 | 27.8 | 106 | 41.1 |
| 25 | -3.9 | 58 | 14.4 | 82.4 | 28 | 107 | 41.7 |
| 30 | -1.1 | 59 | 15 | 83 | 28.3 | 107.6 | 42 |
| 32 | 0 | 60 | 15.6 | 84 | 28.9 | 108 | 42.2 |
| 33.8 | 1 | 60.8 | 16 | 84.2 | 29 | 109 | 42.8 |
| 35.6 | 2 | 61 | 16.1 | 85 | 29.4 | 109.4 | 43 |
| 37.4 | 3 | 62 | 16.7 | 86 | 30 | 110 | 43.3 |
| 38 | 3.3 | 62.6 | 17 | 87 | 30.6 | 111 | 43.9 |
| 39 | 3.9 | 63 | 17.2 | 87.8 | 31 | 111.2 | 44 |
| 39.2 | 4 | 64 | 17.8 | 88 | 31.1 | 112 | 44.4 |
| 40 | 4.4 | 64.4 | 18 | 89 | 31.7 | 113 | 45 |
| 41 | 5 | 65 | 18.3 | 89.6 | 32 | 114 | 45.6 |
| 42 | 5.6 | 66 | 18.9 | 90 | 32.2 | 115 | 46.1 |
| 42.8 | 6 | 66.2 | 19 | 91 | 32.8 | 116 | 46.7 |
| 43 | 6.1 | 67 | 19.4 | 91.4 | 33 | 117 | 47.2 |
| 44 | 6.7 | 68 | 20 | 92 | 33.3 | 118 | 47.8 |
| 44.6 | 7 | 69 | 20.6 | 93 | 33.9 | 118.4 | 48 |

# SUN EXPOSURE SAFETY CHART

| UV INDEX | BURNING TIME WITHOUT PROTECTION | SENSITIVE-SKINNED CHILDREN AND ADULTS | SUN PROTECTION FACTOR NEEDED |
|---|---|---|---|
| **9+** **EXTREME** | **LESS THAN 15 MINUTES** | Do not expose yourself. Wear clothing, a broad-brimmed hat, sunglasses, and frequently apply sunblock cream with sun protection factor 40. | **SPF 40** **EVERY HALF HOUR** |
| **7-8** **VERY HIGH** | **20 MINUTES** | Do not expose children. Favor staying in the shade. Wear a hat, sunglasses, a shirt, and apply sunblock cream with sun protection factor 40. | **SPF 40** **EVERY HOUR** |
| **5-6** **HIGH** | **25 MINUTES** | Do not expose young children. Wear a hat, sunglasses, a shirt, and apply sunblock cream with sun protection factor 25. | **SPF 25** **EVERY HOUR** |
| **3-4** **MEDIUM** | **40 MINUTES** | Wear a hat, sunglasses, and apply sunblock cream with sun protection factor 15. | **SPF 15** **EVERY HOUR** |
| **1-2** **LOW** | **60 MINUTES** | Wear sunglasses, and apply sunblock cream with sun protection factor 8. | **SPF 8** **EVERY HOUR** |

NOTE: Sunblock and sunscreen products are not meant to allow for longer exposures.

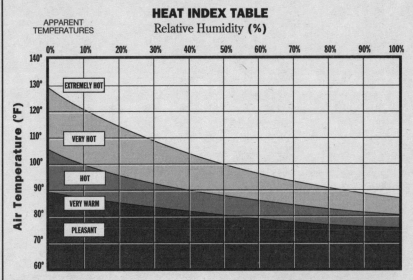

**HEAT INDEX TABLE**
Relative Humidity **(%)**

APPARENT TEMPERATURES

**80° to 90°** Fatigue possible with prolonged exposure and physical activity.

**90° to 105°** Sunstroke, heat cramps and heat exhaustion possible with prolonged exposure and physical activity.

**105° to 130°** Sunstroke, heat cramps, or heat exhaustion likely. Heatstroke possible with prolonged exposure and physical activity.

**130° and higher** Heatstroke or sunstroke imminent.

# TORNADO SURVIVAL TIPS

**When a tornado is coming, you have only a short amount of time to make life-or-death decisions. Advance planning and a quick response are the keys to surviving a tornado.**

Courtesy of the National Oceanic and Atmospheric Administration

## BEFORE

Conduct tornado drills each tornado season. Designate an area in the home as a shelter, and practice having everyone in the family go there in response to a tornado threat. Discuss with family members the difference between a "tornado watch" and a "tornado warning."

■ **Have disaster supplies on hand.** Flashlight and extra batteries, portable, battery-operated radio and extra batteries, first-aid kit and manual, emergency food and water, nonelectric can opener, essential medicines, cash and credit cards, sturdy shoes.

■ **Develop an emergency communication plan.** In case family members are separated from one another during a tornado (a real possibility during the day when adults are at work and children are at school), have a plan for getting back together. Ask an out-of-state relative or friend to serve as the "family contact." After a disaster, it's often easier to call long distance. Make sure everyone in the family knows the name, address, and phone number of the contact person.

## TORNADO WATCHES AND WARNINGS

A tornado watch is issued by the National Weather Service when tornadoes are possible in your area. Remain alert for approaching storms. This is time to remind family members where the safest places within your home are located, and listen to the radio or television for further developments. **A tornado warning is issued when a tornado has been sighted or indicated by weather radar.**

## DURING

■ **If at home:** Go at once to the basement, storm cellar, or the lowest level of the building. If there is no basement, go to an inner hallway or a smaller inner room without windows, such as a bathroom or closet. Get away from the windows. Go to the center of the room. Stay away from corners because they tend to attract debris. Get under a piece of sturdy furniture such as a workbench, heavy table or desk and hold on to it. Use arms to protect head and neck. If in a mobile home, get out and find shelter elsewhere.

■ **If at work or school:** Go to the basement or to an inside hallway at the lowest level. Avoid places with wide-span roofs such as auditoriums, cafeterias, large hallways, or shopping malls. Get under a piece of sturdy furniture such as a workbench, heavy table or desk and hold on to it.

■ **If outdoors:** If possible, get inside a building. If shelter is not available or there is no time to get indoors, lie in a ditch or low-lying area or crouch near a strong building. Be aware of the potential for flooding.

■ **If in a car:** Never try to outdrive a tornado in a car or truck. Tornadoes can change direction quickly and can lift up a car or truck and toss it through the air. Get out of the car immediately and take shelter in a nearby building. If there is no time to get indoors, get out of the car and lie in a ditch or low-lying area away from the vehicle. Be aware of the potential for flooding.

## FUJITA AND PEARSON TORNADO SCALE

| | | |
|---|---|---|
| F-0 | 40-72 mph | Chimney damage, tree branches broken |
| F-1 | 73-112 mph | Mobile homes pushed off foundations or overturned |
| F-2 | 113-157 mph | Considerable damage, mobile homes demolished, trees uprooted |
| F-3 | 158-206 mph | Roofs and walls torn down, trains overturned, cars thrown |
| F-4 | 207-260 mph | Well-constructed walls leveled |
| F-5 | 261-318 mph | Homes lifted off foundations and carried considerable distances |

## TORNADO DANGER SIGNS

An approaching cloud of debris can mark the location of a tornado even if a funnel is not visible. Before a tornado hits, the wind may die down and the air may become very still. Tornadoes generally occur near the trailing edge of a thunderstorm. It is not uncommon to see clear, sunlit skies behind a tornado.

# MARINE WEATHER WARNINGS

## SMALL CRAFT ADVISORY

To alert mariners to sustained (more than two hours) weather or sea conditions, either present or forecast, that might be hazardous to small boats. If a mariner notices a Small Craft Advisory pennant displayed, he should determine immediately the reason by tuning his or her radio to the latest marine broadcast. Decision as to the degree of hazard will be left up to the boatman, based on his or her experience and size and type of boat. The threshold conditions for the Small Craft Advisory are usually **18 knots** of wind (less than 18 knots in some dangerous waters) or hazardous wave conditions.

## GALE WARNING

To indicate winds within the range **34 to 47 knots** are forecast for the area.

## STORM WARNING

To indicate winds **48 knots and above**, no matter how high the speed, are forecast for the area. However, if the winds are associated with a tropical storm or hurricane, this warning indicates that winds within the range **48-63 knots** are forecast.

## HURRICANE WATCH

An announcement issued by the National Weather Service via press and television broadcasts whenever a tropical storm or hurricane becomes a threat to a coastal area. It indicates that a hurricane is near enough that everyone in the area covered by the "Watch" should listen to their radios for subsequent advisories and be ready to take precautionary action in case hurricane warnings are issued.

## HURRICANE WARNING

Issued only in connection with a tropical storm or hurricane to indicate that winds **64 knots and above** are forecast for the area.

## A SPECIAL MARINE WARNING

Is issued whenever a severe local storm or strong wind of brief duration is imminent and is not covered by existing warnings or advisories. No visual displays will be used in connection with the Special Marine Warning Bulletin; boaters will be able to receive these special warnings by keeping tuned to a NOAA Weather Radio station or to Coast Guard and commercial radio stations that transmit marine weather information.

# WINTER PREPAREDNESS SAFETY TIPS

**Before severe winter weather arrives:** Know safe routes from home, work, and school to high ground.• Know how to contact other household members through a common, out-of-state contact in the event you have to evacuate and become separated. • Know how to turn off gas, electric power, and water before evacuating. • Know ahead of time what you should do to help elderly or disabled friends, neighbors, or employees. • Keep plywood, plastic sheeting, lumber, sandbags, and hand tools on hand and accessible. • Winterize your house, barn, shed, or any other structure that may provide shelter for your family, neighbors, livestock, or equipment. Install storm shutters, doors, and windows; clear rain gutters; repair roof leaks; and check the structural ability of the roof to sustain unusually heavy weight from the accumulation of snow—or water, if drains on flat roofs do not work. • Store drinking water, first-aid kit, canned/no-cook food, non-electric can opener, radio, flashlight and extra batteries where you can get them easily, even in the dark. • Keep cars and other vehicles fueled and in good repair, with a winter emergency kit in each. Get a NOAA weather radio to monitor severe weather.

## WINTER WEATHER WARNINGS

### WINTER WEATHER ADVISORY
Winter weather conditions are expected to cause significant inconveniences and may be hazardous, especially to motorists.

### WINTER STORM WATCH
Be alert, a storm is likely.

### WINTER STORM WARNING
Take immediate action, the storm is in or entering the area.

### BLIZZARD WARNING
Snow and strong winds combined will produce blinding snow, near-zero visibility, deep drifts, and life-threatening wind chill–seek refuge immediately.

### FROST/FREEZE WARNING
Below freezing temperatures are expected and may cause damage to plants, crops, or fruit trees.

### FLASH FLOOD OR FLOOD WATCH
Be alert to signs of flash flooding and be ready to evacuate on a moment's notice.

### FLASH FLOOD WARNING
A flash flood is imminent. Act quickly to save yourself. You may have only seconds.

### FLOOD WARNING
Flooding has been reported or is imminent take necessary precautions at once.

Reprinted with permission from FEMA Federal Emergency Management Association.

## WIND CHILL TABLE

Dry Bulb Temperature (°F)

| Wind Speed (MPH) | 45° | 40° | 35° | 30° | 25° | 20° | 15° | 10° | 5° | 0° | -5° | -10° | -15° | -20° | -25° | -30° | -35° | -40° | -45° | |
|---|---|---|---|---|---|---|---|---|---|---|---|---|---|---|---|---|---|---|---|---|
| 4 | 45 | 40 | 35 | 30 | 25 | 20 | 15 | 10 | 5 | 0 | -5 | -10 | -15 | -20 | -25 | -30 | -35 | -40 | -45 | 4 |
| 5 | 43 | 37 | 32 | 27 | 22 | 16 | 11 | 6 | 0 | -5 | -10 | -15 | -21 | -26 | -31 | -36 | -42 | -47 | -52 | 5 |
| 10 | 34 | 28 | 22 | 16 | 10 | 3 | -3 | -9 | -15 | -22 | -27 | -34 | -40 | -46 | -52 | -58 | -64 | -71 | -77 | 10 |
| 15 | 29 | 23 | 16 | 9 | 2 | -5 | -11 | -18 | -25 | -31 | -38 | -45 | -51 | -58 | -65 | -72 | -78 | -85 | -92 | 15 |
| 20 | 26 | 19 | 12 | 4 | -3 | -10 | -17 | -24 | -31 | -39 | -46 | -53 | -60 | -67 | -74 | -81 | -88 | -95 | -103 | 20 |
| 25 | 23 | 16 | 8 | 1 | -7 | -15 | -22 | -29 | -36 | -44 | -51 | -59 | -66 | -74 | -81 | -88 | -96 | -103 | -110 | 25 |
| 30 | 21 | 13 | 6 | -2 | -10 | -18 | -25 | -33 | -41 | -49 | -56 | -64 | -71 | -79 | -86 | -93 | -101 | -109 | -116 | 30 |
| 35 | 20 | 12 | 4 | -4 | -12 | -20 | -27 | -35 | -43 | -52 | -58 | -67 | -74 | -82 | -89 | -97 | -105 | -113 | -120 | 35 |
| 40 | 19 | 11 | 3 | -5 | -13 | -21 | -29 | -37 | -45 | -53 | -60 | -69 | -76 | -84 | -92 | -100 | -107 | -115 | -123 | 40 |
| 45 | 18 | 10 | 2 | -6 | -14 | -22 | -30 | -38 | -45 | -54 | -62 | -70 | -78 | -85 | -93 | -102 | -109 | -117 | -125 | 45 |
| | 45° | 40° | 35° | 30° | 25° | 20° | 15° | 10° | 5° | 0° | -5° | -10° | -15° | -20° | -25° | -30° | -35° | -40° | -45° | |

Temp. 10°   -10°   -25°   -65°   -90°

| Not pleasant for outdoor activities on overcast days. | No longer pleasant for outdoor activities on sunny days. | Freezing of exposed skin begins depending on the degree of sunshine. | Outdoor travel dangerous. Exposed areas can freeze in less than 1 minute. | Exposed skin will freeze within half a minute. |

## ROMAN AND ARABIC NUMERALS

| | |
|---|---|
| I | 1 |
| II | 2 |
| III | 3 |
| IV | 4 |
| V | 5 |
| VI | 6 |
| VII | 7 |
| VIII | 8 |
| IX | 9 |
| X | 10 |
| XI | 11 |
| XII | 12 |
| XIII | 13 |
| XIV | 14 |
| XV | 15 |
| XVI | 16 |
| XVII | 17 |
| XVIII | 18 |
| XIX | 19 |
| XX | 20 |
| XXX | 30 |
| XL | 40 |
| L | 50 |
| LX | 60 |
| LXX | 70 |
| LXXX or XXC | 80 |
| XC | 90 |
| C | 100 |
| CC | 200 |
| CCC | 300 |
| CD | 400 |
| D | 500 |
| DC | 600 |
| DCC | 700 |
| DCCC | 800 |
| CM | 900 |
| M | 1000 |
| MM | 2000 |

# Why is a foot a foot?

**Many of our linear measurements were originally derived from the human body.**

- At one time, a foot was the average length of a man's foot. In nearly all languages, a word signifying the human foot is used for the primary linear measure.
- The word "inch" is derived from the Latin word "uncia," meaning "the twelfth part." An inch was simply one-twelfth the length of a human foot.
- Oddly enough the word "ounce," was also derived from the Latin "uncia," with an ounce being one-twelfth of a Roman pound.
- The word "yardstick" is really a redundancy, as "yard" originally meant "a stick." King Henry I of England decreed that the ulna, or yard of his time, should be the length of the distance between the tip of his own nose and the end of his thumb. "Ell" and "ulna," which were early names of the modern yard, literally mean elbow.
- Fathom (6 feet) is derived from a word meaning "the outstretched arms," and the original fathom was the distance that a man could extend his arms.
- The hand (4 inches), now used chiefly in measuring the height of horses, formerly was the average width of a human hand.
- Acre itself is derived from a root word meaning "to do" or "work," and the acre as a measure was originally the area a yoke of oxen could plow in one day.

## What is Indian Summer?

The term Indian Summer is used when we experience a little revival of summer after it should have finished. The sky is usually cloudless, but hazy or even smoky looking, especially toward the horizon.

In England this warming trend used to be called Little Summer of St. Luke if it happened in October, or St. Martin's Summer if it happened in November. Today, everyone refers to it as Indian Summer, although no one seems to know the reason for the name.

There are several stories, however, that tell about how early settlers mistook the haze of late New England autumn air for the campfires of Indians, thus the name Indian Summer.

## First Class

Letters and all other written matter, whether sealed or unsealed, and all other matter sealed, nailed, sewed, tied or fastened in any manner, so that it cannot be easily examined, 2 cents an ounce or fraction thereof.

## Second Class

Newspapers or periodicals sent by publishers and news agents, 1 cent a pound; sent by others, 1 cent for every four ounces, fully prepaid by stamps affixed to the matter.

## Third Class

Printed matter, unsealed, (matter in notched envelopes must pay letter postage) 1 cent for every two ounces, fully prepaid. This includes books, circulars, chromos, engravings, music, proof sheets, with accompanying manuscript, reproductions by electric-pen, hektograph, or other similar process easy of recognition, seeds, plants, etc. Limit of weight, 4 lbs., except for single book which may weigh more. Productions by copying press or typewriter are first-class matter.

## Fourth Class

Matter not included in the three preceding classes, so put up as to be easily examined, 1 cent an ounce. Limit of weight, 4 lbs. Full prepayment compulsory.

# 1900 POSTAGE RATES

### As published in the 1900 FARMERS' ALMANAC

## Special Delivery

Every article of mailable matter bearing a 10-cent special delivery stamp, in addition to postage, is entitled to immediate delivery by special messenger, on arrival at any post office. Extent of delivery, the carrier limits of letter carrier offices; other offices, one mile from the post office. Hours of delivery, 7 A.M. to 11 P.M. at carrier offices; at others, 7 A.M. to arrival of last mail before 9 P.M.

## Postal Cards

Single, 1 cent; double, or reply, 2 cents. Nothing may be attached except a label of address, and no writing on address side beyond the superscription.

## Unmailable

Obscene books, letters, or other matter, or matter relating to lotteries; matter bearing on the outside indecent, injurious and threatening language; liquors, poisons, explosives, live animals or other articles liable to injure the mails or the persons who handle them.

## Permissible Writing

No writing is permitted on third- or fourth-class matter, beyond the superscription, except the name and address of sender preceded by the word "from." Wrappers of fourth-class matter may bear names and number of articles enclosed; a word or passage in a book may be marked.

## Weighing

To avoid errors, packages should be weighed at the post office.

## Reforwarding

Matter may be forwarded from office of original address to another on request of addressee; no new charge is made on letters and postal cards thus forwarded, but other matter is subject to full additional postage. Undelivered matter is returnable on same terms.

# GLOSSARY OF ALMANAC TERMS

**Aph./Aphelion–**The point at which a body in an elliptical orbit around the Sun is at its greatest distance from the Sun. Earth is in aphelion in early July.

**Apo./Apogee–**The point at which a body moving in an elliptical orbit around the Earth is at its greatest distance from the Earth.

**Ascending Node–** ☊ The point of the Moon's (or planet's) orbit at which it crosses, from south to north, the plane of the Earth's orbit extended to meet the celestial body.

**Combust–**When the Moon, star or planet is not visible due to its proximity to the Sun.

**Conjunction–** ☌ The alignment or close alignment of two or more astronomical bodies.

**Cl./Close–**Used in this Almanac to define a conjunction. Example: Saturn/Moon cl. ev., means that Saturn and the Moon are close (or in conjunction) in the evening.

**Declination–**The angular distance to a specific point on the celestial sphere, measured in degrees either north or south from the celestial equator in a direction perpendicular to the point.

**Descending Node–** ☋ The point at which the Moon's (or planet's orbit) crosses, from north to south, the plane of the Earth's orbit extended to meet the celestial body.

**Dionysian Period–**Named for the monk Dionysius Exiguus who, in the A.D. 500s, introduced the present custom of reckoning time by counting the years from the birth of Christ. The current Dionysian Period began on January 1, 1672.

**Dominical Letter–**Used in reckoning civil calendars. It is determined by the date on which the first Sunday of the year falls. If January 1 is a Sunday, the letter is A; and so on to G when the first Sunday is Jan. 7. Should the year in question be a leap year, the letter applies only through the month of February and then takes the letter before.

**Eclipse, Annular–**Is when a solar eclipse occurs with the apparent size of the New Moon marginally smaller than that of the Sun. As a result, the rim of the Sun's disc remains visible around the dark disc of the Moon.

**Eclipse, Lunar–**When the Moon passes into the Earth's shadow.

**Eclipse, Solar–**When the New Moon orbits between the Earth and the Sun and casts its shadow upon the Earth's surface.

**Ecliptic–**The Sun's apparent path among the constellations.

**El./Elongation–**Apparent angular distance of a member of the Solar System from the Sun as seen from the Earth.

**Epact–**The Moon's age in the lunar cycle at the beginning of each solar year, which begins on January 1, at 0h 00m Greenwich Mean Time. The Moon's age cannot exceed 29 days; however, when it is less than one day old, the Epact is considered to be 30 and not zero.

**Evening Star–**A term that is applied to any planet when the planet is visible in the evening sky and crosses the meridian before midnight.

**Golden Number–**After a period of 235 lunar months or 19 years, the phases of the Moon recur in the same order and on the same dates as the preceding cycle. The Golden Number is used in reckoning civil calendars and represents the year's position in this 19-year cycle.

**Gr. El./Greatest Elongation–**When a planet attains its greatest apparent angular distance from the Sun in the sky.

**Inf./Inferior–**Inferior conjunction is

# GLOSSARY OF ALMANAC TERMS

when an "inferior planet" (Mercury or Venus) passes between the Earth and the Sun.

**Jewish Lunar Cycle**–Similar to the 19-year cycle upon which the Golden Number is based.

**Julian Period**–Devised in 1582 by Joseph Scaliger as a way to measure time. Scaliger had Julian Day (JD) #1, named after his father, Julius Scaliger, which began at noon on January 1, 4713 B.C., the most recent time that three major chronological cycles began on the same day: 1) the 28-year solar cycle; 2) the 19-year lunar cycle; and 3) the 15-year indication cycle used in ancient Rome to regulate taxes. It will take 7,980 Julian years to complete the period, the product of 28, 19 and 15.

**Mer./Meridian**–A great circle on the celestial sphere passing through the north and south celestial poles and the zenith (overhead point) of a given place.

**Moon Highest or Lowest**–The day of the month that the Moon appears at its highest or lowest point on the meridian. Moon highest ⌒ Moon lowest ⌣

**Moon's Southing**–Also known as the Moon's "Meridian Passage" or "Upper Culmination." It's when the Moon appears exactly above the south point of the observer's local horizon.

**Morning Star**–A term that applies to any planet when it is visible in the morning sky and crosses the meridian after midnight.

**Occ./Occultation**–An eclipse of a star or planet by the Moon or another planet.

**Opposition**–☍ The position of an astronomical object when it is opposite the Sun in the sky, and as a consequence, crosses the meridian at midnight.

**Per./Perigee**–The point at which a body moving in an elliptical orbit around the Earth is at its closest approach to the Earth.

**Peri./Perihelion**–The point at which a body in an elliptical orbit around the Sun is at its closest distance to the Sun. Earth is at perihelion in early January.

**Roman Indiction**–A 15-year cycle used in reckoning ecclesiastical calendars. It was established in ancient Rome on January 1, 313 A.D. as a fiscal term to regulate taxes. In order to figure out the Roman Indictions, add 3 to the number of years in the Christian era and divide by 15. The remainder of the year is Roman Indiction–no remainder is 15.

**Solar Cycle**–A 28-year cycle used in reckoning civil calendars. At the end of the cycle, it restores the first day of the year to the same day of the week.

**Tears of Saint Laurence**–During the 19th century, Irish farmers, as well as Catholics in England and Germany, noted an annual shower of shooting stars around the night of the Feast of St. Laurence (August 10 on the Catholic calendar). Today, the display is better known as the Perseid Meteors.

**Zodiac**–Greek, zöon, "animal" (all but one of the 12 zodiacal constellations represent living creatures); the circular zone on the celestial sphere, centered on the ecliptic and extending in width to about 9 degrees on either side. Within this zone, the motion of the visible planets, the Sun and the Moon take place. It is divided into 12 zones, each 30 degrees long, called the signs of the zodiac. It was (and still is) highly regarded in astrology.

## THREE YEARS' WORTH OF

# FARMERS' ALMANACS™

## for only

# $11⁹⁹

### SAVE ALMOST 20% OFF THE COVER PRICE!

Sign up for a three-year subscription today (includes the 2002, 2003, and 2004 editions). You'll save almost 20% off the cover price and avoid any increase that may occur within the next three years. Cover price is $4.99, but if you take advantage of our three-year subscription, you'll pay only $11.99 for all three years! There are 3 easy ways you can order. Then sit back and wait for your yearly Almanac to be mailed to your house. It's that easy. (Each new edition will be mailed to you in September of the previous year.)

### To order by phone call: 1-888-222-4276
### To order online visit our store: www.farmersalmanac.com
### ———————— To order by mail: ————————

**MAIL TO:** *Farmers' Almanac* Subscription, Box 1609, Lewiston, ME 04241.
Make check payable to *Farmers' Almanac*.

❑ CHECK OR MONEY ORDER ENCLOSED    ❑ *VISA*    ❑ *MasterCard*    ❑ *AMERICAN EXPRESS*

Credit Card Number _____    Expiration Date _____

Signature _____

Name _____

Address _____

City _____ State _____ Zip _____

Phone _____

| 3-YEAR SUBSCRIPTION STARTING WITH 2002 ITEM # FA-2 SFARET | $ . |
| APPLICABLE SALES TAX | $ |
| SUBTOTAL | $ . |
| SHIPPING AND HANDLING ($5.85 for each 3-year subscription) | $ . |
| TOTAL | $ . |

# EASY WAYS TO HELP KEEP THE EARTH GREEN

## OUTDOOR TIPS

* Water your lawn only when absolutely necessary. On an average, lawns only need water every 3 to 5 days.

* If you have to water, water during the coolest part of the day, before 10:00 in the morning or after 5:00 in the evening.

* Instead of using insecticides, try planting marigolds, basil, savory, horseradish, mint, onions, garlic, and chives near your garden. These plants' (and many others) natural odors and root secretions repel some insects.

* Participate in the many organized litter cleanup days, or organize one yourself.

## CAMPING TIPS

* Make sure you take everything you brought into the wilderness out of the wilderness.

* Use biodegradable soap when camping. Don't wash yourself, your clothes, or your dishes in a lake or stream. Use a dishpan of water, then discard the water away from any natural water source.

* Protect your food and garbage from wildlife. Never feed wildlife as this disrupts their natural feeding habits.

* When camping, remember you are a guest. Don't disturb the wildlife, especially nesting birds and young animals.

* Use existing campsites and trails. Don't cut new trails or pull out vegetation to make an existing site bigger.

* Teach your family, friends, and children to respect the world in which we live. If we respect something, we are less likely to harm it.

# 2000

### JANUARY
```
 S  M  T  W  T  F  S
                   1
 2  3  4  5  6  7  8
 9 10 11 12 13 14 15
16 17 18 19 20 21 22
23 24 25 26 27 28 29
30 31
```

### FEBRUARY
```
 S  M  T  W  T  F  S
       1  2  3  4  5
 6  7  8  9 10 11 12
13 14 15 16 17 18 19
20 21 22 23 24 25 26
27 28 29
```

### MARCH
```
 S  M  T  W  T  F  S
          1  2  3  4
 5  6  7  8  9 10 11
12 13 14 15 16 17 18
19 20 21 22 23 24 25
26 27 28 29 30 31
```

### APRIL
```
 S  M  T  W  T  F  S
                   1
 2  3  4  5  6  7  8
 9 10 11 12 13 14 15
16 17 18 19 20 21 22
23 24 25 26 27 28 29
30
```

### MAY
```
 S  M  T  W  T  F  S
    1  2  3  4  5  6
 7  8  9 10 11 12 13
14 15 16 17 18 19 20
21 22 23 24 25 26 27
28 29 30 31
```

### JUNE
```
 S  M  T  W  T  F  S
             1  2  3
 4  5  6  7  8  9 10
11 12 13 14 15 16 17
18 19 20 21 22 23 24
25 26 27 28 29 30
```

### JULY
```
 S  M  T  W  T  F  S
                   1
 2  3  4  5  6  7  8
 9 10 11 12 13 14 15
16 17 18 19 20 21 22
23 24 25 26 27 28 29
30 31
```

### AUGUST
```
 S  M  T  W  T  F  S
       1  2  3  4  5
 6  7  8  9 10 11 12
13 14 15 16 17 18 19
20 21 22 23 24 25 26
27 28 29 30 31
```

### SEPTEMBER
```
 S  M  T  W  T  F  S
                1  2
 3  4  5  6  7  8  9
10 11 12 13 14 15 16
17 18 19 20 21 22 23
24 25 26 27 28 29 30
```

### OCTOBER
```
 S  M  T  W  T  F  S
 1  2  3  4  5  6  7
 8  9 10 11 12 13 14
15 16 17 18 19 20 21
22 23 24 25 26 27 28
29 30 31
```

### NOVEMBER
```
 S  M  T  W  T  F  S
          1  2  3  4
 5  6  7  8  9 10 11
12 13 14 15 16 17 18
19 20 21 22 23 24 25
26 27 28 29 30
```

### DECEMBER
```
 S  M  T  W  T  F  S
                1  2
 3  4  5  6  7  8  9
10 11 12 13 14 15 16
17 18 19 20 21 22 23
24 25 26 27 28 29 30
31
```

# 2001

### JANUARY
```
 S  M  T  W  T  F  S
    1  2  3  4  5  6
 7  8  9 10 11 12 13
14 15 16 17 18 19 20
21 22 23 24 25 26 27
28 29 30 31
```

### FEBRUARY
```
 S  M  T  W  T  F  S
             1  2  3
 4  5  6  7  8  9 10
11 12 13 14 15 16 17
18 19 20 21 22 23 24
25 26 27 28
```

### MARCH
```
 S  M  T  W  T  F  S
             1  2  3
 4  5  6  7  8  9 10
11 12 13 14 15 16 17
18 19 20 21 22 23 24
25 26 27 28 29 30 31
```

### APRIL
```
 S  M  T  W  T  F  S
 1  2  3  4  5  6  7
 8  9 10 11 12 13 14
15 16 17 18 19 20 21
22 23 24 25 26 27 28
29 30
```

### MAY
```
 S  M  T  W  T  F  S
       1  2  3  4  5
 6  7  8  9 10 11 12
13 14 15 16 17 18 19
20 21 22 23 24 25 26
27 28 29 30 31
```

### JUNE
```
 S  M  T  W  T  F  S
                1  2
 3  4  5  6  7  8  9
10 11 12 13 14 15 16
17 18 19 20 21 22 23
24 25 26 27 28 29 30
```

### JULY
```
 S  M  T  W  T  F  S
 1  2  3  4  5  6  7
 8  9 10 11 12 13 14
15 16 17 18 19 20 21
22 23 24 25 26 27 28
29 30 31
```

### AUGUST
```
 S  M  T  W  T  F  S
          1  2  3  4
 5  6  7  8  9 10 11
12 13 14 15 16 17 18
19 20 21 22 23 24 25
26 27 28 29 30 31
```

### SEPTEMBER
```
 S  M  T  W  T  F  S
                   1
 2  3  4  5  6  7  8
 9 10 11 12 13 14 15
16 17 18 19 20 21 22
23 24 25 26 27 28 29
30
```

### OCTOBER
```
 S  M  T  W  T  F  S
    1  2  3  4  5  6
 7  8  9 10 11 12 13
14 15 16 17 18 19 20
21 22 23 24 25 26 27
28 29 30 31
```

### NOVEMBER
```
 S  M  T  W  T  F  S
             1  2  3
 4  5  6  7  8  9 10
11 12 13 14 15 16 17
18 19 20 21 22 23 24
25 26 27 28 29 30
```

### DECEMBER
```
 S  M  T  W  T  F  S
                   1
 2  3  4  5  6  7  8
 9 10 11 12 13 14 15
16 17 18 19 20 21 22
23 24 25 26 27 28 29
30 31
```

# 2002

### JANUARY
```
 S  M  T  W  T  F  S
       1  2  3  4  5
 6  7  8  9 10 11 12
13 14 15 16 17 18 19
20 21 22 23 24 25 26
27 28 29 30 31
```

### FEBRUARY
```
 S  M  T  W  T  F  S
                1  2
 3  4  5  6  7  8  9
10 11 12 13 14 15 16
17 18 19 20 21 22 23
24 25 26 27 28
```

### MARCH
```
 S  M  T  W  T  F  S
                1  2
 3  4  5  6  7  8  9
10 11 12 13 14 15 16
17 18 19 20 21 22 23
24 25 26 27 28 29 30
31
```

### APRIL
```
 S  M  T  W  T  F  S
    1  2  3  4  5  6
 7  8  9 10 11 12 13
14 15 16 17 18 19 20
21 22 23 24 25 26 27
28 29 30
```

### MAY
```
 S  M  T  W  T  F  S
          1  2  3  4
 5  6  7  8  9 10 11
12 13 14 15 16 17 18
19 20 21 22 23 24 25
26 27 28 29 30 31
```

### JUNE
```
 S  M  T  W  T  F  S
                   1
 2  3  4  5  6  7  8
 9 10 11 12 13 14 15
16 17 18 19 20 21 22
23 24 25 26 27 28 29
30
```

### JULY
```
 S  M  T  W  T  F  S
    1  2  3  4  5  6
 7  8  9 10 11 12 13
14 15 16 17 18 19 20
21 22 23 24 25 26 27
28 29 30 31
```

### AUGUST
```
 S  M  T  W  T  F  S
             1  2  3
 4  5  6  7  8  9 10
11 12 13 14 15 16 17
18 19 20 21 22 23 24
25 26 27 28 29 30 31
```

### SEPTEMBER
```
 S  M  T  W  T  F  S
 1  2  3  4  5  6  7
 8  9 10 11 12 13 14
15 16 17 18 19 20 21
22 23 24 25 26 27 28
29 30
```

### OCTOBER
```
 S  M  T  W  T  F  S
       1  2  3  4  5
 6  7  8  9 10 11 12
13 14 15 16 17 18 19
20 21 22 23 24 25 26
27 28 29 30 31
```

### NOVEMBER
```
 S  M  T  W  T  F  S
                1  2
 3  4  5  6  7  8  9
10 11 12 13 14 15 16
17 18 19 20 21 22 23
24 25 26 27 28 29 30
```

### DECEMBER
```
 S  M  T  W  T  F  S
 1  2  3  4  5  6  7
 8  9 10 11 12 13 14
15 16 17 18 19 20 21
22 23 24 25 26 27 28
29 30 31
```